East Coast Pilot

Lowestoft to Ramsgate

Colin Jarman, Garth Cooper and
Dick Holness

Imray Laurie Norie & Wilson

Published by
Imray Laurie Norie & Wilson Ltd
Wych House St Ives
Cambridgeshire PE27 5BT England
☎ +44 (0)1480 462114 *Fax* +44 (0)1480 496109
Email ilnw@imray.com.
www.imray.com
2005

1st edition 2005

ISBN 0 85288 834 1

British Library Cataloguing in Publication Data.
A catalogue record for this book is available from the British Library.

PLANS
The plans in this guide are not to be used for navigation. They are designed to support the text and should at all times be used with up to date navigational charts.
The plans and tidal information have been reproduced with the permission of the Hydrographic Office of the United Kingdom (Licence No. HO151/951101/01) and the Controller of Her Britannic Majesty's Stationery Office.

CAUTION
Whilst every care has been taken to ensure accuracy, neither the Publishers nor the Authors will hold themselves responsible for errors, omissions or alterations in this publication. They will at all times be grateful to receive information which tends to the improvement of the work.

CORRECTIONAL SUPPLEMENTS
This pilot book will be amended at intervals by the issue of correctional supplements which will be published on our website www.imray.com and may be downloaded free of charge. Printed copies are also available on request from the publishers at the above address. Further information may also be found at www.eastcoastpilot.com

Printed in Great Britain at The Bath Press, Glasgow.

East Coast Pilot

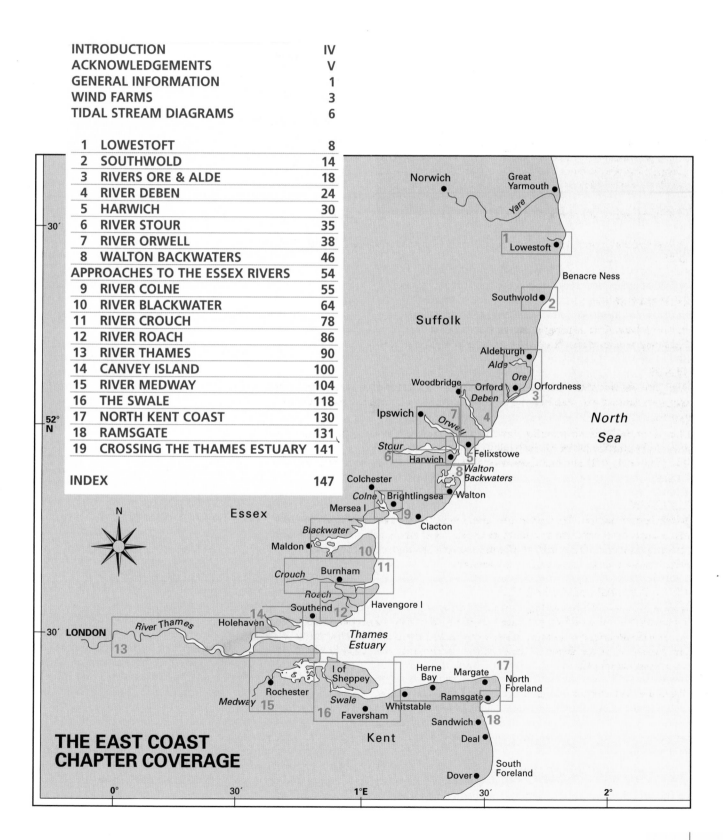

THE EAST COAST
CHAPTER COVERAGE

Introduction

Aim

East Coast Pilot is an aid to pilotage in the waters of the Thames Estuary, its creeks and harbours. It is an adjunct to the chart, providing detail and information in areas that a chart cannot, but it is not a replacement for navigation.

The information in each chapter of *East Coast Pilot* is laid out for an approach from seaward and we designed it to be left open in the cockpit for immediate reference during the approach and entry to your chosen destination. We have tried to present information in a logical and realistic sequence so that the helmsman can refer to the book for guidance from a safe point outside the river, creek or port, right in to the chosen anchorage, marina or berth. It's meant to be a working item in the boat's inventory; not a closely researched guide to pubs and restaurants around the coast that will be referred to only when the crew wants a run ashore. Nor is it a history book or filled with anecdotes. Indeed, it is rather short of anything more than straight pilotage information. We don't apologise for that, because experience has shown that wading through pages of such material, however interesting, in order to reach the nub of what buoy to look for next is not what the anxious pilot wants to do.

Coverage

The area covered by *East Coast Pilot* is from Lowestoft to Ramsgate, reaching far into the many creeks and harbours that lie in between.

When making an offshore passage from port to port across the area, very careful navigation is required to cope with the tides, weather and the intervening banks and deeps, plus the fact that you will be out of sight of land for some distance. Even for experienced skippers these are challenging passages not to be undertaken lightly or without due preparation.

By contrast, once inshore and within the seaward limit of many of the rivers and creeks, actual navigation will give way to the American concept of the 'MkI eyeball', which is where *East Coast Pilot* will come into its own.

Accuracy and updates

The East Coast and Thames Estuary is an area of huge and frequent change. A heavy gale, particularly in winter, combined with spring tides can radically change seemingly immovable bars and swatchways in a few hours. Over time channels move and buoys have to be moved to follow them. Facilities change and information goes out of date. All of these things make *East Coast Pilot* very much a 'work in progress'. We have done our best to ensure accuracy at the time of writing, but even by the time of publication there will have been changes, particularly with regard to the establishment of the offshore wind farms, and in entrance channels and river mouths like the Ore and Deben. We must, therefore, caution you to watch for changes and alterations and to exercise seamanlike commonsense, always referring to the most up-to-date charts and published corrections. The advice and guidance in *East Coast Pilot* is given in good faith and is as accurate as we can make it, but neither the authors nor the publisher can accept responsibility for any errors or omissions in the published material.

What we would really appreciate is being informed by readers of any changes they discover so that we can provide updates on the dedicated website www.eastcoastpilot.com and, later, in new editions of the printed *East Coast Pilot*. The best way to contact us is by email via the website.

Our East Coast

All three of us love the East Coast. We have all sailed in many other areas, not only of the British Isles, but of the world, yet each of us has returned to our home waters with exactly that feeling – we've come home.

Yet we often wonder what it is that we enjoy about slopping around in this area of the cold, grey North Sea, where the waves always seem to be the wrong length and made of concrete. Probably it's that time when we drop anchor in some quiet hole up a secluded creek, snug the boat down and go below to a warm cabin where, with dram in hand, we yarn about the fun we've had that day and about other times in other creeks.

There's something special about the creeks and inlets, the swatchways and gutways, the fleets and deeps. When the sun, tide and wind all go down together and the boat floats on her reflection, swinging quietly to her anchor, a peace descends and if it doesn't take your breath away, it certainly makes you hold it in for fear of breaking the calm and dispelling the magic.

It's completely relaxing, just looking and watching as the mud is revealed and the birds - curlew, oystercatcher, redshank, whimbrel, gull, shellduck, heron, white egret - begin to strut, prod, poke and peck, contentedly calling, chirping and crying. The long, mournful wails of the curlew and trilling of the oystercatcher are guaranteed to draw you back, again and again, to these muddy waterways.

On some days the sun will be bright, the breeze ruffling the water, the swiftly running tide chuckling and chirruping about the cable and hull calling 'Come on, lets go' and you'll be away on the tide bound for – where? Does it matter? You're underway and the whole estuary is there to be sailed.

ACKNOWLEDGEMENTS

Our sincere thanks go to the many people who have, one way or another, contributed to this book. We hope that now it exists, many more will contribute their knowledge, advice and expertise.

Thanks to Alec Williamson and *Second String*, Bernard Neal and *Bella Sufili*, and Bill Ewen and *Excelsior* for their help afloat.

We are grateful also to Chris Edwards, RYA Regional Environmental Co-ordinator, for his advice regarding offshore wind farms.

We are grateful too for the help given by Don Cockrill, John Feltham, Colin Overington, Don Smith and Steve Rivers. We must thank also John White for information about the Deben entrance.

Within Imray Laurie Norie & Wilson we are indebted to Willie Wilson for his enthusiastic support for the project, from the earliest discussions, hunched over a coffee in a dark corner of the London Boat Show, right through to the book going on sale. We would also like to mention the terrific help provided by the editorial and production team at Imray, without whose unstinting help and patience *East Coast Pilot* would not have seen the light of printed day.

Colin Jarman, Garth Cooper, Dick Holness
May 2005

Dedication

For Angela, Liz and Mary, not forgetting *Cornsilk*, *Jumblie* and *Ngaire* – the project would have failed without any one of them.

ABBREVIATIONS

Bn	Beacon	LWN	Low Water Neaps	S	South, Southwards, Southerly
By	Buoy	LWS	Low Water Springs	s	second(s)
CC	Cruising Club	M	Mile (nautical mile)	SC	Sailing Club
CG	Coastguard	m	metre	SCB	South Cardinal Buoy
Ch	Channel	MHWS	Mean High Water Springs	SCM	South Cardinal Mark (e.g. beacon)
Conspic	Conspicuous	min, mins	Minute, minutes		
DSC	Digital Selective Calling	MLWS	Mean Low Water Springs	SHB	Starboard Hand Buoy
E	East, eastwards, easterly	MMSI	Maritime Mobile Service Identity	SHM	Starboard Hand Mark (e.g. beacon)
ECB	East Cardinal Buoy				
ECM	East Cardinal Mark (e.g. beacon)	MSI	Maritime Safety Information including inshore waters forecast, gale warnings and navigational warnings	SW	Southwest, Southwestwards
				SWB	Safe Water Buoy
F	Fixed light			SWly	Southwesterly
Fl	Flashing light			SWM	Safe Water Mark
ft	Foot, feet	Mo	Morse	TSS	Traffic Separation Scheme
G	Green	N	North, Northwards, Northerly	UKHO	United Kingdom Hydrographic Office (the Admiralty)
H	Hour, e.g. H+15 is 15 minutes past the hour	NCB	North Cardinal Buoy		
		NCM	North Cardinal Mark (e.g. beacon)	UTC	Universal Time Corrected (same as GMT Greenwich Mean Time)
hr	Hour, hours				
HW	High Water	NE	Northeast or Northeastwards		
HWN	High Water Neaps	NEly	Northeasterly	vert	vertical
HWS	High Water Springs	NW	Northwest, Northwestwards	VQ	Very Quick flashing light
IQ	Interrupted Quick flashing light	NWly	Northwesterly	VTS	Vessel Traffic Service
		Oc	Occulting light	W	West, Westwards, Westerly, White
Iso	Isophase light	PHB	Port Hand Buoy		
kn	Knot, knots	PHM	Port Hand Mark (e.g. beacon)	WCB	West Cardinal Buoy
LFl	Long flash	PLA	Port of London Authority	WCM	West Cardinal Mark (e.g. beacon)
LOA	Length Overall	Pt	Point		
LPG	Liquefied Petroleum Gas	PWC	Personal Water Craft (jet ski)	Y	Yellow
LW	Low Water	Q	Quick flashing light	YC	Yacht club
		R	Red		

General information

Chart datum

The charts used in this pilot are based on UK Hydrographic Office (Admiralty) data and, therefore, drawn to Lowest Astronomical Tide (LAT). This means, in essence, that they show a 'worst case scenario' and that there will normally be more water in an area than is shown.

The horizontal datum is WGS84, which complies with modern GPS equipment.

Courses and bearings

We have applied the general pilot book convention of providing courses and bearings in degrees True, but have used the qualifier 'about' or 'approximately'. This is because it is the skipper/navigator's responsibility to confirm such courses and bearings with regard to tide, wind and sea conditions as well as applying corrections unique to the particular boat. We also believe that to steer a course in a seaway to within ±10° is acceptable; to steer within ±5° is good; to steer a precise course of (say) 241° is impossible. That impossibility makes it reasonable to quote a course of 'about 240' and let the reader make the necessary corrections.

Tides

In order to keep everything uniform and to provide a universal datum, all tides are based on HW Dover. Differences in time are given before (–) or after (+) in hours and minutes, e.g. HW Dover +0120 is 1hr 20mins after HW Dover.

Landfall waypoints

In order to provide a starting point for the pilotage notes, we have selected a point in the offing and called it the 'landfall waypoint'. It is a point in clear water, which we feel can be approached safely and from which pilotage can reasonably begin. You are strongly advised to plot the waypoint and decide for yourself whether you actually wish to use it. You may well decide on another position nearby. Do not just put our chosen waypoint into your GPS and passage plan without checking it and agreeing with it.

Chart lists

We have given the numbers of paper charts covering a particular area published by Imray and the Admiralty (UKHO). We have not attempted to list electronic charts, because there are too many permutations of publisher and chart 'packages' and the list would be too long.

Coastguard stations

The Thames Estuary is covered by Yarmouth and Thames Coastguard centres, with London CG specifically responsible for the River Thames, and an overlap into Dover CG around the North Foreland to Ramsgate.

If calling the coastguard it is best to use their MMSI from a DSC VHF set, but with non-DSC sets they can all be contacted via Ch 16 using their name as the call sign, e.g. *Thames Coastguard*.

With the exception of London, which does not make MSI broadcasts, all the CG stations announce these useful broadcasts on VHF Ch 16 and give the channel on which they will be made.

Dover CG DSC MMSI 002320010 ☎ 01304 210008.
Covers area including Ramsgate to Reculver Towers. MSI announcements on Ch 16 at 0105, 0505, 0905, 1305, 1705, 2105 UT.

London CG DSC MMSI 002320063 ☎ 0208 312 7380.
Covers area from Shell Haven Point (N bank) and Egypt (S bank) to Teddington.

Thames CG DSC MMSI 002320009 ☎ 01255 675518.
Covers area from Reculver Towers to Southwold. MSI announcements on Ch 16 at 0010, 0410, 0810, 1210, 1610, 2010 UT.

Yarmouth CG DSC MMSI 002320008 ☎ 01493 851338.
Covers area from Southwold northwards. MSI announcements on Ch 16 at 0040, 0440, 0840, 1240, 1640, 2040 UT.

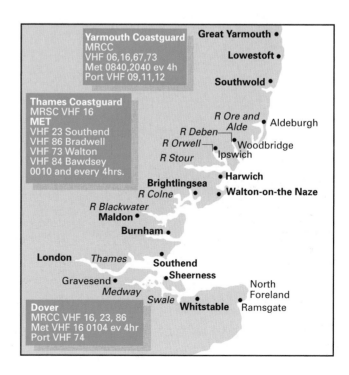

Danger – pot markers

There are more pot markers and fishing floats in the Thames Estuary than ever and they are, generally, very poorly marked or not marked at all. There is even an area between The Naze and Harwich where there is a printed warning on Imray charts.

Although some fishermen do mark their gear carefully, with decent flags on upright poles, it generally requires a very sharp lookout to spot small floats or empty drinks containers, which may be half submerged in a strong tide. At night it is all but impossible to see them until it's too late.

All of this makes motoring or motorsailing a time for extreme caution, especially at night. Indeed such is the problem that it may sometimes be wise to take a longer route or remain further offshore so as to be sure of going round infested areas.

Medical help

For emergency medical help make a VHF call to the Coastguard when at sea or call 999 by phone when in harbour.

For non-emergency help and advice, when in harbour, call the NHS Direct helpline ☎ 0845 4647, available 24hr. For more information about NHS Direct visit www.nhsdirect.nhs.uk

Riding lights

The International Regulations for Preventing Collisions at Sea, 1972 (COLREGs), require vessels of more than 7m length to display a black ball during the day and an all round white light at night when riding to an anchor.

In these days of crowded anchorages and heavy traffic, our advice would be for ALL vessels to display these signals, particularly at night.

Macwester *Calizmar* beating in from the Spitway towards the Colne on a day of sunshine and showers. A sharp lookout in these waters is essential at all times

Pot markers may be good, bad or non-existent, but there are lots of them to be avoided

Windfarms – a feature of the future

The Thames Estuary is the most crowded sailing area in the UK after the Solent. Its rivers, creeks, channels, guts and swatchways have a charm and character that make them unique, but the commercial traffic using the Thames is so continuously heavy that the Port of London Authority (PLA) is the largest port authority in the country.

The Estuary is going to be even more crowded with the development of the Scroby Sands, Gunfleet, Kentish Flats, Thanet Array, Greater Gabbard (Inner Gabbard and Galloper) and the mighty London Array wind farms.

While the Scroby, Greater Gabbard, Gunfleet and Thanet farms are likely to have only limited impact on navigation, the London Array, consisting of up to 300 tower-mounted generators with a total power output of 1,000MW, will have a huge effect. Under current plans it will straddle the Long Sand and Knock Sands and the Knock Deep, which will shut off virtually the entire central area of the Thames approaches from the East and North. Meanwhile, to the South, the Kentish Flats farm lies on or close to some of the most popular sailing routes across the North Kent coastal margin.

Effects

The PLA has said that present yacht routes through the sands keep small craft out of the way of big commercial ships and argues they shouldn't be interfered with. They also point out that, in some cases, the proposed developments would add time to commercial shipping trips, which would add to costs.

The Royal Yachting Association (RYA) and Cruising Association (CA) produced a chart-based diagram showing the widely used yachting routes (published in a document called *Sharing the Wind*), together with their requirements for safe navigation in and around all offshore wind farms. They pointed out, for example, that the SE boundary of the London Array skirts Fisherman's Gat, where yachtsmen are encouraged to navigate just outside the main channel used by commercial traffic, but that the proximity of the array wouldn't leave yachts room to tack.

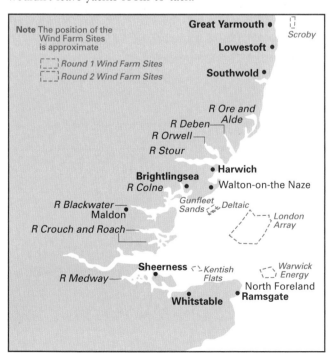

Note The position of the Wind Farm Sites is approximate

▢ Round 1 Wind Farm Sites
▢ Round 2 Wind Farm Sites

With this problem in mind and to avoid possible commercial traffic congestion in Fisherman's Gat and the Black Deep, the PLA is seeking to have a large section of the SW corner of this development moved to make room for yachts to use Fisherman's Gat clear of the marked commercial channel.

It was only in 2003 that Trinity House buoyed Foulger's Gat and encouraged recreational sailors to use this route through the Long Sand rather than mixing it with the commercial big boys in Fisherman's Gat. The original London Array plans showed Foulger's Gat completely obliterated by the wind farm, but the RYA negotiated with the developer and a 1km wide passageway through the array will be provided to let yachts continue using the buoyed Foulger's Gat.

Facts and fears

The effect of wind farms on navigation instruments and aids is a concern to many and trials at the first wind farm constructed at North Hoyle off the North Wales coast have produced mixed results. They have shown that wind farm structures interfere with even high definition radars, but the same trials showed that VHF radio communications, GPS systems and even mobile phones are not affected.

Fears have also been expressed that the cables, carrying the wind-generated electricity from the central collecting sub-station in each wind farm to the shore-side connection point to the National Grid, won't be buried deep enough in the seabed and could be dredged up by vessels fishing or anchoring. With the strength of tidal flows through the Thames Estuary, sand banks not only move, but the beds of the channels are also changed frequently by scouring.

There are concerns too that the large electrical currents involved might affect magnetic compasses. The PLA has raised this with the Maritime and Coastguard Agency (MCA) on behalf of commercial navigators.

Considerable concern has also been expressed about the risks these farms could present to yachts navigating at night and in bad weather. The towers are painted yellow up to 12m above sea level and the corner towers, plus those at some key points down the sides of the farm, will have yellow flashing lights, also at 12m. There is, however, doubt that, at this height, these lights will be visible to crews of recreational craft navigating in fog. The farms will have fog sound signals.

It has been generally agreed that the rotor tip clearance will be 22m above MHWS and at this height 96 per cent of yachts will, if forced into the arrays, get underneath without being struck by a rotor. Unfortunately, on the Gunfleet, just off Clacton, the clearance will be only 20m, bringing the percentage of yachts able to go through without being struck by the rotor tips down to 88 per cent.

Looking ahead

The Government has dictated that after the first round of wind farm building (which includes the Gunfleet, Scroby Sands and the Kentish Flats), no wind farm development will take place inside an 8km band round the coast. This is referred to as the 'Wind Farm Exclusion Zone' and should not be confused with proposals to put exclusion zones round each wind farm. This latter proposal is strongly opposed as making no useful contribution to small craft safety and it is hoped that it will sensibly be dropped.

Building the Kentish Flats windfarm. Such work will become increasingly familiar to East Coast sailors

Statistically, there are 92 clubs, 14 marinas and 73 RYA training centres that have regular access to the Thames Estuary. It's estimated that there are 22,500 moorings and around 6,900 marina berths, and the RYA estimates the number of its members with access to the area to be around 55,000. Cruising Association records show that approximately 30 per cent of its national UK membership is based within 40 miles of the area. These figures boil down to the fact that a huge number of people and boats use the Thames Estuary and will, therefore, be affected by future developments.

Refuges and passages

The whole estuary is subject to strong tidal streams, the vagaries of wind strength and direction, and is well known for being rough in wind-against-tide conditions. There are also a number of uncomfortable overfalls.

So what ports of refuge are there in stress of weather and how will passages across the Estuary be affected by the wind farms?

To the South, the nearest all-weather havens are Ramsgate, Dover and Calais. Within the northern part of the area safe haven can be found in Harwich Harbour, via Goldmer Gat and the Medusa Channel from the south, or from the east and north by entering from north of the Cork Sand alongside the deep water commercial shipping channel.

The Ore and Deben could possibly provide refuge, however entry to these two rivers is difficult and not to be attempted in heavy weather or on-shore winds above Force 4. Further north there is no reliable refuge nearer than Lowestoft or, at a pinch, Yarmouth, neither of which can be counted as an all-weather refuge. They should not be considered in NE to E by SE winds of much over Force 4.

Yachts on passage right across the Estuary will generally try to follow a straight line outside all the sandbanks between Orfordness and a position either inshore at North Foreland or outside the Goodwin Sands, or the Sandettie

area. Many will use the Kentish Knock and Long Sand Head light buoys as waypoints.

The Knock Deep passage inside the Kentish Knock is regarded as a potentially useful area for shelter in strong weather from certain directions, but the current proposals for the London Array would straddle the Knock Deep, prohibiting its use.

Yachts heading for the Swale, Medway or Thames areas from the S largely use the inshore passage round North Foreland, then W along the 'Overland Route' through the Gore and Horse Channels and the Four Fathoms Channel, passing to the S of the Kentish Flats wind farm. However, in some circumstances they might have preferred the deeper water of the Queen's Channel before heading across the Kentish Flats towards the Spaniard. The wind farm means that these will now have to divert further N and use the

Past and present: boats of all ages happily share East Coast waters

Princes Channel towards the Medway and Thames, or at least pass around the N side of the wind farm before turning SW for the Swale.

The Princes route means mixing with major shipping, which has the potential to be hazardous for both recreational craft and commercial vessels. The Horse Channel Overland route requires accurate timing over the shallows close to the Kent coast. Use of all these routes will also be restricted by tidal flow.

Yachts from the East have to cross the Traffic Separation Scheme (TSS) that extends across the whole mouth of the Thames Estuary. The tracks of these yachts will change as they keep clear of commercial shipping and avoid the Gabbard and Galloper banks or head for the Falls Gap when conditions make the North and South Falls areas inadvisable.

Yachts entering the strategic area at North Foreland and heading north to the Deben and Crouch, as well as yachts entering from the North and heading for the Swale or Medway, all cross the wind farm areas.

Nine major rivers flow directly into the Thames Estuary and, during a normal summer sailing season, there is constant yacht traffic between every combination of origin and destination - some 110 combinations in total, although no one really knows how many boats are out at a given time and using which route. In addition to the passage routes there is a large amount of day sailing within the Thames Estuary, some of which covers sea areas where there are or will be wind farms. One way or another, many thousands of people will be affected by these developments.

Wings at sunset – a gull flies ahead of the rain

Pyefleet at night

Tidal streams

The figures against the arrows denote mean rates in tenths of a knot at neaps and springs. Thus 06.11 indicates a mean neap rate of 0·6 knots and a mean spring rate of 1·1 knots.

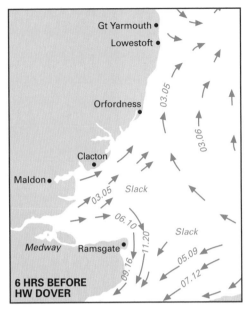

6 HRS BEFORE HW DOVER

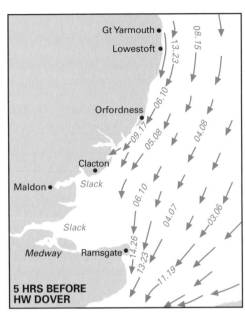

5 HRS BEFORE HW DOVER

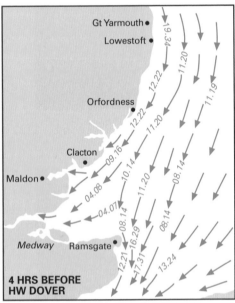

4 HRS BEFORE HW DOVER

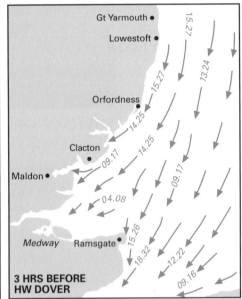

3 HRS BEFORE HW DOVER

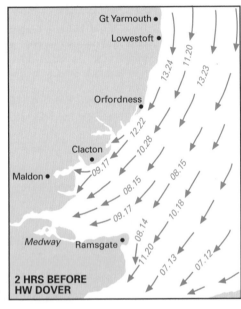

2 HRS BEFORE HW DOVER

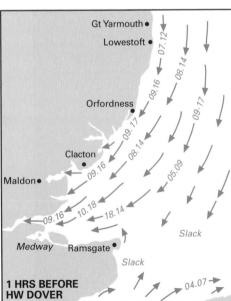

1 HRS BEFORE HW DOVER

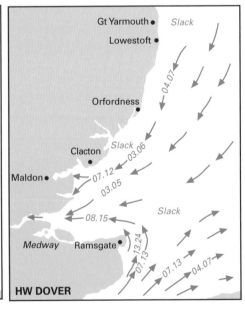

HW DOVER

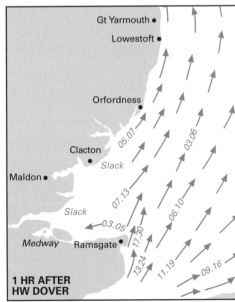

1 HR AFTER HW DOVER

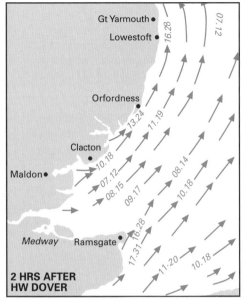

2 HRS AFTER HW DOVER

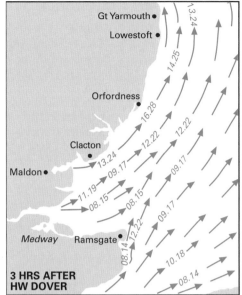

3 HRS AFTER HW DOVER

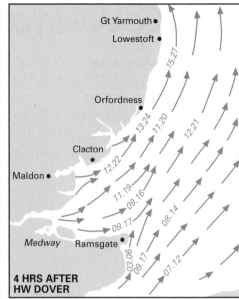

4 HRS AFTER HW DOVER

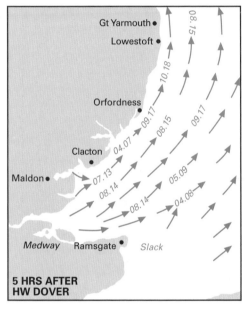

5 HRS AFTER HW DOVER

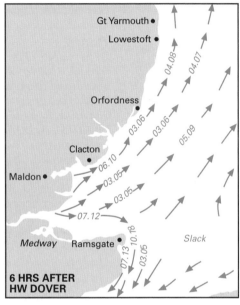

6 HRS AFTER HW DOVER

1. Lowestoft

⊕ **Landfall waypoint**
52°28'.26N 001°46'.00E
(⅓M E of entrance)

Charts
Imray *C28, 2000* series
Admiralty *1536, 1543*

Tides
HW Dover –0133

Harbourmaster
Lowestoft Port Control
VHF Ch 14
Call sign *Lowestoft Port*

Harbourmaster
☎ 01502 572286

Port Control Lights
Three vertical reds –
Do not enter

Green, white, green vertical –
Clear to enter (or depart)

Before entering or leaving,
permission must be requested
on Ch 14

Main hazards

Shifting sand banks make it imperative to stay in the marked channels. With wind against tide heavy seas can build off the entrance, which is quite narrow and marked by two lighthouses on the pier ends.

Unless urgent, do not attempt an entrance during strong E or NE winds, especially on a foul tide when the wind is hard against the flow. It gets rough in anything over F4 especially with wind against the tide, which sets strongly across the entrance.

Landmarks

The entrance to Lowestoft is marked by two pagoda-shaped lighthouses on the pier ends. To N are factory-type buildings and at times it is possible to see huge turbine blades in for repair from a wind farm, jutting up against the skyline. Most of the town is low-lying, but a good reference point is the top of the grain silos S of, and behind, the harbour.

Approaches

From E

Make for the East Newcome PHB (Fl(2)R.5s). Although this buoy lies E of the entrance to Lowestoft, a direct course in is blocked by the shallow ground of the tail of the Holm Sand.

From the E Newcome head S to round South Holm SCB (VQ(6)+LFl.10s) before turning NW. Follow Stanford Channel towards the harbour, passing between Stanford PHB (Fl(2)R.2.5s) and SW Holm SHB (Fl(2)G.5s). On reaching the Newcome PHB (Fl(4)R.15s) turn due W towards the entrance piers with their twin white pagoda lighthouses.

From S

Pick up the East Barnard ECB (Q(3)10s) on the 10m contour marking the edge of the Newcome Sand. To the N lies the Newcome Sand PHB (Q.R), which marks the N extremity of the sands and is the S gate to the Stanford Channel.

Follow the Stanford Channel, passing between Stanford PHB (Fl(2)R.2.5s) and SW Holm SHB (Fl(2)G.5s). On reaching the Newcome PHB (Fl(4)R.15s) turn due W towards the entrance piers with their twin lighthouses.

From N

Keep within sight of the shore in the buoyed channel through Corton Roads and inside the Holm Sand until abreast the entrance piers.

Watch out for a pair of cardinal buoys about ½M off the end of Lowestoft Ness - ECB (VQ(3)5s Bell) and SCB (Q(6)+LFl.15s Bell). On the chart they mark an obstruction, so do not try to pass between them, as they guard shallow, foul ground. In fact, the whole seabed around the area is littered with wrecks, sewer outlets and submarine cables.

Against wind and tide, make the final approach to the piers from S, keeping the South Pier almost in line with the North one. Watch out for an eddy in the entrance.

The South Pier shows a set of international port control lights: G over W over G meaning clear to enter; 3 vert R meaning do not enter. Both pierheads are lit: the North Pier (Oc.G.5s), the South Pier (Oc.R.5s).

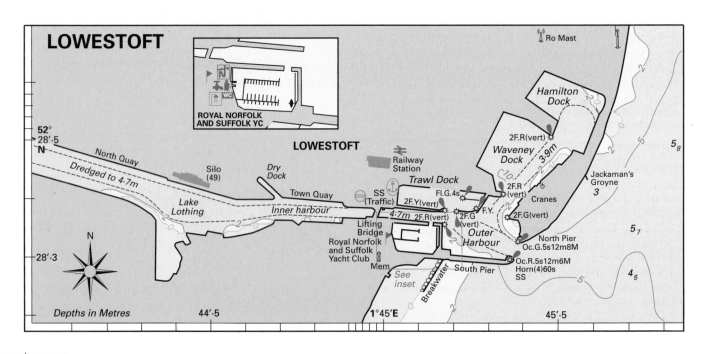

Traffic lights   S pier   N pier

Approaching Lowestoft from the North, close inshore. Entrance lighthouses stand up to left of tall light standards

Traffic lights

Lowestoft entrance. The three vertical reds on the post on the port or South pier forbid entry

RN & SYC Marina   Trawl Dock   Waveney Dock

Grain silo

Once inside, Lowestoft's outer harbour opens out. The tall granary building to the left of centre is a good landmark. Keep just to the right of it as you come in

Entry

The entrance is narrow (maximum commercial ship beam is 22m) and canted at an angle so that vessels leaving or entering cannot see each other. This makes it essential to call Harbour Control on Ch 14 or ☎ 01502 572286 for permission to enter. The narrowness and the angle of the entrance prevent very heavy S swells driving in, but it's open to NE winds and seas.

Strictly observe the Narrow Channels Rule 9(b) of Col Regs. There is a minimum of 4.3m of water, although 6m is more generally found.

Once inside, the harbour opens out into a series of basins.

Lowestoft lighthouse N

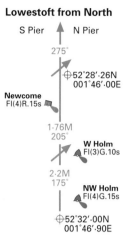

Lowestoft from North

S Pier   N Pier

275°

⊕52°28'·26N
001°46'·00E

Newcome
Fl(4)R.15s

1·76M
205°

W Holm
Fl(3)G.10s

2·2M
175°

NW Holm
Fl(4)G.15s

⊕52°32'·00N
001°46'·90E

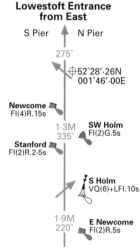

Lowestoft Entrance
from East

S Pier   N Pier

275°

⊕52°28'·26N
001°46'·00E

Newcome
Fl(4)R.15s

1·3M
335°

SW Holm
Fl(2)G.5s

Stanford
Fl(2)R.2·5s

S Holm
VQ(6)+LFl.10s

1·9M
220°

E Newcome
Fl(2)R.5s

⊕52°28'·64N
001°49'·20E

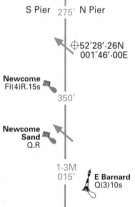

Lowestoft from South

S Pier   275°   N Pier

⊕52°28'·26N
001°46'·00E

Newcome
Fl(4)R.15s

350°

Newcome
Sand
Q.R

1·3M
015°

E Barnard
Q(3)10s

⊕52°25'·00N
001°46'·56E

Lowestoft harbour from the E. Note narrow entrance. RN&SYC marina is first enclosed dock to port. Waiting pontoon for bridge opening is in bottom left of Trawl Dock the enclosed dock opposite RN&SYC

Lowestoft harbour from SW. Note wind turbine at N end of industrial sector is a new landmark

LOWESTOFT HARBOUR

The harbour entrance widens into the main or outer harbour, from which a number of lesser basins branch off.

There is a shallow area in the SW corner of the outer harbour. Off to starboard are the Waveney and Hamilton Docks, both having charted drying areas on the E or NE sides. Up river to starboard is the etrance to the Trawl Dock where oil rig and wind farm support vessels moor. Opposite that dock, to port, is the yacht basin at the head of which stands the Royal Norfolk and Suffolk YC (RN&SYC).

The RN&SYC marina has visitors' berths on the N side of the first pontoon and on the W of the cross pontoon in front of the clubhouse. Call the yacht harbourmaster on Ch 80 for directions before entering. Yachts over 12m LOA should moor against the large bumper tubes against the outer wall and guard against warps chafing on the rough stone quay.

Just up river from the yacht harbour is the Haven Road Bridge. Passage through is free, but opening times are strictly observed (see page 12). Vessels waiting to go up river may get permission to wait in the Trawl Dock if they can't get into the yacht basin. Do not approach the bridge unless the green light on the N wall is showing.

Beyond the road bridge is the Inner Harbour, which swells out into Lake Lothing. The channel is buoyed and dredged to 4.7m up to a point abreast the Lowestoft Cruising Club pontoons on the starboard hand. It shelves to 1.8m from there to the Carlton Road railway swing bridge.

Opposite the Lowestoft CC is the Lowestoft Haven Marina. Although the general environment is that of an industrial area, visitors are welcome at all three of Lowestoft's yacht basins, which are in the forefront of the redevelopment of Lowestoft into a major yachting centre.

ROYAL NORFOLK & SUFFOLK YC

Contact
VHF Ch 80
Call sign *Royal Norfolk Harbourmaster*
Contact ☎ 01502 566726 (0730–1930)
Email rnsyc@ctc-net.co.uk
www.rnsyc.org.uk

Facilities WC. Showers. Launderette

Fuel Diesel from berth at head of marina alongside the slip and under marina office

Electricity On pontoons

Water On pontoons. Launching slip (trailers). Launching crane (2.5 ton). Pump out, berth near slipway

Provisions Shops nearby. Pubs/restaurants nearby and in town

Chandlery nearby

Taxi ☎ 01502 511615, 565656.

Entrance to RN & SYC Marina with the club in the background to the right

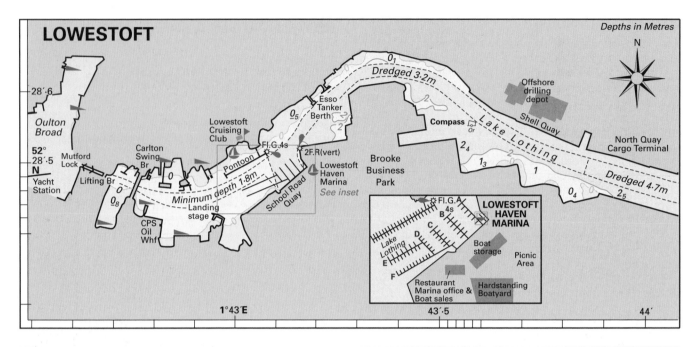

Lowestoft harbour bridge

LOWESTOFT HARBOUR BRIDGE

The Lowestoft Harbour Bridge, between the outer and inner harbours, is only opened on demand to commercial shipping. And then not between 0815 and 0900, 1230 and 1300, 1700 and 1730 to allow commuter traffic unimpeded access.

Small craft may pass through at the time of opening for commercial shipping, so long as Port Control has agreed beforehand. If yachts give at least 20 minutes' notice of passage, the bridge can be opened for them at 0700, 0930, 1100, 1600, 1900 and 2100 on weekdays and 0745, 0930, 1100, 1400, 1730, 1900 and 2100 at weekends and Bank Holidays.

Call Port Control on Ch 14.

Approaching the bridge from the E there are traffic lights on the N quay.

There is a pontoon in the SE corner of the Trawl Dock (opposite RN&SYC) to use while waiting for the bridge.

Looking S across Lake Lothing, with Lowestoft Haven Marina on S side. Long pontoon on N side is Lowestoft CC

Mutford Lock

Lowestoft is one of the gateways to the Broads. To make the final transition from Lake Lothing into Oulton Broad itself, boats have to go through (in order from the E) Carlton Railway Bridge, Mutford Road Bridge and Mutford Lock.

It is advisable to book transits in advance with the lock master. VHF Ch 9, 14. ☎ 01502 531778 or 01502 523003. The lock is operated by the Broads Authority and is 22m long and 6.5m wide with a minimum 2m depth (plus state of tide).

The bridges and lock open on request during the following hours: Daily April-October 0800–1130, 1330–1630; Sat, Sun and Bank Holidays, May–September 0800–1130, 1430–1930. The lock is crowded at weekends and bank holidays.

LOWESTOFT CRUISING CLUB

Contact
  ☎ 01502 574376
Facilities WC. Showers
Water At each berth
Electricity At each berth
Berths To book phone John Cooper, LCC moorings office
  ☎ 01502 511156 Mobile 07810 144362
  Email MooringsOfficer@LowestoftCruisingClub.co.uk
Provisions 15 mins' walk.

LOWESTOFT HAVEN MARINA

Contact
  VHF Ch 80
  Call sign *Lowestoft Haven Marina*
  Contact ☎ 01502 580300 (0730–1930)
Facilities WC. Showers. Launderette. Still under development at time of writing.

Lowestoft Ness from the south. Port radio mast to left of block of flats. Crane is part of support complex for Scroby Sands wind farm

2. Southwold

⊕ **Landfall waypoint**
52°18′.75N 001°40′.7 E (About ½M E of entrance)

Charts
Imray *C28*
Admiralty *2695*

Tides
HW Dover –0105

SOUTHWOLD HARBOUR

Contact
VHF Ch 12 or 09 (0900–1700)
Call sign *Southwold Port Radio*
Out of hours call Great Yarmouth Coastguard on Ch 67
Harbourmaster ☎ 01502 724712 (0900–1700)

Access 24hr depending on tide, draught and weather

Facilities WC. Showers. (Both at caravan site, accessed with mooring receipt.)

Electricity Connection points on staging. £2 a night to HM

Water Tap at each end of staging, use cans or own hose

Gas Calor and Gaz at chandler next to boatyard at seaward end of foreshore

Repairs 30-ton travel-hoists and large slip

Fuel Arrange with boatyard

Phone At pub. Emergency phone at RNLI centre

Provisions Some from café. Shops 1M in town

Pub/restaurant The Harbour Inn ☎ 01502 722381 and town

Taxi ☎ 01502 722111.

Main hazards

There are shifting sand banks close to and within the entrance. With wind against tide heavy seas can build up off the entrance and the depth over the bar can alter drastically after E gales.

Do not attempt an entrance during strong E or NE winds, especially against the tide.

Strong tides run athwart the entrance and in some conditions a 'bore' wave runs in between the piers.

The visitors' berths are alongside staging opposite the Harbour Inn pub. There are 16 berths, but boats form rafts up to four deep. Shore lines are obligatory to cope with the 6kn ebb tide. Because departure should always be on the flood, the suggestion is to moor with the boat facing down the harbour so that she can be eased out into the stream and motored away cleanly.

There's usually around 2m of water at low tide and the bottom is hard and steeply shelving. There are ladders on the staging and the harbour authority thoughtfully supplies fender boards to straddle the piles. Remember to leave them behind on departure.

Take care turning round. There are stagings on both sides of the river and full power plus propeller kick will be needed to turn tightly in the narrow space. A local trick is to shove the stem into the muddy bank opposite and let the tide swing the boat round.

Above the moorings is a low bridge taking the road from Southwold across to the village of Walberswick. Be careful because boats have been known to end up against the bridge, carried there by the fierce tide.

Approaching Southwold from the south, the first landmark is the white lighthouse on the low cliff on which the town stands, centre is the larger of the two churches and far left is water tower at the edge of the marshes. The end of the north pier is just to the left of the centre church and the south pier to the right of the smaller church.

The entrance to Southwold and the river Blyth. The post on the end of the north pier is the traffic light. Watch out for strong cross currents sweeping across the mouth of the entrance

Southwold from the southeast showing recommended track

Labels on photograph: Visitors' berths · The Knuckle · N Pier traffic lights · South Pier

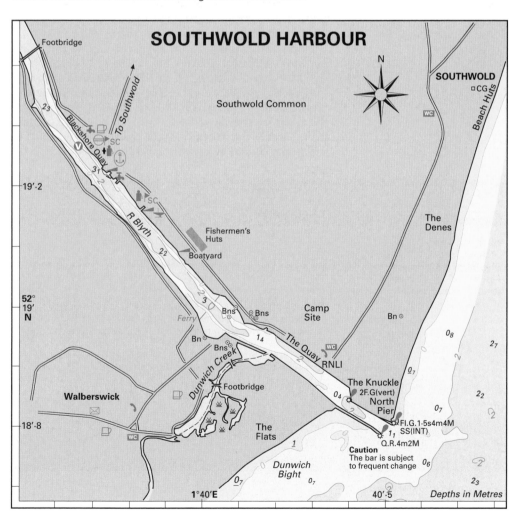

SOUTHWOLD HARBOUR

Footbridge

To Southwold

Blackshore Quay

SC

SC

R Blyth

Fishermen's Huts

Boatyard

Ferry

Bns · Bns

Bn

Bns

Dunwich Creek

Footbridge

Walberswick

The Quay

RNLI

Camp Site

Bn

The Knuckle
2F.G(vert)
North Pier

Fl.G.1·5s4m4M
SS(INT)

Q.R.4m2M

Caution
The bar is subject to frequent change

The Flats

Dunwich Bight

1°40'E

Southwold Common

N

SOUTHWOLD

□CG

WC

Beach Huts

The Denes

Bn

WC

WC

23
31
22
3
14
04
2
1

08
07
07
06
07
1
27
22
2
23

40'·5

Depths in Metres

19'·2

52°
19'
N

18'·8

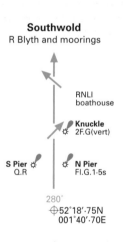

Southwold
R Blyth and moorings

RNLI boathouse

Knuckle
2F.G(vert)

S Pier
Q.R

N Pier
Fl.G.1·5s

280°

⊕52°18'·75N
001°40'·70E

Southwold harbour looking inland up the River Blyth

Landmarks

The town of Southwold lies 1M N of the harbour entrance, which forms the entrance to the River Blyth. It is prominently marked by a white lighthouse (Fl(4)WR.20s37m16/12M) perched on top of the low cliff and surrounded by the bulk of the town. Also prominent is a Norman-style church built by wealthy local wool merchants. The seafront is marked by rows of highly coloured beach huts and further inland, at the back of the marshes, is a large concrete water tower.

Approach

From any seaward direction there is clear and deep water to within a short distance of the entrance. Along the coast in both directions the depth runs from 5m close in to 10m or more ½M out. There are no off-lying marks or buoys, so aim for an offing waypoint at 52°18´.75N 001°40´.7E. This is approximately ½M E of the entrance piers.

Entry

Entry signals

Three vertical F.R lights mounted on a pole at the end of the N Pier indicate 'Harbour Closed'. If displayed, contact Southwold Harbourmaster or, if outside listening hours, contact Yarmouth Coastguard for advice. Two red flags flown from the same pole dictate closure in daylight. Three vertical greens or no flags means it's clear to enter

Entrance is best attempted at HW±30min or, if there is sufficient depth, near LW when the coastal stream is slackest. Recommended timing would be on the second half of the flood.

Visiting vessels should contact the harbourmaster for entry and berthing instructions before approaching the entrance and before leaving their berth on departure.

North Pier is marked with a light (Fl.G.1.5s) and South Pier with a Q.R. Do not stray into the bay to N of the North Pier, the water is shallow and the sand bank keeps moving.

Approach parallel to the S pier. The entrance is narrow, 36m, and the stream runs hard both ways – 3-4kn on flood and 5-6kn on ebb. In addition, the main tide flows at right angles across the entrance, both rising (southward) and falling (northward) at anywhere between 2.5 and 4kn.

Southwold entrance – The Knuckle. Turn hard to starboard towards the RNLI building to find the safe water

Southwold. View to seaward

Keep straight down the middle between the piers as far as the Knuckle (2F.G(vert)), at the landward end of the N Pier, which is marked with a 4kn speed limit sign mounted on a post, which is in turn mounted on an iron frame jutting out into the entrance.

Just past this turn hard to starboard and aim to be close alongside the concrete retaining wall on the starboard side of the river just before the RNLI shed and RIB launching crane. Follow this wall almost to its end then head back into the middle of the river. Hugging the wall avoids sand and shingle building up on the S side of the entrance, but take care to maintain steerage way above the tidal flow, otherwise eddies can swing the boat and push her against the wall. Usually there's at least 2m of water along the wall.

At the far end of the wall is a sand spit jutting out to catch the unwary.

Approaching Orfordness Lighthouse from the north

Sizewell Power Station is a prominent landmark on a flat coastline

3. Rivers Ore & Alde

⊕ **Landfall waypoint**
52°01′.60N 001°28′.20E
(S of Orford Haven SWB)

Charts
Imray *2000 series, C28*
Admiralty SC *5607, 2052, 2695*

Tides
Orford Haven Dover +0010
Orford Quay Dover +0100
Slaughden Dover +0155
Snape Dover +0225

Main hazards

The entrance to the Ore and Alde is subject to frequent changes, especially following E gales. Latest information is available on chartlets published by Small Craft Deliveries ☎ 01394 382600, by visiting the Woodbridge CC website www.woodbridgecruisingclub.co.uk or the specialist site for the Ore and the Deben at www.debenentrance.com

The Orford Haven SWB (LFl.10s Bell) was at 52°01′.62N 001°28′.00E in the second half of the 2004 season, but may have been moved since if there have been major changes to the banks. It is essential to obtain current information before approaching the entrance.

The inner marks, Oxley and Weir are removed in late Autumn and replaced in early Spring.

Ideal time to enter the Ore is about HW-2hr.

Streams in the river can run strongly.

Entry should not be attempted in strong SE or E winds when seas can break heavily.

Landmarks

Orfordness Lighthouse is prominently conspicuous, especially from N, while the bluff of Bawdsey cliff, topped with a lattice radar tower, stands out to the S.

Approaching the landfall waypoint, the Shingle Street bay opens up with a Martello Tower on the left and a series of low buildings with the CG radio mast prominent on the right.

Entry

From both N and S

There's clear and deep water to within a short distance of the entrance. Along the coast in both directions the depth runs from 5m close in to 10m or more only ½M offshore.

Crossing Hollesley Bay, N of the entrance, keep in at least 7m of water. At night follow the border of the G and the W

Entrance to river Ore from the SE. Main channel is S of the shoals and close in under the W bank

Looking north across Hollesley Bay, Orfordness lighthouse stands out against the threatening skies

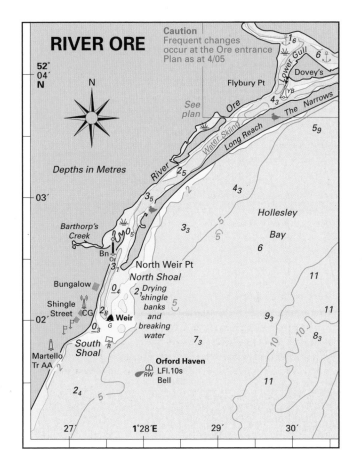

sectors of Orfordness Light (Fl.5s20M & F.WRG.17-12M). Outside this area (in the R sector) lies the Whiting Bank, which is buoyed.

Pick up the unlit Orford Haven SWB and make for the CG Mast to the left of the bungalow on the shore to find the best water through the entrance channel. The actual course will depend on the current position of the offing buoy, but aim directly for the Oxley PHB and then to port of the Weir SHB.

Hug the port hand bank going in until well past the bar, before taking a centre of the river course.

With wind against tide heavy seas build up off the entrance and the depth over the bar can alter drastically after SE gales. Obtain the latest available information about the entrance before attempting it and avoid it entirely in strong onshore winds.

ORE ENTRANCE

The entrance to the River Ore is subject to major changes, especially after SE winds. The buoys may be moved several times during a season and it is essential to obtain the latest information before entering.

For chartlet:
  www.debenentrance.com
  Small Craft Deliveries ☎ 01394 382600
  Local chandlers

For last minute information and immediate aid:
  VHF Ch 08 callsign *Chantry*
  Orford Port Trust ☎01354 45950

The Orford Haven offing buoy with, in the middle background, the Oxley (red) buoy with Shingle Street behind. The bar itself is midway between the second red buoy and the shoreline

Shingle Street hamlet identifies the Ore entrance

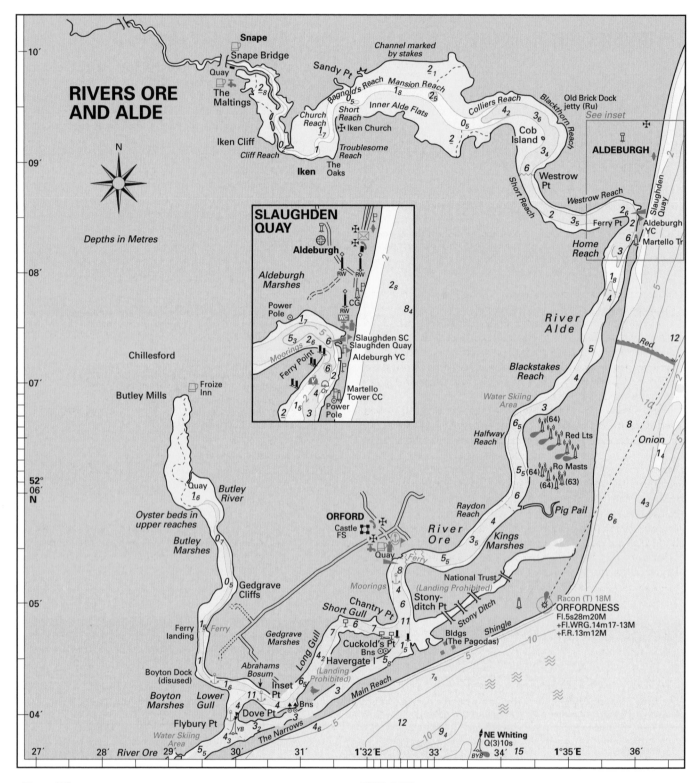

Two Rivers

Although one long river, navigable from the entrance right up to Snape Bridge alongside the famous Snape Maltings concert hall, it's a waterway with two names. From the entrance to about 1M up from the village and quay at Orford it's the Ore; from this point in Halfway Reach up to Snape it's the Alde.

THE ORE

For much of its length, the Ore divides around Havergate Island, a bird sanctuary, which is home to a great variety of wading and marsh birds, including one of the of the biggest breeding colonies of Avocets in Britain. Landing is prohibited.

Having successfully negotiated the entrance to the Ore, the first major landmark is the incinerator chimney and buildings of the Hollesley Bay Prison on the W bank. There is a short drying creek called Barthorp's Creek in the W

Entering the River Ore. The line of rough water is a mid-stream sand bank. Keep well over to port and close under the shore where it's steep to

bank, which was used by barges taking produce from the prison farm to London.

The rather featureless Long Reach is a straight stretch of water running NE inside Orford Ness and is a favourite area for water skiing. At the top end of the reach is a SCB marking the end of Havergate Island. Leaving the buoy to starboard leads into the Lower Gull where there is a good anchorage under the port bank.

The Butley River branches off N just beyond the Lower Gull anchorage, but there's a sand spit jutting out from the W bank and the entrance to the creek is well over against the N shore. The channel is marked with withies and there are oyster beds in the top half of the creek, above the ferry landings, but there's a good anchorage in a bit over 2m of water at LW in the lower reaches of the creek below the disused Boyton Dock.

Past the Butley River entrance, the river runs through Long Gull and Short Gull before joining once more with the other part that flows E of Havergate Island through Main Reach. This reach is virtually a straight cut through the marshes and forms a shorter route to Orford.

ORFORD

Contacts
Harbourmaster ☎ 01394 450481.
Orford Port Trust VHF Ch 08, call sign *Chantry*
☎ 01394 459950.
Quay Warden ☎ 01394 450713

Water From a standpipe at the back of the quay.

Fuel In cans from Friend's Garage 1½ miles on road out of village

Provisions In village

Pubs/restaurant Jolly Sailor near Quay ☎ 01394 450243
Crown and Castle in Market Hill ☎ 01394 450205
King's Head on Front Street ☎ 01394 450205
Butley Orford Oysterage in Market Hill ☎ 01394 450277

Post office On Market Hill

Crane On quay, contact HM

Scrubbing posts Near quay

Telephone Pay phone in car park at back of Orford SC

ORFORD

Approaching Orford from S, the Norman Keep (commonly called Orford Castle) stands out to the left of the village, in the centre of which stands the church on the crown of the hill.

Approaching Orford from downriver. Quay in centre and Orford SC the white building to right of blue boat

The main channel is clearly marked by two lines of moorings each side of the river. There are two moorings laid for visitors, each with a topmark showing a 'V'. To find a vacant mooring is difficult and if you do pick one up, don't leave the boat unattended.

Don't anchor within the area of the moorings, the bottom is foul. It's best to anchor above or below the main areas of moorings and go ashore by dinghy, but be careful of the swiftly flowing tide. You can stay for a short time alongside the quay for an hour or so either side of HW. A ferry runs from the quay across to the landing stage on the Ness and other river boat trips also use the quay.

Continuing up river from Orford, the next prominent feature is the nest of large BBC World Service radio transmitter masts to starboard. The marshes surrounding them are owned by the National Trust and landing is strictly forbidden. It is here that the Ore becomes the Alde.

THE ALDE

Under its new name, the Alde continues in a winding, but generally N direction up to Slaughden Quay, which is on the outside of a hairpin bend inland. The first prominent landmark is a Martello Tower on the starboard side where

SLAUGHDEN QUAY (ALDEBURGH)

Contact
Harbourmaster VHF Ch 80; ☎ 01728 452896/453047
Boatyards:
Upson's Boatyard ☎ 01728 452896
Aldeburgh Boatyard ☎ 01728 452019

Fuel From boatyards

Chandler Aldeburgh Boatyard

Rigger Aldeburgh Boatyard

Visitors' moorings Contact HM ☎ 01394 452896 or David Cable ☎ 01394 452569

Electrical engineer Upson's Boatyard

Facilities (all at Aldeburgh YC) WC. Showers. Telephone

Aldeburgh YC Bar/food. Water

Standpipe On quay and Aldeburgh YC terrace

Provisions Aldeburgh (about 1M)

Taxi ☎ 01728 833621 and 833311

Landing is possible on Orford Quay at half tide

The Norman Keep dominates Orford's skyline

the shingle bank between the river and the sea is hardly more than 50 yards wide. The tower is known as 'CC'.

Slaughden Quay

Slaughden is sited on a sharp bend in the river, which, having run NNE now swings almost due W as it heads inland.

Anchoring at Slaughden is not advisable within the areas of the moorings. However, an anchorage can be found in the bay 150 yards S of the club.

From Slaughden up to Westrow Point the river is lined on either side with moorings and, at the point itself, is crossed by an underwater power cable. Above that, the river turns NE in Island Reach and a good place to anchor can be found between Cob Island to port and the Old Brick Dock to starboard. Half a mile or so further on, the river runs W and widens out into a shallow lake with the channel marked by withies.

Boats of medium draught can anchor off Iken Church, The Oaks, and Iken Cliff in about one and half metres of water at low tide. Landing on the Iken shore is restricted and there's only a footpath along the bank to Snape. Further up in the next reach there's a long hole with a good two metres of water, but the mud flats make landing impossible.

At the top of this reach lies the world famous Snape Maltings concert hall, where it is possible to lie alongside the quay, which dries at low tide. Do not moor outside a barge or other flat-bottomed boat, because the ground here slopes and if the inner boat slides you could be pushed over.

When planning a trip up river above Cob Island, aim to begin as early on the flood as possible. By doing so, the channel can be picked out most easily and the channel markers understood. Note that these markers come and go from season to season, so once the mud is covered, there may be no marks to guide you or they may be confusing. Starting early may also make a stop at Snape for lunch and a drink possible before hurrying back down to deeper water.

Aldeburgh Church   *Aldeburgh YC*

The approach to Slaughden Quay with Aldeburgh town beyond

The Aldeburgh YC at Slaughden Quay with all tide landing pontoon

Iken church looking down river with Black Heath House in the trees

The river Alde at Snape can only be reached at high water

4. River Deben

⊕ **Landfall waypoint**
51°58´.54N 001°24´.30E
(immediately E of
Woodbridge Haven SWB)

Charts
Imray *2000 Series, C28*
Admiralty *SC 5607, 2693*

Tides
Woodbridge Haven
Dover +0025
Waldringfield
Dover +0100
Woodbridge
Dover +0105

Hazards

The Deben entrance is subject to violent changes, especially following E gales. It is essential to obtain the latest information from chartlets published by Small Craft Deliveries ☎ 01394 382600 and sold at many chandlers, or by visiting the Woodbridge Cruising Club website (www.woodbridgecruisingclub.co.uk) or the specialist site for the Deben at www.debenentrance.com.

The Woodbridge Haven SWB was at 51°58´.54N 001°24´.25E at the end of 2004, but may have been moved since if there have been major changes to the banks. It is essential to obtain current information before approaching the entrance.

The first time visitor is recommended to call up Felixstowe Ferry Harbourmaster John White for pilotage or advice on VHF Ch 08, call sign *Odd Times*, ☎ 01394 270106, mobile 07803 476621; or Deputy Harbourmaster Stephen Read on mobile 07803 476621 and Ch 08 call sign *Odd Times*. The boatyard now runs the ferry, which will act as a water taxi to and from the moorings as well (VHF Ch 08, call sign *Deben Ferry*) between its runs across the river.

The ideal time to enter is about HW–2hr. Streams in the river mouth are quite strong. Entry should not be attempted in strong SE or E winds, or at night.

DEBEN ENTRANCE
The Deben entrance changes frequently and sometimes drastically. It is essential to obtain the latest information before entering

For chartlet:
www.debenentrance.com
Small Craft Deliveries ☎ 01394 382600
Local chandlers

For last minute information and immediate aid:
VHF Ch 08 callsign *Odd Times*
Mobile ☎ 07803 476621
☎ 01394 270106

Entrance to River Deben from S. Approximate track (May 2005) shown above

Woodbridge Haven – rough water indicates ebb tide overflow across the bar

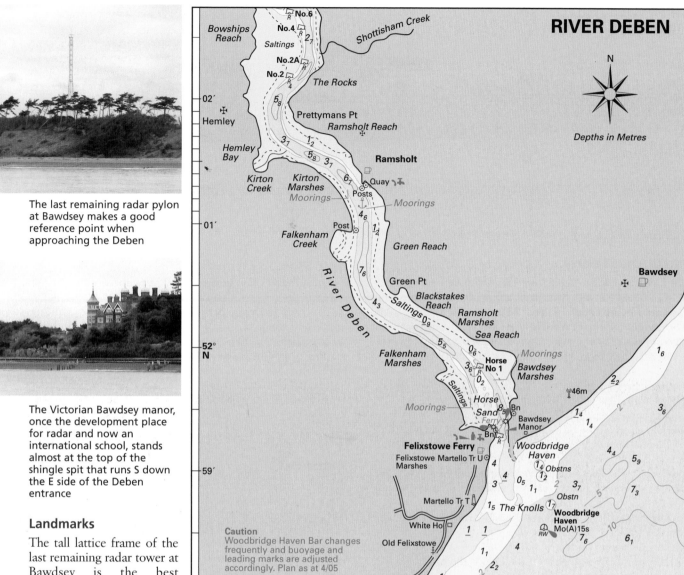

The last remaining radar pylon at Bawdsey makes a good reference point when approaching the Deben

The Victorian Bawdsey manor, once the development place for radar and now an international school, stands almost at the top of the shingle spit that runs S down the E side of the Deben entrance

Landmarks

The tall lattice frame of the last remaining radar tower at Bawdsey is the best landmark close to the entrance to what is arguably Suffolk's most beautiful river. The entrance lies between Bawdsey Manor, visible in the trees on the N bank and two Martello Towers on the S side of the river.

Entry

From the Woodbridge Haven SWB Mo(A)15s steer a line to leave the East Knolls PHB to port and aim roughly for a spot halfway between the Mid Knolls SHB and the stone flood defences on the shore. When close to the beach, make a hard turn to starboard and keep close in under the shingle bank until at least halfway to the large PHB marking a shingle bank off the Felixstowe Ferry SC.

After passing the buoy, head across to the starboard bank for the deeper water and slightly less fierce tidal stream. The relatively narrow entrance channel between the shingle banks then opens out into Felixstowe Ferry itself.

Felixstowe Ferry from the bar. Enter close along W shore

Felixstowe Ferry SC

Ferryman runs a water taxi service between crossings

FELIXSTOWE FERRY

On the left bank lies Felixstowe Ferry with Felixstowe Ferry SC prominent on the bank, just below the ferry steps and slipway to Felixstowe Ferry Boatyard. Close by is an assortment of shacks, mostly used by local fishermen for gear storage. There's also a pair of scrubbing posts on the upstream side of the slipway. There is no public access to the river, launching licenses are available either from the harbourmaster, John White ☎ 01394 270106 or mobile 07803 476621 or from the boatyard office.

The famous Ferry Café, reputed to serve some of the best fish and chips on the East Coast, stands behind the boatyard.

On the opposite bank is Bawdsey and Bawdsey Manor, which is now a school but was at one time the centre of radar research. There's a jetty and dinghy slipway. The one-time servicemen's houses along the front are now holiday homes.

Above the Ferry, just about in mid-stream, lies the Horse Sand. The deep water channel is on the E side and the shallower channel on the W side is crammed with moorings.

The stretch of water above the last of the moorings and almost as far as the next bend in the river is the only section to which a universal 8kn speed limit does not apply. It is a designated water ski and speed boat area and on the W bank is a semi-pontoon and ski ramp.

The river is clearly defined by the banks here, and any buoys are racing marks for either FFSC or the up river Waldringfield SC. This section of the river is also the least exciting as it runs between high sea defence banks through Falkenham Marsh to port and low-lying arable land to starboard.

At Green Point, where the river turns N and the view of Ramsholt opens out, the Deben reveals its true character with gently rolling slopes covered in woodland and well tended farmland.

RAMSHOLT

Ramsholt stands on the E bank and consists of an old stone barge jetty and a pub, the Ramsholt Arms ☎ 01394 411229, plus a red telephone box. There are no services there, but it's a pleasant spot to stretch the legs and 'take refreshment'. For information about moorings contact the harbourmaster, George Collins, mobile 079303 04061 (day), when he's usually to be found on his own boat, or ☎ 01394 334318 (evenings).

FELIXSTOWE FERRY

Contact
Harbourmaster VHF Ch 08
Call sign *Odd Times*
☎ 01394 270106 or mobile 07803 476621

Facilities WC behind FFSC

Water From standpipe by the telegraph post at top of slip

Fuel In cans from boatyard

Chandler Nearby (limited stock)

Provisions Some at café, otherwise shops in Felixstowe 3M

Pubs/restaurant Ferry Boat Inn ☎ 01394 284203
Victoria Inn ☎ 01394 271636
Ferry Café ☎ 01394 276305 for fish and chips and all-day breakfasts

Repairs Felixstowe Ferry Boatyard ☎ 01394 282173

Crane At head of slip, contact boatyard

Scrubbing posts close to slip. Contact boatyard

Telephone Pay phone near Ferry Boat Inn

Visitors' moorings Contact harbourmaster

Taxi ☎ 01394 277777, 275555.

Ramsholt. A good pub and public telephone box but no services

There are over 200 moorings at Ramsholt and the fairway is sometimes difficult to identify, but there is good anchorage in the middle, so long as you don't mind the wash from passing craft.

WALDRINGFIELD

Above Ramsholt, the channel swings W round Kirton marshes, where the drying Kirton Creek joins the river, before heading NE round Prettyman's Point into an area known as The Rocks, because the river bed is strewn with them, beneath Ramsholt Woods. There is a low sandy cliff forming a sheltered anchorage with a sandy beach for swimming and picnicking, but it's often crowded at weekends. There are no roads or facilities and visitors are requested not to cut down trees to make fires.

Opposite The Rocks is the first of the river buoys, which continue right up to Woodbridge.

The first four buoys are PHBs marking the edge of mudflats extending out from the W shore, pushing the channel well over to the E side of the river until it sweeps back to the W side above No.1 SHB below Waldringfield. Give Nos.4 and 6 a good berth as the mud and sand spit they mark is growing. Note that all the buoys above Felixstowe Ferry are·unlit.

WALDRINGFIELD

Boatyard Waldringfield Boatyard ☎ 01473 736260

Water From taps at boatyard quay or outside sailing club

Fuel Diesel at boatyard (HW only). Other fuels in cans from garage 1M up the Woodbridge road

Boat repairs Slipway and 40-ton crane

Scrubbing posts In front of sailing club

Chandler At boatyard

Telephone Public box near inn

Pub/restaurant The Maybush ☎ 01473 736215

Club Waldringfield SC ☎ 01473 736633

Stores None

Bus or taxi Into Woodbridge or Martlesham.

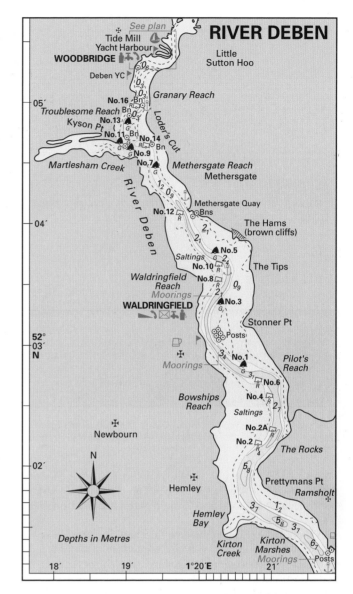

Waldringfield – looking upstream through the moorings, main channel is quite narrow

Looking N from the Woodbridge CC with the club dinghy pontoon in the foreground; the entrance to Bass's Dock (drying) just past the shelter and with the masts of yachts in the Tide Mill Harbour showing behind the Woodbridge Tide Mill

No.1 SHB marks the downstream extremity of Stonner Island where the main channel bears to port and is marked by triple lines of moorings all the way through Waldringfield itself.

Visitors' moorings are hard to find here, but there is good holding in a gap in the moorings immediately off the beach in front of Waldringfield SC. Take care, however, not to obstruct the club's start line. Anchoring in the main channel is not recommended as it is quite narrow and there is much traffic both up and downstream.

If there is not a vacant mooring, go up as far as No.3 SHB, at the top of the moorings, and anchor roughly in line with it.

There is clean landing on the beach at Waldringfield and there are some pretty walks around the area, but services are limited.

WOODBRIDGE

Above Waldringfield the river becomes increasingly attractive and wooded. It also shallows and below half tide, great care is needed not to touch. From No.3 SHB, at the N end of Stonner Island, the river runs into a bay called Ham Tips. A spit from the opposite, W, bank is marked by Nos.8 and 10 PHBs. Landing at The Tips is possible, but only for a short period either side of HW.

The river swings hard over to the other shore just above The Tips and then straightens for the run up past Methersgate on the starboard side. There's another stone jetty here originally used for loading local farm produce into barges. Landing at Methersgate Quay is discouraged.

From the Quay and No.12 PHB, almost all the way to Woodbridge, the river is clearly marked with both buoys and moorings. At No.14C PHB the river turns 90° to port in Troublesome Reach and heads W towards Kyson Point, which also marks the entrance to Martlesham Creek (drying), before swinging 90° back N again. The saltings that caused these violent changes in direction were cut through in the 1890s to accommodate barges. The cut, called Loders Cut, can be used by shallow draught craft at about HW±1hr.

There is a small local boatyard sited on the S bank of the W-running Martlesham Creek with pontoons, which dry out, and fresh water and power, but little else for visitors.

Roughly half way up Granary Reach, between No.13 SHB and No.16 PHB the river dries at LW, but deepens again as

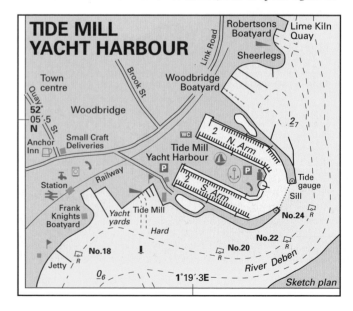

it passes the Deben YC and Eversons Boatyard. From there, through Woodbridge and right up to Wilford Bridge just above Melton, the river dries to a mere trickle at low water.

Boats unable to take the ground can find a least depth of 2m inside the Tide Mill Yacht Harbour at Woodbridge, but the cill restricts entrance and exit to HW±1½hr. Those happy to take the mud can moor at the quay at Bass's Dock, behind which can be seen the railway station, or along the front of the old Tide Mill Granary. On the end of the dock is the workshop of Frank Knights and round the corner the now derelict Whisstock's Boatyard and slipway, with the old Ferry Hard stretching right down to the middle of the river bed, and then up the other side to Sutton Hoo.

Woodbridge is an historic town and much of the surrounding countryside is well worth a visit and the Sutton Hoo burial site is just across the river opposite the quayside. There's a good shopping centre and easy access via bus, taxi or train to Ipswich.

WOODBRIDGE
TIDE MILL YACHT HARBOUR
Contact
> VHF Ch 80
> Call sign *Tide Mill Yacht Harbour*
> Contact ☎ 01394 385745
> *Email* info@tidemillyachtharbour.co.uk
> www.tidemillyachtharbour.co.uk
> Access HW±1½hr

Facilities WC. Showers
Water On pontoons
Electricity On pontoons
Telephone At railway station
Boat repairs Several boatyards, see below
Fuel Diesel on berth at entrance
Chandler Classic Marine ☎ 01394 380390
Sailmaker Suffolk Sails ☎ 01394 386323
Rigger Atlantic Rigging ☎ 01394 610 324
Electronics Suffolk Yacht Services ☎ 01394 279129
Provisions In town, 10 mins
Pubs/restaurants In town; café beside Tidemill
Taxi ☎ 01394 380034, 386661
YACHT CLUBS AT WOODBRIDGE
Deben YC ☎ 01349 386504
Facilities WC. Showers. Bar.
Woodbridge CC ☎ 01394 382028
Facilities WC. Showers. Bar
BOATYARDS AROUND WOODBRIDGE
Everson & Sons ☎ 01394 385786 Crane, slipway
Frank Knights ☎ 01394 382318 Crane, engineer
Robertsons ☎ 01394 382305
Boat repairs Slipway, crane
Facilities WC
Water On quay
Electricity On quay. Gas
Chandler On site
Granary Yacht Harbour ☎ 01394 386327
Located up river from Woodbridge at Melton
Boat repairs 36-ton boat hoist
Berthing By prior arrangement
R Larkman, Melton ☎ 01394 382943
Wintering yard with small chandler
Crane 9-ton crane for lifting boats over sea wall
Facilities Limited

Tide Mill Yacht Harbour, Woodbridge

Looking down to Woodbridge from small dock up river

Woodbridge Tide Mill with berths against quay

5. Harwich

⊕ **Landfall waypoint**
51°55′.20N 001°18′.50E (on recommended yacht track, 0.3M SW of Landguard NCB)

Charts
Imray *2000 series*
Admiralty *SC 5607, 1491, 2693*

Tides
Dover +0040

Harbourmaster
Harwich Port Control
Ch 71
Call sign *Harwich VTS*
Harbourmaster
☎ 01255 243030

Port Control
Harwich Harbour is accessible at all times, but it is imperative that small craft keep clear of the main shipping channels and berthing manoeuvres of container ships. The harbour authority maintains a 24hr radar and radio watch, Ch 71, and all yachts are requested to keep a radio watch on this channel from Landguard to Fagbury, on the River Orwell, and to the Ramsey buoys on the Stour. Call on Ch 71 only in an emergency, such as being unable to get out of the way of an announced shipping manoeuvre.
The authority also produces an excellent yachtsman's guide detailing the recommended yacht tracks (available from local marinas and chandlers or by writing to Harwich Haven Authority, Harbour House, The Quay, Harwich CO12 3HH or ☎ 01255 243030). Harbour launches also patrol the harbour.

Landmarks

Harwich Harbour is the largest container port in the UK and it is set to become even bigger and busier. The most prominent landmarks are the huge blue cranes on the Trinity Quay to starboard of the entrance.

On a clear day, from the landfall waypoint, the disused lighthouse on the Dovercourt Beach should be visible, looking rather like a pale coloured over-large dovecote on stilts at the back of the beach. The tall steeple of Harwich Town church will also be seen, together with the white roof of the Ro-Ro shed on the end of Harwich Quay. On the E side of the entrance is a beacon (SCM) on the tip of Landguard with, just inland, the lower fortifications of Landguard Fort, and then one of the several radar towers (white) that are dotted about the harbour.

Main hazards

Big ships and ferries, including a High Speed Ferry (HSS) whose movements are announced on Ch 71.

Areas of shallow water need care and attention. These include the Harwich Shelf on the port side of the entrance and the Shotley Spit on W side of the Orwell mouth.

When entering Harwich, keep at least a cable clear of the end of Dovercourt Breakwater where the bottom is foul at low tide and there are strong eddies. Also keep to starboard of the seasonal (April to October) Harwich Shelf ECB, which marks the E limit of the Harwich Shelf.

Approaches

The approaches to Harwich are well marked. In particular, the deep water shipping channel is heavily buoyed, but, because of the number, tonnage and size of shipping using the channel, there are recommended yacht entry tracks shown on charts, which must be used. All of them converge on the landfall waypoint roughly halfway between the Landguard NCB (Q) and Pye End SWB (LFl.10s).

From seawards

After a North Sea crossing, yachts will pick up the Cork Sand Bn (Fl(3)R.10s) or the nearby Cork Sand Yacht NCB (VQ) and, keeping S of the deep water channel, proceed to pass well to port of Landguard NCB (Q) to keep well clear of the bend in the shipping lane.

From N

Perhaps having departed the Rivers Ore and Alde or Deben, pass close to Wadgate Ledge SHM (Fl(4)G.15s) and cross the deep water channel at right angles between the Platters SCB (Q(6)+LFl.15s) and the Rolling Ground SHB (Q.G) to join the recommended yacht track coming in from E.

Harwich Haven Authority recommends crossing the deep water channel between waypoints 51°55′.80N 001°20′.40E and 51°55′.20N 001°20′.20E to give the shortest right-angle crossing.

Harwich harbour from S. Advisory waypoint lower, centre. To N lies the Orwell to W is the Stour. From Landguard Point (right) to entrance of Orwell will soon be all container berths.

Approaching Harwich from E or N the cranes of the container port stand out clearly

Approaching from S

Follow a course of about 345° from the Medusa SHB (Fl.G.5s) through the Medusa Channel to pass close to the Stone Banks unlit PHB and join the recommended yacht track at the landfall waypoint or, at most, three cables S of Landguard NCB (Q).

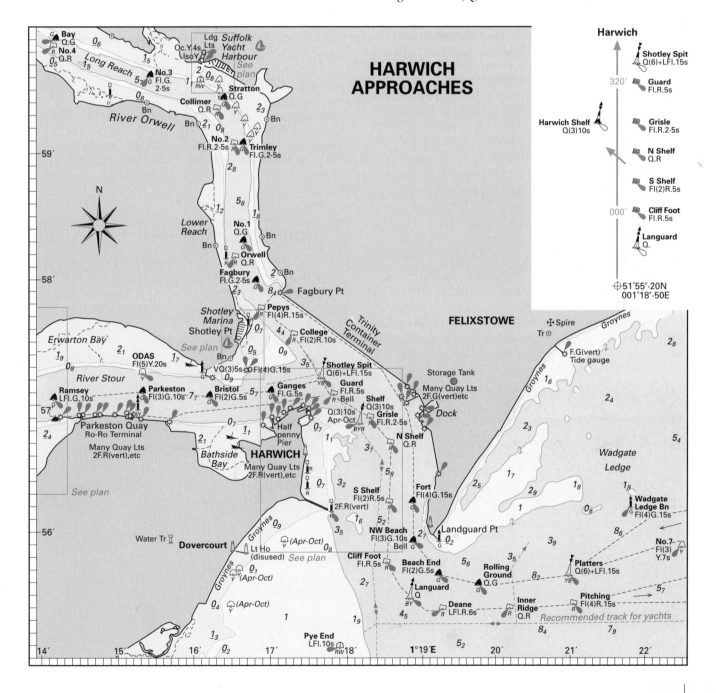

| Stour | Shotley | Green water tower conspic | Guard buoy | Orwell |

Sailing in through Harwich Harbour in the late evening with the Felixstowe container cranes on the right, the River Orwell between the cranes and the red buoy, then Shotley Point and the River Stour opening on the left

Entry

Progress through the harbour must be via the recommended yacht tracks shown on charts. At the Guard PHB (Fl.R.5s. Bell) either turn W along the Harwich waterfront to reach the moorings at Halfpenny Pier, or cross the mouth of the Stour to Shotley Spit SCB (Q(6)+LFl.15s).

At that buoy, either turn W to enter Shotley Point Marina or to proceed on up the River Stour, keeping to the Shotley side until clear of Parkeston Quay, or continue N from Shotley Spit into the River Orwell. Keep close watch on the depth anywhere near Shotley Spit.

HARWICH HARBOUR

Harwich Harbour itself has no facilities for yachts. There are two yacht clubs based at Harwich: Harwich Town SC, which is a dinghy racing club with a clubhouse overlooking the main harbour, and Harwich and Dovercourt SC, which is a cruising club. Its headquarters are at the top of Gashouse Creek, a drying gutway between the Trinity House jetty and Bathside Bay.

Halfpenny Pier

From the Guard PHB make W past the Ro-Ro terminal and Halfpenny Pier comes up to port. Approach is clear, but beware swell from passing ships while going alongside.

Beware the HSS. Times are announced on VHF Ch 71

HALFPENNY PIER

Contact
　Harbourmaster ☎ 01255 243030
Berth Alongside pontoons. Watch for swell off passing ships. No charge for short stay, but charges apply overnight
Facilities Water on pontoons
Electricity On pontoons
Provisions In town
Pubs/restaurants Nearby in town
Sailmaker Dolphin Sails ☎ 01255 243366
Taxi ☎ 01255 503000
Note Harwich Navy Yard has no facilities for yachts. It is used by the pilots and harbour launches.

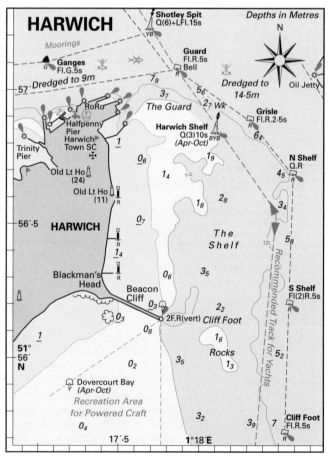

Harwich Halfpenny Marina – free berthing for short stays during the day

HARWICH AND DOVERCOURT SC

Contact
☎ 01255 551153
Access HW±2hr
Visitors' moorings Two
Facilities WC
Water On quayside
Telephone In club
Provisions In nearby town centre.

Downriver from Halfpenny Pier is the new RNLI lifeboat station and the yellow pontoon of the Harwich Ro-Ro berth

Shotley Point Marina

On entering Harwich Harbour, a low building will be seen off the port bow, which carries the word 'Marina' in large letters. It's at Shotley Point Marina. Other landmarks are the tall white mast at the old HMS *Ganges* naval base and a huge water tower.

Entry to Shotley Marina is via a dredged channel (2m at MLWS) and a lock providing 24hr access. Approach from Shotley Spit SCB, running parallel to the deep water channel towards Ganges SHB (Fl.G.5s). When close to the buoy, turn

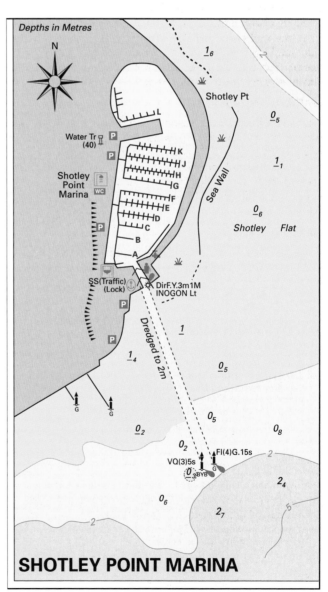

SHOTLEY POINT MARINA

Looking straight in along Shotley Marina entrance channel between channel marker beacons to motor cruiser at waiting pontoon to left of lock gates. Glass control tower and distinctive green water tower behind marina. Red traffic light outside control tower

to starboard and pass between a pair of top-marked beacons, which are lit Fl(4)G.15s on the starboard post and VQ(3)5s on the port hand post. From the posts, the channel into the lock runs on a bearing of about 340°.

Locking into the marina is governed by traffic lights (red and green) and there is a pontoon outside the entrance for boats to wait at. There is also an INOGON directional leading light mounted on the starboard lock knuckle with arrows to keep approaching craft on 339.5° up the narrow dredged approach channel.

HARWICH AREA CONTACTS

Harwich Haven Authority ☎ 01255 243030
Harwich Harbour Control ☎ 01255 243000

HM Customs and Excise
Harwich ☎ 01255 244700
Ipswich ☎ 01473 235700
Felixstowe ☎ 01394 303030

Radio watch

Inbound to Harwich from the landfall waypoint or the Pye End buoy, yachts should monitor VHF Ch 71 and maintain a listening watch until they pass Fagbury (Fl.G.2.5s) on the Orwell or Erwarton Ness beacon beacon on the Stour.

SHOTLEY MARINA

Contact
☎ 01473 788982
VHF Ch 80
Call sign *Shotley Marina*
Website www.shotley-marina.co.uk
Email sales@shotley-marina.co.uk

Facilities WC. Showers and baths. Launderette

Water On pontoons

Electricity On pontoons

Gas Calor and Gaz

Fuel From berth immediately to starboard inside lock (24hr)

Provisions From local shop at Shotley Gate 5 mins' walk

Bar/restaurant The Shipwreck ☎ 01473 788865

Boat repairs Shotley Marine Services ☎ 01473 788982.
40-ton boat-hoist, 20-ton crane

Transport Water taxi to Harwich and Felixstowe. Bus service from Shotley gate (10 mins' walk) to Ipswich.

The lock at Shotley Marina. Traffic lights on the left control vessel movements, while the INOGON panel on the right indicates correct alignment for entry. Secure to cleats on the top of the floating fenders

6. River Stour

⊕**Landfall waypoint**
51°55′.20N 001°18′.50E (On recommended yacht track, 0.3M SW of Landguard NCB)

Charts
Imray *2000 Series, C28*
Admiralty *SC 5607, 1491, 1594, 2693*

Tides
Harwich Haven
HW Dover +0040
Mistley Quay
HW Dover +0105

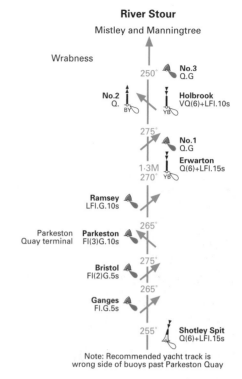

Landmarks and approach

After crossing to N side of the main shipping channel at the Guard PHB (Fl.R.5s Bell), turn W at Shotley Spit SHB (Q(6)+LFl.15s). Pass Shotley Point Marina control and workshop buildings to starboard below the Ganges Cliff, on top of which is a conspicuous pale green water tower.

The next landmark to starboard is the old Ganges jetty with a white radar tower on the seaward end. Over on the S side of the river is the Harwich International Port (Parkeston Quay), where the ferries and HSS catamaran berth. This area marks the change from Harwich Harbour to the River Stour proper.

River Stour to Erwarton Ness

Continue W outside the N edge of the deepwater channel, leaving the two SHBs Parkeston and Ramsey to port. This course gives any ships room to swing when entering or leaving their berths.

The river is both broad and straight for nearly 3M; the deepest water is to N of the centre line with only one particular hazard to watch for – a line of large ship mooring buoys on the S side of the channel opposite No.1 buoy (Q.G), which have the Harwich Harbour oil spill boom slung between them. Give them a good berth, but there is enough water to pass either side of them.

RoRo ferry passing Harwich town, making up the River Stour to her berth close to the passenger ferry terminal

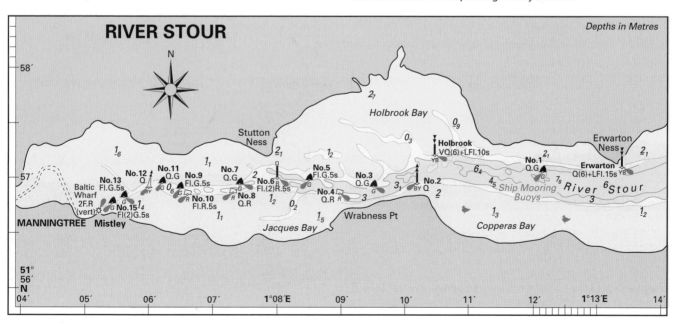

On the starboard side is Erwarton Ness with its SCM (Q(6)+LFl.15s). Erwarton is a popular anchorage with good holding, and it gives good shelter in N winds. There's good clean landing on a sand and shingle beach at HW±1½hr, and a slightly muddy landing can be made using an old barge hard that extends out from the shore to the base of the Ness Bn, almost to LW. There are several footpaths along the foreshore, one of which goes N across the fields to The Queen's Head pub a mile away at the village of Erwarton.

In S winds, if the Erwarton anchorage becomes uncomfortable, it is possible to find more shelter across on the S shore in Copperas Bay.

Erwarton to Wrabness

About ¾M W of Erwarton Ness SCM is the first SHB, No.1 (Q.G), which is positioned N of the ship mooring buoys warned of above. Around 1M further W there's a pair of beacons. One is the Holbrook Beacon SCM (VQ(6)+LFl.10s) to starboard and the other is No.2 Beacon NCM (Q) to port. The pair act as a gate to Wrabness and the Holbrook Beacon also marks the entrance to the drying Holbrook Creek. This little waterway meanders N across Holbrook Bay towards the palatial buildings and prominent clock tower of the Royal Hospital School standing on the N shore.

Anchorage is possible in the entrances to either Holbrook Creek or Shallager Creek just W. Positions are best found below half tide and by careful depth sounding.

WRABNESS

There are many moorings at Wrabness, which is marked by a plethora of beach huts under a low cliff on the wooded S bank. It is usually possible to pick up an empty mooring for a short stay and anchoring in the main channel is not recommended, because the bottom has been heavily dredged for gravel in the past and the holding is suspect. The channel is also used by shipping bound to or from Mistley Quay. Most other parts of the river offer good holding in some wonderfully glutinous East Coast mud and some of this can be found above the Wrabness moorings towards No.4 PHB.

Wrabness to Mistley

The river is well marked all the way to Mistley, largely to assist the coasters that use the waterway, and it is essential to avoid sailing too far away from the buoyed channel as the whole area dries extensively. This is another East Coast area where visitors are advised to set off up river before the mud banks are covered and to be aware that buoys can be blown across the banks they are marking.

The No.6 beacon (Fl(2)R.5s), about ¾M above Wrabness moorings, marks the N edge of the Smith Shoal, which moves the channel and best water well towards the N side of the river at Stutton Ness.

Having run W for most of its length, the channel dives SW towards Mistley Quay at the No.12 NCB (Q) at Ballast Hill. Head for Nos.13 and 15 SHBs and the quay lies straight ahead.

Wrabness Point. Try to find a mooring as holding is suspect for anchoring

Mistley Marina Conspic chimney Public quay Mistley church

Approaching Mistley. From No.12 keep roughly in line with the centre chimney for the best water. Don't stray too far beyond the channel marks, as there's not much water even at high tide

Mistley Town Quay

Tide gauge shows depth against wall at Mistley quay

Yachts can lie alongside at HW±1½hr, depending on draught, but the quayside berth dries at LW to fairly level, soft mud. Beware a steep-to sand bank immediately opposite the quay, which can impede manoeuvring. There is considerable redevelopment work going on at Mistley Quay, which has restricted the length of quay available for public mooring. There are no facilities, but there's a good pub, The Thorn ☎ 01206 392821, at the top of the quay together with local shops. Local yachtsmen work the tide to stay for lunch and then drop back down river to anchor at Erwarton or across on the S side of the river in Copperas Bay for the night.

Mistley Marine ☎ 01206 392127, mobile 07850 208918, VHF Ch 71 is developing a small drying marina on the S bank just downriver from Mistley Quay. The company runs a small boatyard and marine engineering works and operates a dredging barge. River moorings and quayside moorings dry out. There are no toilet or shower facilities.

With care and an adventurous spirit, it's possible to reach ½M beyond Mistley to Manningtree at HW and visit the Stour SC ☎ 01206 393924 www.stoursailingclub.co.uk with its waterfront clubhouse, small hard jetty, and slipway. Visitors are few, but increasing, as they get to know about this small, attractive town that has all a crew needs close to hand, including pubs, restaurants, shops, banks and a train service to London.

Approach Manningtree by following the channel buoys carefully and remember that the whole area dries soon after HW. Boats with a draught greater than 1.5m need to avoid a nasty sand bank some 50m in front of the Stour SC clubhouse and quay. The advice is to skirt along the line of moorings.

Manningtree is the head of the navigable river and is also on the doorstep of the Dedham Vale and 'Constable country'. Above Manningtree the river becomes non-tidal.

Well known watering hole The Thorne public house

7. River Orwell

Quay extension means even bigger container ships

⊕ **Landfall waypoint**
51°55'.20N 001°18'.50E
(On recommended yacht
track, 0.3M SW of
Landguard NCB)

Charts
Imray *2000 Series, C28,*
Y16
Admiralty *SC 5607, 1491,*
2693

VHF Channels
Monitor port operations
Ch 71 from Pye End to
Fagbury
Monitor port operation Ch
68 from Fagbury to
Ipswich

Hazards

The Orwell is in 24hr use by large cargo ships and RoRo
ferries. They are very quiet and a sharp lookout must be kept
astern. They are constrained by draught and yachts must
keep well clear. If a ship is manoeuvring near docks it is
frequently best for yachts to heave to and wait until passage
is again clear.

If anchoring anywhere in the Orwell, keep clear of the
main channel. Remember to display a black ball during the
day and a riding light at night, but it is advisable to do the
same if lying to a mooring, because it tells the skippers and
pilots of passing ships that there are people aboard. This
advice is the result of some 'incidents' between ships and
moored and anchored yachts.

Tides

Harwich Haven	HW Dover +0040
Pin Mill	HW Dover +0100
Ipswich	HW Dover +0115

The Orwell – lower reaches

The River Orwell, or the Ipswich River as it often known
locally, is attractive and remarkably unspoilt, yet increasingly
commercial. It is 9M from the end of the Trinity Quay at
Harwich to the lock gates into Ipswich Wet Dock and
getting on for ½M wide in places at HW.

Because of the commercial shipping, the main channel
has been dredged to a depth of nearly 12m and is about
400m (2 cables) wide. Gently rising mudflats merge into
either narrow sandy beaches or heavily wooded banks on
either side.

Entering the Orwell from Harwich Harbour, stay W
outside the dredged channel, leaving the Guard PHB
(Fl.R.5s) to starboard and, after crossing the narrowest part
of the deep water channel leave the Shotley Spit SCB
(Q(6)+LFl.15s) to starboard. From there make about N
towards the College PHB (Fl(2)R.10s).

Leave College to starboard. It marks the W edge of the
deep water channel opposite the Trinity container berths
quay and is there for big ships. There's plenty of depth
between the buoy and the Shotley Spit, which runs out from
Shotley Point (roughly half way along the marina retaining
wall) to Shotley Spit SCB.

When entering the Orwell from the Stour, it is not
necessary to go all the way down and round the Shotley Spit
SCB. There is generally sufficient depth to cross the Spit
itself at all states of the tide about 200m N of Shotley Spit
SCB.

The changeover from Harwich Harbour Authority to
Ipswich Port Authority is at the Fagbury SHB (Fl.G.2.5s) off
Fagbury Point, close N of the container berths. Nearby is a
clearly marked underwater cable, which must be avoided if
anchoring to await the tide.

Entrance to the Orwell proper with inbound yachts passing the
last of the Felixstowe container terminals

The river is extremely well buoyed and generally there is plenty of room and water outside the channel to avoid large vessels (which have total right of way and often use their horn to assert it). Remember most of them have to do 10–12kn just to maintain steerage way in what is quite a winding and confined channel.

The deep water channel has been pushed further over to the Shotley bank by recent developments and extensions of the Trinity Quay and a new PHB Babergh (Fl.R.2.5s), has been installed between Pepys PHB (Fl(4)R.15s) and the first SHB, Fagbury (Fl.G.2.5s). Once past the end of Trinity Quay you are in the Orwell proper.

Note: Recommended yacht track is wrong side of PHBs opposite container berths

To port, a little N of Shotley Marina, the river opens out into a gentle bay, called Stone Heaps, the name being a legacy from the old barging days, which offers a very good anchorage, if a little rough when ships pass. The holding is good, water is plentiful at all states of tide and a shingle beach offers clean landing for a walk round the back of the marina to shops at Shotley Gate.

Trimley Marshes

Trimley Marshes lie on the E side behind a raised flood protection bank. Once a marshy bird sanctuary they have been excavated and flooded by breaching the sea wall to make a proper wetland for wading birds. A walk along the wall with binoculars is always rewarding for birdwatchers.

The Babergh PHB, which emphasises the deep water channel.
The boundary between Harwich harbour and the Orwell proper
lies about 100m this side of the next red buoy, Orwell PHB

Just above the newly opened gap in the wall is the start of a line of small boat moorings, which lead into Trimley Bay. Landing is possible at HW on a sandy beach backed by cliffs. It's a popular place to picnic and for kids to swim, but the bay is also a designated speedboat and water-ski area.

The down-river end of Trimley Bay is marked by the Trimley SHB (Fl.G.2.5s) and on the opposite (W) side of the channel is No.2 PHB (Fl.R.2.5s), which marks the start of the bend NW in the river round Collimer Point.

Off Collimer Point itself is Collimer PHB (Q.R) and Stratton SHB (Q.G). On the W bank also is a tidal gauge giving the depth of water over the natural riverbed. Inshore of it is the remains of one of the many old barge hards once in regular use on the river. The river turns NW at this point.

Suffolk Yacht Harbour (SYH)

The first major landing point on the river is at Suffolk Yacht Harbour (frequently referred to as Levington Marina), a few hundred yards downriver from the entrance to Levington Creek (drying) on the starboard bank. The entrance to the marina is a well dredged, 30m wide by 2m deep (at LWN) channel, marked with a SWB at the start of the approach channel and port and starboard hand posts with top marks in the channel. Tides set across the channel and care is required not to be pushed down on them, especially at Springs. They are substantial steel tubes and will do serious damage to topsides.

At night there are leading lights (outer Iso.Y and inner Oc.Y.4s); the lower light is sited on a post behind and slightly to port of the visitor's berths and the upper on a taller post near the head of the West Dock, the alignment giving a centre-line approach through the entrance channel. Visitor's berths and the after hours harbour master's office lie directly opposite the entrance with the fuel berth just to starboard.

SYH is in an isolated location 1M from nearest bus stop to Ipswich and Felixstowe, but food and drink are available to visitors on LV87, the lightship home of the Haven Ports YC. There is also the Ship Inn at the village of Levington 1M away.

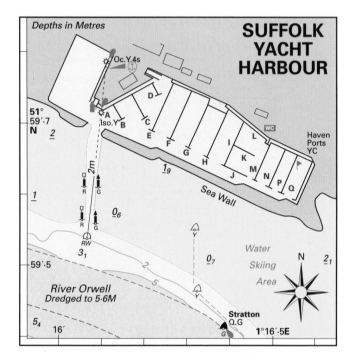

Entrance to SYH. Pontoons for visitors and fuel berth are
straight ahead by berthing master's hut

Suffolk Yacht Harbour

Contact
VHF Ch 80
Call sign *Suffolk Yacht Harbour*
Harbourmaster ☎ 01473 659465 *Email* info@syh.co.uk
www.suffolkyachtharbour.ltd.uk
Access 24hr

Facilities WC. Showers. Launderette

Water At each berth

Electricity At each berth

Fuel Diesel and petrol from berth at entrance

Chandler On site

Provisions Some on site

Gas Calor and Gaz

Telephone Next to chandler/office

Showers and toilets Yes (3 blocks)

Boat repairs Slipways (2), 60-ton boat-hoist, 20-ton crane

Scrubbing posts At head of West Dock, turn to port at entrance

Shipwrights On site

Sailmaker On site

Electrical engineers On site

Rigger On site

Engineer On site

Electronics On site

Pub/restaurant Haven Ports YC (in old light vessel in marina)
☎ 01473 659658.
Ship Inn ☎ 01473 659573.

Levington Creek

Leaving SYH and travelling up river, the next buoy, No.3 SHB (Fl.G.2.5s), lies off the entrance to Levington Creek. At HW it's worth going up in the dinghy to the old barge quay at the top. From there it's a short walk to the Ship Inn at Levington. The channel in the creek is marked with withies.

Above the creek, almost as far as the high level Orwell Road Bridge, both shores of the Orwell are lined with moorings between the deep water channel and the drying banks.

Nacton

The Nacton foreshore runs between Levington Creek and Potter Point, the next major landmark on the N side. The flat mud runs up into a narrow sandy beach, popular for picnics and teaching youngsters to swim, because the water gets very warm as it comes in over the mud in mid-Summer. It's a good place to see Cormorants standing on mud humps at LW with their wings held outspread to dry.

Butterman's Bay

On the charts Butterman's Bay is correctly shown as the reach up to Pin Mill itself. However, locals usually refer to Butterman's Bay as being the wider stretch of river opposite Levington Creek (properly Colton Creek), on the W side, where there are a number of yacht moorings and a recognised anchorage for sailing barges. During the summer there is often one or more of these stately craft anchored there.

At the top end of the Bay, nestling under the end of a wooded cliff sits a prominent, solitary white cottage, called

Barge *Thalatta* sailing down the Orwell towards Pin Mill with Butt & Oyster the pale building at left

Clamp House, which was reputed to be a smuggler's den. Off the cottage is No.4 PHB (Q.R) on the W side of the deep-water channel and, opposite that, the Bay SHB (Q.G). Upriver from both these buoys are double and triple rows of moorings. At the heart of which, on the S bank, lies one of the Mecca's of East Coast sailing, Pin Mill.

Pin Mill

Much has been written about Pin Mill and the famous building yards of Harry King and Frank Ward. Though even more column inches have probably been given over to the riverside pub the Butt and Oyster, which has one of the finest views from the bar window.

Getting ashore at Pin Mill requires a dinghy and a pair of boots, because there's a lot of mud. A long hard is laid out from the shore almost to LW mark, so landing is possible at most states of the tide, but, if you go ashore at LW or early on the flood, pull the dinghy all the way up. There's a small rill called the Grindle that runs along the up stream side of the hard, enabling dinghies to float a long way up. Similarly, if landing at HW or on the ebb, be prepared for a long drag back down. A vacant mooring may usually be used for an hour or two, if one can be found, but for longer stays, seek out the harbourmaster Tony Ward, at the chandler.

Pin Mill is a small, unspoilt hamlet that lies in a steep valley running back from the shoreline up to the nearby village of Chelmondiston, from where buses to and from Ipswich run regularly. There's a grocery store, a butcher and post office at 'Chelmo', as it's called locally. Apart from the Butt and Oyster, Pin Mill hard offers a chandler with fuel and water (cans needed), a small general store and, across the rill, the Pin Mill SC.

The barge hard and posts are still used by Thames barges and almost invariably there is one being worked on at weekends. The Pin Mill barge match held each June starts off the end of the hard.

From Pin Mill, the river turns more N up Potter Reach, and then back NW at Hall Point between the Park Bight SHB (Q.G) and the No.6 PHB (Q.R) into Cathouse Reach with the channel tucking under the wooded slope that shields Woolverstone Marina and the Royal Harwich YC from SW winds.

Opposite the marina is the Cathouse SHB (Fl.G.2.5s).

WOOLVERSTONE

Woolverstone Marina is an open-river 200-berth marina with pontoons held by massive piles driven into the riverbed in a deep pool S of the main channel. Its situation under the wooded shore is attractive, but it suffers from strong tidal streams through the berths and almost constant swell from passing traffic. Down river is a short pier with a barge pontoon moored across the end, which is the fuel berth, and alongside a wide slip called the Cathouse Hard, also belonging to the marina.

Adjacent to the marina down stream is the Royal Harwich YC, which recently installed its own jetty and 40 deep water pontoon berths. During the summer the club welcomes visitors, who can use the showers, bar and restaurant in the clubhouse.

Snuggled into the trees between the club and the marina lies the fabled Cathouse, another smugglers den. It is reputed that, when the coast was clear a lamp was shown, but when the Revenue men were prowling, a black cat sat in the window as a warning.

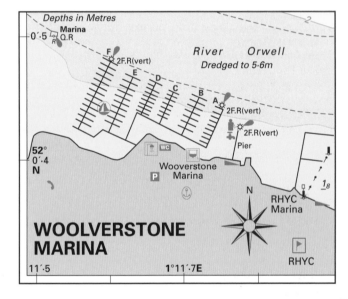

PIN MILL

Contact
  HM Tony Ward ☎ 07714 260568, mobile 077142 055686
  Swinging moorings only.

Pub/restaurant Butt and Oyster ☎ 01473 780764

Fuel In cans at top of hard

Chandler Yes

Gas Calor and Gaz from chandler

Provisions Some from chandler also shops in Chelmondiston. EC Weds

Water Taps at Pin Mill SC and near chandler at top of hard

Boat repairs Two boatyards Frank Ward (near chandler) and Harry King ☎ 01473 780258, near sailing club

Scrubbing post Contact HM

Telephone In car park 100 yards up road

Club Pin Mill SC ☎ 01473 780271
  www.pinmillsc.plus.com/Homepage.htm

Royal Harwich YC

Woolverstone Marina

Freston tower on S bank of Orwell

From Woolverstone up river, leave the No.7 SHB (Q.G) to starboard and the Marina PHB (unlit can) to port into Downham Reach. Here the channel begins to narrow markedly with unspoilt Suffolk parkland to be seen on either shore. Up ahead and spanning the river is the high level Orwell Road Bridge.

On the W shore of Downham Reach stands Blackwood Cottage, nestling in the woods with its own landing stage, and then the Stoke SC clubhouse and moorings providing a foreground to a Victorian folly. Called Freston Tower, the folly is reputed to have been built by one of the Paul family (famous for their barge fleet) as a garden dining room for entertaining guests to fine food and wine and fine views of the company's vessel's passing up and down the river.

The channel here is quite narrow but extremely well buoyed. When a ship is sighted, keep just outside the line of buoys on either side until it passes. At the bridge itself the channel narrows down to 92m (300ft) between the artificial islands that protect the bases of the eight piers, which carry the bridge. The air draught is 43m (141ft).

Do not attempt to pass under the bridge at the same time as a ship, whatever her size.

ROYAL HARWICH YC

Marina Master ☎ 07742 145994
Visitors' berths By arrangement
Access 24hr

Facilities WC. Showers
Water On pontoons
Electricity On pontoons
Scrubbing posts By arrangement
Bar/Restaurant In clubhouse
Security Pontoons gated.

WOOLVERSTONE MARINA

Contact
VHF Ch 80.
Call sign *Woolverstone Marina*.
Harbourmaster ☎ 01473 780206/780354.
Visitors' berths on ends of pontoons as available.
Access 24hr

Security Pontoons gated
Facilities WC. Showers
Water On pontoons
Electricity On pontoons
Fuel Diesel from barge at downstream end of marina
Chandler On site
Boat repairs Crane, boat hoist, slip
Engineer On site
Pub/restaurant On site
Provisions On site.

Orwell Bridge from downriver. Keep clear when commercial ships are passing through

Ostrich Creek

Once through the Orwell bridge – and do look up when passing under it, the deck is made in two sections with a considerable gap between them – there is a SHB E Fen (Fl.G.5s) marking the E side of the channel between the bridge and the down river end of the Cliff Quay complex. Opposite is the West Power PHB (Fl.R.5s) and this should be left very close to starboard to stay just W of the deep water channel and clear of the shipping activities at Cliff Quay – if ships are on the move. About ¼M further N is the No.12 PHB Cliff Reach (Q.R), which also marks the entrance to Ostrich Creek where both Fox's Marina and the Orwell YC are to be found.

Enter Ostrich Creek from the No.12 PHB, passing between the piles topped with R and G markers. The Orwell YC, on the N shore, has some drying moorings and water can be obtained from the clubhouse or from a floating pontoon. Fuel and oil are available at a garage adjacent to the clubhouse. There's a regular bus service into the centre of Ipswich.

Opposite Orwell YC, on the downriver side of Ostrich Creek, lies Fox's Marina and boatyard, home of Oyster Yachts. The yard has one of the largest chandlers on the East Coast, a club and a restaurant.

FOX'S MARINA

Contact
VHF Ch 80
Call sign *Fox's Marina*
Harbourmaster ☎ 01473 689111
Access 24hr, dredged to 2m MLWS

Facilities WC. Showers

Water On pontoons

Electricity On pontoons

Telephone On corner of YC at head of pontoon gantry

Security Pontoons gated

Chandler On site

Gas Calor and Gaz

Fuel Diesel and petrol from fuel berth on S side of entrance

Provisions Shops near by

Boat repairs and all services Up to 70 tonnes, masts to 110ft.

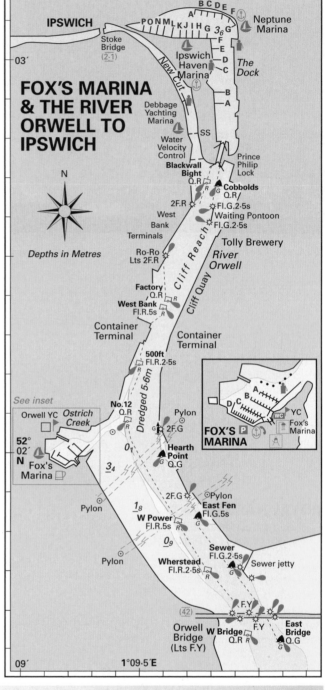

FOX'S MARINA & THE RIVER ORWELL TO IPSWICH

The entrance to Ostrich Creek with Fox's Marina on the left and Orwell Yacht Club on the right

Entrance lock to Ipswich Wet Dock, Neptune and Ipswich Haven marinas

Ipswich Wet Dock

Although there are a number of buoys on the approach to the lock gates into the Ipswich Wet Dock, there is deep water from quayside to quayside and sufficient lighting to see when going in at night. The port's working channel is VHF Ch 68 and the call sign is *Ipswich port radio*. Call from about buoy No.9 (below the Orwell Bridge) if wishing to enter.

Although originally designed for commercial shipping, and some still uses it, the lock has been refurbished and fitted with rope travellers on the port side and a floating pontoon to starboard for yachts to moor against as they progress through. Ships have priority for the lock and when one is about to use it, the pontoon is slipped and towed out while the ship passes through. There is a pontoon jetty to starboard on the approach to the lock to moor against if you have to wait long.

Visual signals for entering or leaving the lock, which these days opens virtually on request, are a set of red and green traffic lights located above the Orwell Navigation Service's building on the E side of the lock.

Debbage's yard and marina in The Cut at Ipswich, close beside the Wet Dock

NEPTURE MARINA

Contact
VHF Ch 80.
Call sign *Neptune Marina*.
Harbourmaster ☎ 01473 215204
Security Pontoons gated
Facilities WC. Showers
Boat repairs Crane, 40-ton boat-hoist
Water On pontoons
Electricity On pontoons
Diesel From fuel berth by hoist and workshop to starboard of final approach
Provisions Shops nearby
Taxi ☎ 01473 256666, 257777.

IPSWICH HAVEN MARINA

Contact
VHF Ch 80.
Call sign *Ipswich Marina*.
Harbourmaster ☎ 01473 236644
Security Main gate plus pontoons gated
Facilities WC. Showers
Boat repairs Crane, 70-ton boat-hoist
Fuel Diesel and petrol from fuel berth between pontoons A and B
Gas Calor and Gaz
Telephone In office lobby
Electronics On site
Engineers On site
Chandler On site
Bar/restaurant On site and nearby
Provisions Shops nearby
Taxi ☎ 01473 256666, 257777.

Once inside the Wet Dock, aim for the far end (it's actually a dogleg) where the Neptune Marina lies on the starboard side, with the new Haven Marina to port. Both offer the usual facilities and shops are 10 minutes walk away in the town itself. Haven Marina has its own restaurant, but there are also a couple of pubs and a café on the waterfront. It is a pleasant walk around the dockside to the Tollemache & Cobbold brewery/pub/musem. Ipswich itself boasts restaurants, pubs, cinemas, and a highly respected theatre.

The New Cut

To port of the entrance to the Wet Dock is a stretch of water called The New Cut. It is the point at which the river Gipping (from which Ipswich got its orginal name of Gyppiswick) joins the Orwell. Here Debbage Yachting has a yard and small marina situated about halfway between the entrance and the Wherstead Road road bridge, above which navigation is by dinghy only. Boats lie alongside stagings and dry out. You can obtain fuel and water.

A flood relief gate crosses New Cut. Normally it lies on the river bed, but when required it is raised to close the Cut. There are large warning signs and three vertical red traffic lights indicate when it is raised and that access to boats is denied.

8. Walton Backwaters

⊕ **Landfall waypoint**
51°55´.1N 001°17´.9E (Close
N of Pye End buoy)

Charts
Imray *2000 series*
Admiralty SC *5607, 2695*

Tides
Stone Point
HW Dover +0040

Main hazards

The Walton Backwaters lie S of Harwich, well protected by the Pye Sand and Sunken Pye on the seaward side of the narrow Pye Channel approach. This sand is very hard and grounding must be avoided, particularly in onshore winds or when a swell is running. In fact it would be very unwise to attempt entry to the Backwaters in strong NE winds when big seas are running.

Approaches

It is imperative that the Pye End SWB (LFl.10s) is located and identified before approaching the Backwaters.

Nowadays the buoy is of good size and, with the help of GPS, is fairly easy to find, even in choppy seas, although a good pair of binoculars will be useful. This is especially true at night when the light may be hard to identify against the background of Felixstowe and the deepwater channel marks if an approach is made from SE.

The two main landmarks when approaching the Harwich area are the cranes of Felixstowe container terminal and the Naze Tower just N of Walton on the Naze. Either or both is likely to be in sight from several miles, but in misty conditions they may quickly disappear.

From N

When approaching the Backwaters from Harwich, it is best to follow the charted yacht track to stay W of the deep water channel until near Cliff Foot (Fl.R.5s) before turning more SWly towards the Pye End buoy. This course avoids the Cliff Foot Rocks and the shallow waters over the Halliday Flats off Dovercourt Bay.

From NE

Following the coast from the Deben or Ore, cross the Harwich Deep Water Channel by way of the charted yacht track to arrive at Inner Ridge PHB (Q.R) on the S side, then alter course W for the Pye End buoy.

From E

If arriving from across the North Sea, the likely approach to Harwich is via the Sunk, so continue to parallel the deep water channel, on the S side, until reaching the Inner Ridge (Q.R) or Deane (LFl.R.6s) PHBs or even Landguard NCB

High Hill   Heather J   Crab Knoll

Looking into Walton Backwaters along Pye Channel with No.3 Crab Knoll buoy at right, then No.5 Heather J and No.4 High Hill by motorboat's bow wave

No.6   No.7

Entering Walton Backwaters along Pye Channel with No.4 High Hill on left, No.7 green between black and white yachts and red No.6 right beside boat with tan sails

Entering Walton Backwaters from Pye Channel with Macwester *Merrimack* coming out past No.10 Baines. Derelict lighters are on foreshore of Horsey Island

Island Point (Q.)

No.10	
Pickard	
	195°
RNLI	RNLI Fl.G.10s
	220°
No.4 High Hill Fl.R.10s	Heather J No.5
	225°
	Crab Knoll-No.3 Fl(2)G.10s
	220°
Orwell YC No.2	
	240°
Pye End LFl.10s	

⊕51°55'·1N
001°17'·9E

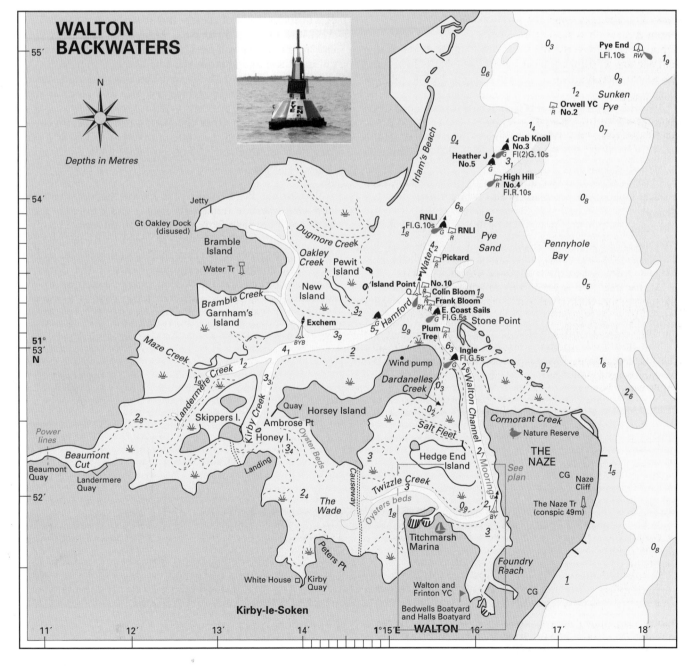

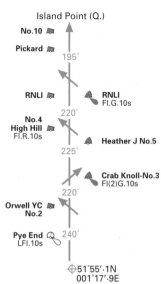

WALTON BACKWATERS

N

Depths in Metres

- 55'
- 54'
- 51° 53' N
- 52'

Pye End
LFl.10s
RW

Sunken Pye

Orwell YC
No.2
R

Crab Knoll
No.3
Fl(2)G.10s

Heather J
No.5
G

High Hill
No.4
Fl.R.10s

Pennyhole Bay

Pye Sand

RNLI
Fl.G.10s

RNLI
R

Pickard
R

Irlam's Beach

Jetty

Gt Oakley Dock
(disused)

Bramble
Island

Water Tr

Dugmore Creek

Oakley
Creek

Pewit
Island

New
Island

Bramble Creek

Garnham's
Island

Exchem
BYB

Island Point

No.10
Colin Bloom
Frank Bloom
E. Coast Sails
Fl.G.5s

Stone Point

Hamford

Water

Plum
Tree

Ingle
Fl.G.5s

Maze Creek

Landermere Creek

Kirby Creek

Skippers I.

Quay

Ambrose Pt

Honey I.

Horsey Island

Oyster Beds

Wind pump

Dardanelles
Creek

Salt Fleet

Walton Channel

Cormorant Creek

Nature Reserve

THE
NAZE

Power
lines

Beaumont
Cut

Beaumont
Quay

Landermere
Quay

Landing

The
Wade

Causeway

Oysters beds

Twizzle Creek

Hedge End
Island

Moorings

See
plan

CG

Naze
Cliff

The Naze Tr
(conspic 49m)

Titchmarsh
Marina

Foundry
Reach

Peters Pt

White House

Kirby
Quay

Walton and
Frinton YC

CG

Kirby-le-Soken

Bedwells Boatyard
and Halls Boatyard

WALTON

1°15'E

Naze Tr   Island Point NCB

The Walton Channel as approached from seaward, looking past Island Point north Cardinal to red and green channel buoys and Stone Point with Naze Tower beyond

(Q), which is sometimes the easiest to sight. From there make a turn SW towards the Pye End buoy.

From S

When arriving from the Blackwater or Crouch via the Wallet and Medusa Channel in clear weather, the Naze Tower and the cranes of Felixstowe docks will be sighted while still S of Walton Pier.

Pass the Medusa SHB (Fl.G.5s), which is positioned 2¼M seaward of Walton Pier, and Stone Banks PHB (Fl.R.5s), while aiming for the Felixstowe cranes. This course should keep you E of the Pye End buoy but bring you close enough to spot it and identify it.

Once N of Walton Pier, all the way to Pye End buoy, keep a sharp lookout for pot markers and fishing floats.

Entry

Although the Pye End is a safe water buoy, it is usual, when entering the channel, to pass it on the landward side leaving it close to port. From the buoy shape a course of about 240° for just under 1M to reach the No.2 Orwell YC PHB.

At this stage a look ahead will show no sign of a break in the coast; the Backwaters do not reveal themselves until much closer in. Not for nothing did Arthur Ransome name his famous book *Secret Water*.

The next buoy to make for is Crab Knoll No.3 SHB (Fl(2)G.10s), distant ⅓M, followed closely by an unlit SHB No.5 Heather J.

The lit High Hill No.4 PHB (Fl.R.10s) marks the N end of a deeper section of the channel towards the lit SHB No.7 (Fl.G.10s) and unlit PHB No.6. From there pass No.8 PHB Pickard and ahead will be a confusion of PHBs. Keep going towards them and look for the small Island Point NCB (Q), which is not always easy to find and often appears out of place to the W, but everything will fall into place as they come closer.

It is common to enter the Backwaters in the afternoon and the sun's glare on the water at that time can mean a very hard time spotting and identifying buoys until almost upon them. Polarising sunglasses may help and binoculars always do.

Because the Pye Channel is so narrow, between banks of hard sand, the tide funnels through it and can easily reach speeds of more than 2kn, particularly on the early ebb.

Departing the Backwaters at night can also be an interesting experience, because the buoys that are lit tend to be hidden among the background lights of the docks at Felixstowe, while the unlit ones simply disappear in the darkness. It's essential to work out rough courses to steer.

Approaching Stone Point with boats anchored off to enjoy the sandy beach. The Walton Channel goes on round the point

The Walton Channel

When bound up the Walton Channel towards Titchmarsh Marina or Walton town, leave the Island Point NCB (Q) to starboard and bear round SE to follow the line of red PHBs. These and the East Coast Sails SHB (Fl.G.5s) mark the way past Mussel Scarfe where the channel is narrow and, at low tide, the buoys can be blown well out of position over the banks. Careful consideration has to be given to tide and wind direction before deciding how close to pass these buoys and a sharp eye should be kept on the depth.

The channel runs very close in to the beach around Stone Point where that side is steep to and forms a popular anchorage off the lovely sandy beach. The water is relatively deep and tides run fast (2-3kn on a spring ebb), so care must be taken when setting the anchor.

Landing is possible at all states of the tide and the beach is good for swimming or having a picnic, but there is a nature reserve nearby and care must be taken not to disturb birds or damage plant life. Indeed, since the whole of the Backwaters is a Site of Special Scientific Interest (SSSI), such care must be taken throughout the area.

At the S end of the anchorage there is a SHB Ingle (Fl.G.5s) where a drying creek branches off to starboard around the E end of Horsey Island. This buoy marks the start of the Walton Channel with its extensive lines of moorings that show the line of best water and run on S for the best part of 1M to the Marine Store Chandlery NCB. This buoy marks the end of a spit between the Walton Channel, which runs on S past the buoy as Foundry Reach, and The Twizzle, which turns W towards Titchmarsh Marina and Horsey Mere.

Walton and Frinton YC

To reach the Walton & Frinton YC, leave the MarineStore Chandlery NCB to starboard and continue S into Foundry Reach.

There is a landing place about a cable inside the creek on the E bank, which can be used for a seawall walk into town.

Moorings in Foundry Reach indicate the channel, but yachts trying to reach the W&FYC will need to wait until better than half flood. Then, when there is enough water, it's possible to lie alongside a drying quay on the W side of the

Walton yacht basin behind the Walton & Frinton YC. Entrance channel with fold down gate and depth gauge. Gate up shown by triangle on post

Contact
Club Walton & Frinton YC ☎ 01225 675526/678161
Access HW±2hr

Facilities At W&FYC WC. Showers

Water At W&FYC and in basin

Electricity On pontoons in basin

Provisions In town

Telephone At W&FYC

Post office In town

Boat repairs Frank Halls ☎ 01225 675596
Bedwells ☎ 01225 675873
Both located by W&FYC with cranes/slips

Sailmakers East Coast Sails ☎ 01225 678353
Email info@eastcoastsails.co.uk www.eastcoastsails.co.uk

Pub/restaurant W&FYC and many in town

Pharmacy ☎ 01255 675900

Taxi ☎ 01255 675910.

The basin at Walton with Walton & Frinton YC beyond

clubhouse, which stands on a promontory. There is a good concrete landing for dinghies right under the clubhouse and there's a small basin behind it where craft can lie afloat at all times. The end of the concrete landing is marked by a red topped PHM post, which must be left to port when going alongside the club quay.

The basin, the Walton Yacht Basin, is entered through a 12ft wide break in the sea wall from the creek on the E side of the W&FYC. A retaining gate is lowered to the creek bed for entry or exit for a short time at HW when there is between 2 and 2.5m over it. A tide gauge is positioned beside the gate, which will be opened by arrangement. Contact Bedwell & Co ☎ 01255 675873 or W&FYC ☎ 01225 675526. It may not be possible to open the basin's gate on low neap tides.

Titchmarsh Marina

The Twizzle (or Twizzle Creek) runs W from the MarineStore Chandlery NCB, in the Walton Channel, along the S shore of Hedge End Island towards Horsey Mere. Titchmarsh Marina is cut into the S side of the channel.

From the NCB, moorings continue on both sides of the creek and, just over a cable in, there are pontoons on the S side where boats berth alongside. The entrance to Titchmarsh Marina is between the W end of these pontoons and the E end of a second line further up the creek, also on

Approaching entrance to Titchmarsh Marina from eastwards up The Twizzle. Turn in to port this side of the cill depth gauge on the pontoon

the S side. A tide gauge is provided on the E end of the further pontoons showing depth over the marina's cill.

Turn in as soon as the entrance opens up. The seawall banks up to starboard while there's a slipway to port with the fuelling pontoon beside it (at the head of A pontoon) and the marina offices in the building above. Once past the fuelling berth the channel turns hard to starboard past the ends of each pontoon. A is nearest to the marina office, H the furthest away.

It's a fairly long walk into town, but bicycles can be hired from the chandler in the marina.

Horsey Mere

Above Titchmarsh, The Twizzle continues to wind its way NW and W out into the open area of Horsey Mere. It is navigable to the W end of Hedge End Island by shoal draught boats at most states of the tide, but care must be taken to avoid grounding on oyster layings marked by withies.

At HW the Mere is a large expanse of shallow sailing water, but at LW it is just a sea of mud. A causeway, The

Entering Titchmarsh Marina from The Twizzle with fuelling berth to port. Main part of marina lies around the headland to starboard

Chart detail

TITCHMARSH MARINA AND WALTON

Hedge-End Island (floods in part at HWS)

Pontoon

Marine Store Chandlery

Moorings

Twizzle Creek

Colonel's Hard

Titchmarsh Marina

TITCHMARSH MARINA

H-G-F—E-D-C-B-A

Moorings

Foundry Reach

Sole Creek

Walton Mere (Private)

Walton Yacht Basin

Walton & Frinton YC

Depths in Metres

15·5′   01°16′E

TITCHMARSH MARINA

Contact
VHF Ch 80
Call sign *Titchmarsh Marina*
Harbourmaster ☎ 01255 851899
Email info@titchmarshmarina.co.uk
www.titchmarshmarina.co.uk
Access HW±5hr (1m over cill LWS)

Fuel Diesel and LPG at berth in entrance

Facilities WC. Showers. Launderette

Water Taps on pontoons (no hoses, but can be borrowed from office). Also on fuelling berth where hoses are provided

Electricity On pontoons

Gas Calor and Gaz

Phone Overlooking marina by office block

Chandler On site

Bicycle hire From chandler

Provisions In town plus some basics at chandler on site

Post office In town

Boat repairs 35-ton travel-lift, engineers and electronics on site.

Scrubbing berth Near fuel berth

Sailmakers East Coast Sails ☎01225 678353
Email info@eastcoastsails.co.uk www.eastcoastsails.co.uk

Pub/restaurant Harbour Lights on site

Taxi ☎ 01255 675910.

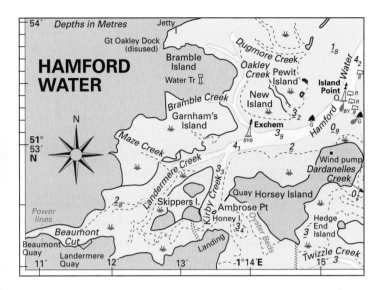

Kirby Quay, Walton Backwaters. Barge yacht in background is *Armadillo*

Wade, crosses the middle of the Mere from the mainland to Horsey Island. This can be crossed by boats with a draught of not much more than 1m, but it must be close to HW, preferably on spring tides.

On the W side of the Wade a creek leads away NW, which becomes Kirby Creek and runs round the W end of Horsey Island to join Hamford Water. A second creek, even less well defined, heads off S towards Kirby Quay. This is really an extension of Kirby Creek, but both the N and S sections fade into the Mere, losing their identity.

Readers of Arthur Ransome's book set in the Backwaters, *Secret Water*, will recognize Kirby Quay as Witch's Quay and Horsey Mere as the Red Sea with Hamford Water as the Secret Water of the title. Unfortunately, Kirby Creek, where it winds S to Kirby Quay is not so well marked as in the book, but it still provides a wonderful area to explore by dinghy.

Hamford Water

Hamford Water runs SW from the Island Point NCB (Q) at the S end of the Pye Channel. Leave the buoy to port and Hamford opens up ahead. It is sometimes known as the West Water.

Depths are good up past the SHB, where the channel bends more to the W, and on as far as the Exchem ECB at the entrance to Oakley Creek. It is a popular stretch in which to anchor, but can be uncomfortable if the wind picks up from NE.

Hamford Water (Westwater), Walton Backwaters. A busy weekend with boats anchored all along the Horsey Island shore

A Dutch visiting yacht creeps up Kirby Creek on the SW corner of Horsey Island with the Naze Tower on the skyline

Oakley Creek

The Exchem ECB, which carries a radar reflector, marks the end of a spit running out from Garnham's Island and also the W side of the entrance to Oakley Creek. Leave the buoy close to port to avoid the mud on the E side when entering Oakley.

The creek runs in a generally N'ly direction between Bramble Island and Pewit Island with a branch, Bramble Creek, turning off W along the S side of Bramble Island, while the main creek rounds the E end of the island and turns NW along its N side. Possible freighter traffic to and from the explosives factory at the top, combined with the narrowness and lack of water above Bramble Creek make Oakley Creek a place where it is inadvisable to anchor. However, if you enjoy exploring creeks and gutways on the tide, with a good chance of seeing plenty of seals, it is worth visiting as the tide rises.

Posts topped with red squares or green triangles mark the winding channel in from the entrance and must be followed carefully. Bramble Creek branches off W about ¼M in with a wooden jetty just inside on the N side of the channel.

Oakley Creek continues to wend its way N with a branch off to starboard where seals often swim and sunbathe on the point of Pewit Island. Above that, the creek tends W and approaches the Great Oakley Dock (landing prohibited) in a short Nly arm and, opposite, a dredger berth where it ends. A large yellow pile stands on a mud spit between the arm to the jetty and the one to the dredger berth. These upper reaches dry and a return down the creek should be made immediately after HW.

Back in Hamford Water, the stretch between Oakley Creek and the entrance to Kirby Creek is a popular anchorage with good depths.

Kirby Creek

Running S from Hamford Water, between Horsey Island and Skipper's Island, Kirby Creek turns SE around the corner of Horsey out into the Mere. One part heads E towards the Wade (and so to The Twizzle), while another winds S to Kirby Quay.

Still in Hamford Water, the stretch between Oakley Creek and the entrance to Kirby Creek is a popular anchorage with good depths.

Looking into Bramble Creek, with its dock, where it branches off from Oakley Creek

When approaching the entrance to Kirby Creek, keep a close eye on the depth, but it is best to enter from E along the Horsey Island shore to avoid the long spit out from the NE corner of Skipper's Island, which is unmarked and seems magnetic to yacht keels.

As the creek opens up, some moorings appear at the S end on either side of Honey Island. A small red buoy with a board topmark labelled 'Fishery Buoy' shortly within the entrance to Kirby Creek marks the start of oyster layings that go right through to the moorings. It is possible to anchor short of the fishery buoy when conditions are rough in Hamford Water, but space is restricted.

Kirby Creek divides around Honey Island (without either branch having a lot of water), before heading E into Horsey Mere. Anchorage is possible on the W side of Honey Island and a dinghy can be taken to a landing on the mainland shore opposite the SE corner of Skipper's Island. From there a sea wall walk of about 1½M goes to Kirby-le-Soken for shops and pubs, The Ship Inn and The Red Lion.

Landermere Creek

Immediately W of the entrance to Kirby Creek there is a mud bar where the spit from Skipper's Island has broadened

Approaching Landermere Quay from Landermere Creek.
Channel on up to Beaumont Quay goes on to the right

across the main channel. Depending upon draught, it may be necessary to wait until above half tide to cross this bar into Landermere Creek itself. Once over it, there is a ½M reach in which to find depth enough to anchor before the creek turns sharply SW around the corner of Skipper's Island towards Landermere Quay.

In the reach down the W side of Skipper's Island there are four or five moorings, but plenty of room to anchor N of them. Immediately S of the moorings the creek divides with one arm rounding the SW corner of Skipper's Island and returning E to join Kirby Creek, and the other continuing W towards Landermere Quay.

For going ashore at Landermere Quay it is best to anchor or borrow one of the moorings then go in by dinghy, because the approach is tortuous and unmarked.

Towards HW it is also possible to explore by dinghy above Landermere Quay, even reaching Beaumont Quay, the most Wly point of the Backwaters. The quay is best approached via Beaumont Cut, a straight, dug channel, but it is crossed by low power cables, preventing anything much larger than a dinghy with a mast from reaching the quay. The stone used to build the solid quay wall is said to have come from an old London Bridge, but the plaque making this statement seems to have disappeared.

The sad bones of the old sailing barge *Rose* lie in a pool just above the quay, providing a reminder of the days when remote docks such as Beaumont provided a vital trade link to the sea.

Beaumont Quay. Looking past the Quay back down Beaumont Cut, the approach channel, with mast height restricted by power cables

The Naze Tower, Walton on the Naze, from seaward when heading S towards Blackwater and Colne

Looking South from Stone Banks buoy with Naze Tower and Walton Pier

Approaches to the Essex Rivers

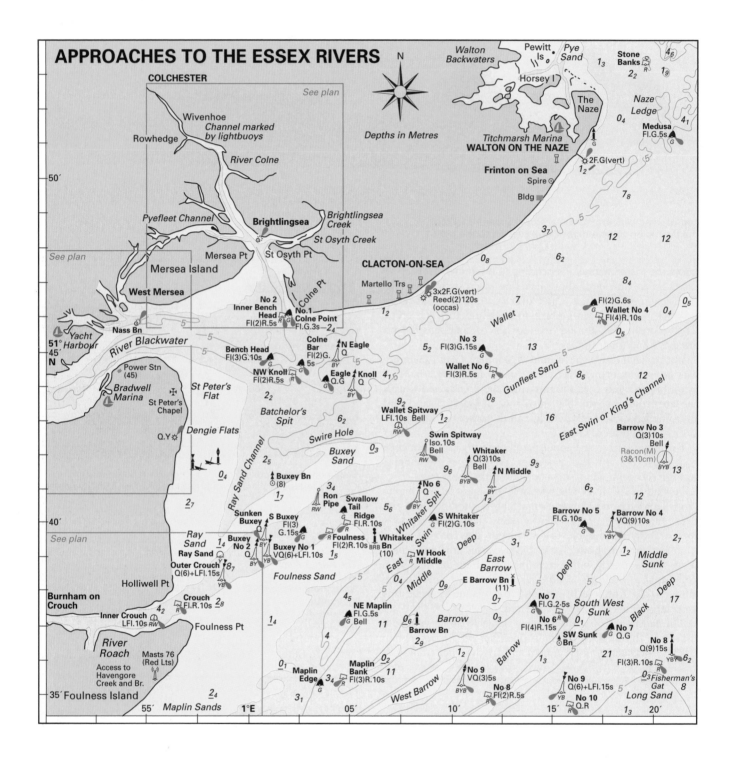

APPROACHES TO THE ESSEX RIVERS

COLCHESTER

Rowhedge
Wivenhoe
Channel marked by lightbuoys

River Colne

Pyefleet Channel

Brightlingsea

Brightlingsea Creek

St Osyth Creek

Mersea Pt
St Osyth Pt

Mersea Island

West Mersea

Nass Bn

Yacht Harbour

51°45'N

River Blackwater

Power Stn (45)
Bradwell Marina
St Peter's Chapel
Q.Y

St Peter's Flat

Dengie Flats

Batchelor's Spit

Swire Hole

Buxey Sand

Buxey Bn (8)

Ron Pipe

Sunken Buxey
S Buxey Fl(3) G.15s

Ray Sand Channel

Ray Sand

Buxey No 2

Buxey No 1 VQ(6)+LFl.10s

Outer Crouch Q(6)+LFl.15s

Holliwell Pt

Burnham on Crouch

Inner Crouch LFl.10s

Crouch Fl.R.10s

Foulness Pt

River Roach
Access to Havengore Creek and Br.

Masts 76 (Red Lts)

Foulness Island

Maplin Sands

Maplin Edge

Maplin Bank Fl(3) R.10s

Depths in Metres

N

Walton Backwaters
Pewitt Is
Pye Sand
Horsey I
Stone Banks
The Naze
Naze Ledge
Medusa Fl.G.5s

Titchmarsh Marina
WALTON ON THE NAZE
2F.G(vert)

Frinton on Sea
Spire
Bldg

CLACTON-ON-SEA

Martello Trs
3x2F.G(vert)
Reed(2)120s (occas)

No 2 Inner Bench Head Fl(2)R.5s
No.1 Colne Point Fl.G.3s

Colne Pt

Colne Bar Fl(2)G. 5s

N Eagle Q

Bench Head Fl(3)G.10s
NW Knoll Fl(2)R.5s
Eagle Q.G
Knoll Q

Wallet

No 3 Fl(3)G.15s
Wallet No 4 Fl(2)G.6s Fl(4)R.10s

Wallet No 6 Fl(3)R.5s

Gunfleet Sand

Wallet Spitway LFl.10s Bell

Swin Spitway Iso.10s Bell

East Swin or King's Channel

Barrow No 3 Q(3)10s Bell Racon(M) (3&10cm)

Whitaker Q(3)10s Bell
N Middle Q

No 6 Q

Swallow Tail Ridge Fl.R.10s

Foulness Fl(2)R.10s

Whitaker Bn (10)

S Whitaker Fl(2)G.10s

W Hook Middle

East Swin

Middle

East Barrow

E Barrow Bn (11)

Barrow No 5 Fl.G.10s
Barrow No 4 VQ(9)10s

South West Sunk

Middle Sunk

No 7 Fl.G.2.5s
No 6 Fl(4)R.15s
No 7 Q.G

SW Sunk Bn

No 8 Q(9)15s
Fl(3)R.10s

Fisherman's Gat

Long Sand

NE Maplin Fl.G.5s Bell

Barrow Bn

West Barrow

No 9 VQ(3)5s
No 8 Fl(2)R.5s
No 9 Q(6)+LFl.15s
No 10 Q.R

9. River Colne

⊕ **Landfall waypoint**
51°44′.0N 001°05′.4E
(immediately NE of Knoll NCB)

Charts
Imray *2000* series
Admiralty SC *5607*, *3741*
for Colne N of
Brightlingsea

Tides
HW Dover +0050

Brightlingsea Harbour Commissioners
Harbourmaster VHF Ch 68
Call sign *Brightlingsea Harbour Radio*
☎ 01206 302200
Mobile 07952 734814

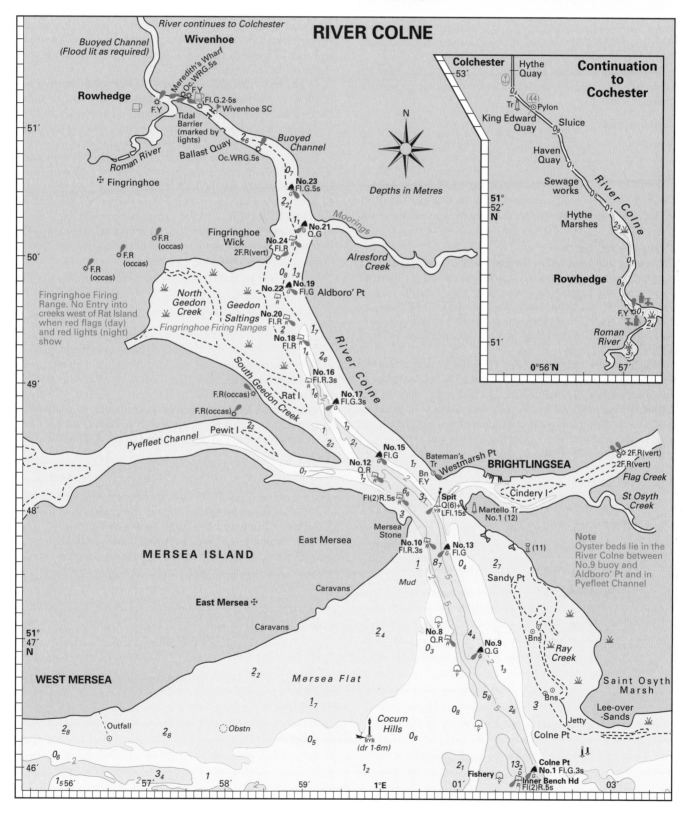

Main hazards

The main hazards to be avoided when approaching the Colne are the long NE-SW stretch of the Gunfleet Sands and Buxey Sand, followed by the shoals of the Knoll, Eagle, Priory Spit, Colne Bar, Bench Head and Mersea Flats.

Channels through or around these hazards are well buoyed, but navigators must identify each buoy carefully and ensure that progress is made from one to the next in the correct sequence. It may be tempting to cut corners, but it's rarely worthwhile. It may appear that you are in clear water with good depth, but wander off course and that can change with little warning.

Buoyage does move and is changed to take account of shifts in banks and shoals. It is wise to maintain up to date charts.

Approaches

Mariners may approach the Colne from the NE (Harwich and rivers to the N), the SE or S (across the Thames Estuary or from the Crouch and Thames), and from the W (River Blackwater). If crossing the North Sea, the likely approach would be via the Sunk, round the NE end of the Gunfleet and through the Wallet, effectively resulting in an approach from NE.

From the NE, SE or S

All routes from seaward converge on the Knoll NCB (Q), which should be left to port. From there, shape a course to leave first the Eagle (Q.G) and then the Colne Bar buoy (Fl(2)G.5s) to starboard with the NW Knoll (Fl(2)R.5s) to port. From the Bar buoy a course of about 345° will take you to Colne Pt No.1 SHB (Fl.G.3s) and the Inner Bench Head No.2 PHB (Fl(2)R.5s).

When sailing coastwise from Harwich a course may be held close to the coast that will enable vessels to pass N (inshore) of the N Eagle NCB (Q) and from there to the Colne Bar buoy. Above half flood a course direct from the N Eagle to the Inner Bench Head buoy may be considered, but this means crossing the Colne Bar, which can be rough in stronger winds and should be avoided on the ebb. Be aware too that the tide sets strongly to the W here on the flood (and E on the ebb).

The Inner Bench Head buoy marks the beginning of the deepwater Colne Channel, which used to be heavily buoyed, but several marks have been removed, making the next PHB No.8.

From W

When approaching from the W (the River Blackwater), sea state, tide and draught will dictate how far off the Mersea Flats you need to stand. With a deep draught and rough seas at low water (last of the ebb out of the Blackwater, first of the flood up the Colne) you may need to sail out round the Bench Head SHB (Fl(3)G.10s), towards the Colne Bar buoy and then N towards the Inner Bench Head to avoid the very extensive Bench Head Shoal.

With less draught or more water and better sea conditions a course across the shoal directly to the Inner Bench Head may be possible. If taking this approach, beware the large unlit 'Fishery' yellow spherical buoy positioned about a cable W of the Inner Bench Head buoy.

Finally, with shallow draught or towards HW with calm water, an inshore course can be set to skirt the Mersea Flats, keeping well S of the ECM *Molliette* wreck beacon on the Cocum Hills. From there a course of about NE will lead to the No.8 PHB (Q.R) and the deep water channel.

Although it may add distance if sailing from the Blackwater, at night approaching the Colne via the Bench Head and Colne Bar buoys provides the certainty of deep water and lit buoys. Similarly, from other directions, finding the Knoll then approaching from there means a lit approach in deep water all the way.

Entry

Once into the Colne deep water channel, it is well buoyed and the sides are steep to (more so on the W side), so if tacking, keep an eye on the depth and it will be quite apparent when you leave the channel across the line of buoys.

Once past No.8 PHB, Mersea Stone will be seen ahead to port, probably with a few craft at anchor there, and the town of Brightlingsea ahead to starboard with a prominent big blue/grey shed.

From No.13 SHB (Fl.G) on there is likely to be much activity, particularly if there are dinghies out racing, so a sharp lookout is needed to avoid other craft as well as pick out the necessary navigation marks. Note also that coasters frequently run up and down the Colne on the tide.

The main place for mooring and re-supplying is Brightlingsea, while the main anchorage is across in the Pyefleet. It is just after No.13 that courses diverge according to destination.

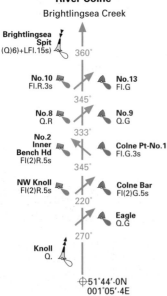

River Colne

Brightlingsea Creek

Brightlingsea Spit
(Q)6)+LFl.15s)

360°

No.10
Fl.R.3s

No.13
Fl.G

345°

No.8
Q.R

No.9
Q.G

333°

No.2 Inner Bench Hd
Fl(2)R.5s

Colne Pt-No.1
Fl.G.3s

345°

NW Knoll
Fl(2)R.5s

Colne Bar
Fl(2)G.5s

220°

Eagle
Q.G

270°

Knoll
Q.

51°44'·0N
001°05'·4E

Looking up the River Colne from the Inner Bench Head buoy with Bateman's Tower immediately to left of the buoy

Bateman's Tower

BRIGHTLINGSEA

Contact
VHF Ch 68
Call sign *Brightlingsea Harbour*
Harbourmaster ☎ 01206 302200
Access 24hr
Water Taxi VHF Ch 37.
Mobile 07733 078 503

Scrubbing posts ☎ 01206 303535

Fuel Diesel and petrol in cans from town

Facilities (at Colne YC) WC. Showers. Launderette

Rubbish disposal At top of CYC jetty

Pump-out At seaward end of pontoons by arrangement (HM)

Water CYC hammerhead. Activated by push button in E end wall of CYC

Gas Calor and Gaz from chandlers

Chandler Two nearby

Provisions In town – 1M.

Post office In town

Boat repairs At nearby yards

Sailmakers In town (Lawrence ☎ 01206 302863)

Pub/restaurant Several nearby and in town and at Colne YC

Pharmacy ☎ 01206 302029

Clubs Colne YC ☎ 01206 302594
Email secretary@colneyachtclub.org.uk
Club Restaurant ☎ 01206 302050
www.colneyachtclub.org.uk
Brightlingsea SC ☎ 01206 303275 www.sailbrightlingsea.com

Taxi ☎ 01255 820123.

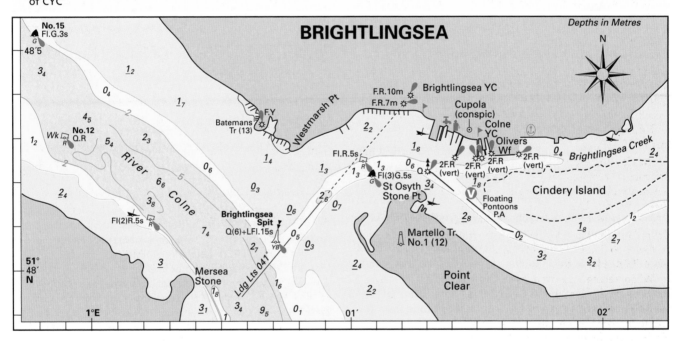

BRIGHTLINGSEA

From No.13 SHB (Fl.G), in reasonable daylight, a tower should be seen on the shore beyond the Brightlingsea Spit SCB on Westmarsh Point – Bateman's Tower (F.Y.12m). Once past No.13 SHB, keep out in the deep water channel with Bateman's Tower clear to the left of the Brightlingsea Spit

River Colne. No.13 buoy with Bateman's Tower and South cardinal buoy marking entrance to Brightlingsea Creek. All Saints Parish Church with square tower on hill behind town

Inset: Brightlingsea Creek in late evening with two dinghies heading for the entrance cardinal mark with Bateman's tower on the shore

Leading lights   *Brightlingsea SC*

Brightlingsea Creek in the evening with the red leading lights showing ashore between the port-hand channel buoy and the church spire. Dinghy park and clubhouse of the Brightlingsea SC

SCB (Q(6)+LFl.15s) until that buoy is almost abeam. Only then is it clear to turn into Brightlingsea Creek. Leave the SCB to port and make a course of about 040° to keep two leading marks on the shore in line. These are lit at night with 2 F.R. lights, but by day they are vertically striped white/red/white. However, this may well look like white/black/white if the light is poor. Spotting the leading marks is made easier by looking for a tall spire that stands up behind them.

Keep the leading marks in line until close to a red PHB (Fl.R.5s), then turn to starboard leaving the PHB to port and a matching SHB (Fl(3)G.5s) to starboard. The entrance should have at least 1m even at LWS, but better water is often found on the S side of the channel.

From the buoys, head E towards Brightlingsea Hard. At night you may have trouble seeing the 2F.R.(vert) lights on either end of the Colne YC hammerhead jetty, but just go towards the main lights and keep an eye out for the NCM (Q) pile on the end of the visitors' pontoon to starboard.

This is a crowded and popular harbour, so it is essential to try, during daylight hours, to make contact with the HM (Ch 68 *Brightlingsea Harbour Radio*) and request a berth on the floating pontoons. Often around HW the HM (or an assistant) will be out and about on the water to help, advise and guide visitors to a berth.

At LW there is limited depth on the inshore side of the pontoons, so be careful when turning. Tides run swiftly in the creek and must be taken carefully into account when berthing alongside or departing.

A well-run water taxi service (Ch 37) makes trips ashore from the pontoons easy and it's much safer than crossing from the shore in a laden dinghy when the harbour is choppy.

Brightlingsea has an attractive waterfront with the Colne YC prominent at the top of the hard (where there is always much activity around tide time) and a lovely timbered building with a cupola (conspic. from seaward) that has been converted to flats. The older part of the town, between the hard and the shopping centre, has retained its nautical air with various marine companies dotted about and boats appearing over garden walls. It is the home of companies as diverse as Sailspar (masts and headsail roller reefing gears), James Lawrence Sailmakers (largely for traditional craft) and the Colne Smack Preservation Society (next to the CYC pontoon) where several smacks are berthed. Sadly the old shipyards are closed and the building of blocks of flats around a yacht basin is due by the big shed below the hard. This will change the character of the waterfront entirely.

The Hard is a popular launching place for all sorts of craft, but is also the location of some of the busiest scrubbing posts on the East Coast. To use them, talk to the hard master ☎ 01206 303535 or make enquiries at the white hut.

Note that anchoring within the harbour is prohibited.

There is commercial shipping traffic through the harbour

Brightlingsea visitors' pontoons in late evening. Be prepared for difficulty finding a berth in high summer

Brightlingsea waterfront. White HM's office behind blue shelter and Sailspar at left, then white hut of Hard Master, scrubbing posts, Colne YC

The Colne YC's pontoon with one boat alongside the hammerhead for water and another jilling about waiting her turn. Looking upstream

and to the N of Cindery Island, going to jetties above the town and further up the drying creek. Keep clear when ships are manoeuvring as they are constrained by draught. There is little or no water above Cindery Island.

St Osyth

St Osyth Creek runs SE off Brightlingsea Creek where the two arms meet at the E end of Cindery Island. It is a narrow, tortuous creek with best water at the entrance between the little Pincushion Island and the S bank of the creek.

The creek is sparsely marked with withies, perches and buoys, but leads to the quay beside a road bridge at St Osyth, which is known to have been a port as far back as 1215. The wooden faced quay is often crowded with craft and there is a line of mud berths at stagings along the waterfront below the boatyard.

Boats of up to 1.5m draught can reach the quay at HW, but must either find a berth alongside and dry out, or return down the creek in good time, as there is little water at LW.

ST OSYTH

Access HW±1½hr
Facilities WC
Water At boatyard
Chandler At boatyard
Provisions In village – ¼M
Post office In village
Boat repairs St Osyth Boatyard ☎ 01255 820005
Pub/restaurant The White Hart ☎ 01255 820318.
    The Kings Arms ☎ 01255 821156

The slipway, scrubbing posts and part of the hard standing and mud berths at St Osyth Boatyard

Looking up the last reaches of St Osyth Creek to the boatyard mud berths at the bridge. Note port-hand channel beacon

The nearby St Osyth Priory, established in the early 12th century, is said to have been named in honour of Osyth, the daughter of an East Anglian King, Redoald. She was beheaded by Danish invaders around 663AD after she refused to worship their Gods. The Priory was built on the site of the earlier nunnery where Osyth had been the first abbess. After her death she was made a saint and the town was named after her.

Mersea Stone Point

Sometimes known as East Mersea Head, the point has a steep shingle beach with clean landing and the attraction of the Dog and Pheasant pub about a mile inland ☎ 01206 383206.

The shore is steep to and if the anchorage is busy it may be necessary to anchor in relatively deep water, but the holding is good and an evening stroll ashore pleasant. It is occasionally useful too as a waiting anchorage if catching a tide early in the morning, but do keep as close to the point as possible, because coasters still run up and down the Colne at night.

The Pyefleet

Pyefleet Creek or The Pyefleet, which runs along the N side of Mersea Island, eventually reaching the Strood, is the main anchorage on the River Colne and is a favourite among East Coast yachtsmen, which means it can become very crowded at weekends in the summer.

The entrance lies about 2 cables N of the wreck of *Lowlands* on the W side of the River above Mersea Stone. Sailing barges often anchor in the mouth and several smacks and bawleys have moorings there. Indeed there are now a lot of moorings in the Pyefleet off the Colchester Oyster Fishery's landing. There is still room, however, to anchor above the moorings between the Mersea shore and Pewit Island. Much beyond that and you come into an area of oyster layings, which, of course, you may not anchor or ground on. The creek shallows too, W of Pewit Island, making it hard to find a hole to lie afloat in clear of the layings.

Barges at anchor around Mersea Stone with its good, steep-to shingle beach

Evening in the Pyefleet

Pyefleet to Alresford

Either leaving the Pyefleet or when continuing up the Colne, leave the No.12 PHB (Q.R) to port.

A short way up the Colne the N and S Geedon Channels open up on the W side to surround Rat Island. These channels lead in towards the Fingringhoe firing ranges, whose activity is indicated by numbers of red flags on the seawall, so cannot be used much, but there is a small hole that local craft sometimes anchor in, just in the mouth of the S channel.

After passing No.17 SHB (Fl.G.3s) it is best to follow the line of red PHBs up to No.22, passing fairly close to each, because they lie along the W edge of the channel while the E side is unmarked and shallows only gradually. When tacking through this area it is not uncommon to have to retreat to deeper water rather swiftly. Beware also the dog leg in the channel around No.18 (Fl.R).

The next SHB is No.19 (Fl.G) Aldboro Point, which is placed at the apex of a long right-hand bend extending from No.22 to No.24 PHBs. On the W bank, at the N end of Geedon Saltings, there is a disused jetty occasionally lit with 2F.R.(vert) lights. Take care to avoid this at night.

The gravel works and jetty in Alresford Creek now appear on the E side of the river.

Alresford Creek

Alresford Creek is entered from No.21 SHB (Q.G) with a line of port hand pillar buoys (red over white) and starboard hand ones (white over green) showing the line of the narrow channel.

Laid and maintained by a group of local yachtsmen who have moorings in the creek, these marks are clear and easy to use, but the creek dries out almost completely and there is little space for visitors to lie.

Within the creek there is a disused jetty on the N side from which ballast was loaded for many years (the ballast is now taken out entirely by road) and a hard landing at a ford. From the landing it is about a mile to Alresford where there's a pub, the Pointer Inn ☎ 01206 822866, and a post office.

Holding in the Pyefleet is good, though in places the mud is very soft and boats do drag their anchors unexpectedly. In fact Pyefleet mud seems to have a character of its own and a delight in sticking firmly and in great quantities to both anchor and chain, making recovery a messy business. It is common to see boats motoring seaward as their crews expend much energy dipping buckets and scrubbing the mud off their ground tackle, decks and topsides.

The Pyefleet has great charm and a place in the heart of most East Coast sailors, but it can also provide a particularly uncomfortable berth in the wrong conditions. Should the wind draw into either the E or W and blow against the tide, the whole creek can cut up rough with boats pitching and tossing all over the place. It can become so bad that a boat will dip her head under at times.

A further attraction for a lot of visitors to the Pyefleet is the presence of the Colchester Oyster Fishery's sheds on the S shore from where it is possible (in the right season) to buy oysters and cooked crabs and lobsters.
☎ 01206 384141
Email info@colchesteroysterfishery.com
www.colchesteroysterfishery.com

Looking into Alresford Creek from No.21 Colne channel buoy. Green and red floats mark channel, which dries

Traffic signals

Alresford to Wivenhoe

The Colne continues above Alresford between wooded banks with Alresford Grange nestling among the trees on the E bank just where the channel runs closest to that shore before taking a long turn NW past a large beacon on the S bank, which displays a directional light for traffic passing downstream through the Wivenhoe tidal barrier, and towards the very active Fingringhoe ballast quay. There coasters load and depart on the tide. When these gravel ships are manoeuvring in the area they take the whole channel and yachts must keep well clear. Remember too that other commercial craft still pass up and down through here to and from Colchester.

There is a line of fore and aft small craft moorings along the E edge of the channel off the ballast quay, making this a busy bottleneck area. It is within sight of the Wivenhoe tidal barrier and Wivenhoe itself.

Looking through the tidal barrier to Wivenhoe waterfront. Church of St-Mary-the-Virgin at right with traffic control lights on east pier head

Immediately below the barrier, on the E bank, is the Wivenhoe SC, which has a slipway and floating pontoon that vessels of under 2m draught can lie alongside at about HW±1hr before drying out in soft mud. Visitors are welcomed and the pontoons are being extended.
☎ 01206 822132 *Email* wsc@hillgf.freeserve.co.uk
www.wivenhoesailing.org.uk

WIVENHOE

Above the ballast quay on the W shore of the Colne the river is spanned by the massive structure of the Wivenhoe tidal barrier. It's an unattractive edifice, but the central section is normally open for vessels to pass through unimpeded.

Once through the tidal barrier, Wivenhoe waterfront opens up with the old Cook's Shipyard and then the town quay

The Rose and Crown on Wivenhoe's waterfront

FINGRINGHOE

As the river bends away from Wivenhoe, another creek opens on the S shore. This is Fingringhoe Creek, commonly known as the Roman River. There are a couple of moorings just inside the mouth of the creek, but it mainly dries and should only be explored by shallow draught vessels near HW. At that time it is an attractive waterway leading up to Fingringhoe, a once thriving port, and home to the Whalebone Inn, which even features on the village sign.

ROWHEDGE

The main river takes a turn to the N above the mouth of the Roman River and Rowhedge appears on the W bank. Once a busy centre for boat building, plus having a large fishing fleet, the Rowhedge waterfront now has a quieter air with few obvious signs of its maritime past.

It's still possible to moor along the quayside at Rowhedge, close outside the waterfront pubs, but timing is dependent upon draught and it's likely that you will only have from perhaps HW-2 to HW+1½hr unless planning to dry out there.

The village, which is right by the river, offers several pubs, including 'Ye Olde Albion' and 'The Anchor' on the quay, as well as a post office and shops.

Rowhedge to Colchester

Although the Colne runs a further two or more miles from Rowhedge to Colchester, there is little to recommend it to the yachtsman other than curiosity. There are tree-lined reaches at first, but then it comes into a run-down industrial area ripe for redevelopment.

The best water is to be found by keeping to the middle of the stream and to the outsides of bends. Near to HW there is enough water for a boat of over 2m draught to creep right up to the Hythe Bridge at Colchester, but this would be within an hour of HW and time must be allowed to return down river to deeper water. It would be possible to lie at the Hythe or King Edward Quay, but it is often occupied by commercial craft and yachts are not welcomed.

There is a winding hole to starboard within sight of the Hythe Bridge. It is intended for turning coasters and consequently has good depth for yachts too.

Approach from No.29 SHB with the open section directly ahead. There's a pair of port and starboard hand buoys, followed by a pair of port and starboard hand beacon piles (Q.R/Q.G) to guide boats into the passageway through. The barrier is marked on each side by 2F.R/F.G(vert) lights. (These signals are also shown on the upstream side for passage down through the barrier.)

Traffic warning signals on the N pier are arranged to show 3F.R(vert) lights, directed both downstream and up. These are lit to indicate that the barrier is closed or that a large vessel is in transit. In either case, do not try to pass through.

Directional lights (DirOc.WRG.5s) are sited on the N bank of the river, at the top end of the waterfront, and on the S bank, below the ballast jetty, to lead through the barrier at night. Upstream traffic should keep to the white sector on a heading of 305° and downstream in the white sector on 125°.

The opening in the barrier is 30m wide, so two-way traffic is practical, but be careful to pass port to port and at less than 5kn.

Once through the barrier, Wivenhoe waterfront opens to starboard with boats berthed bows on in mud berths with all activity watched by visitors to the popular Rose and Crown pub. There is also a line of small craft moorings opposite the quay and, a little higher up, there are new blocks of flats overlooking the quayside where boats can berth on the tide.

There are plenty of shops in Wivenhoe, plus a post office, pubs and restaurants, doctors and dentists, and a chemist.

Finding a mud berth along the quay is a matter of chance and even then an empty berth may not prove comfortable once the tide has gone if your boat's hull does not match the hole made by the resident vessel.

River Colne, Colchester. Hythe Quay and the Hythe road bridge, the effective limit of navigation

10. River Blackwater

⊕ **Landfall waypoint**
51°44′.0N 001°05′.4E
(immediately NE of Knoll NCB)

Charts
Imray 2000 series
Admiralty SC *5607, 3741*

Tides
Maldon HW Dover +0130

Blackwater River Bailiff
Nigel Harmer
☎ 01621 856487
Mobile 07818 013723

Main hazards

The entrance to both the River Blackwater and the River Colne lies W and NW from the Knoll NCB (Q), which in turn stands at the SW end of the Wallet channel, N of the Buxey Sand and W of the Gunfleet Sand. Approaching the buoy is straightforward if arriving from the NE through the Wallet, but from S it means crossing the sand banks, either from the Crouch or Thames. As with everywhere in the Thames Estuary, these banks are hazards to navigation and must be treated cautiously.

From the S, the best approach to the Knoll is via the Spitway between the Swin and Wallet channels, to save a long haul NE to round the NE Gunfleet and return SW through the Wallet.

From the Crouch, small craft may cut through the Rays'n, but even they must cross Swire Hole to avoid drying patches on the Batchelor Spit.

However, once the Knoll is reached, navigation becomes less hazardous although compass courses will be needed in poor visibility.

Approaches

From the Knoll NCB (Q) shape a course to pass the Eagle SHB (Q.G.) close to starboard. Alter course then to pass between the NW Knoll PHB (Fl(2)R.5s) and the Colne Bar SHB (Fl(2)G.5s). From there, steer to leave the Bench Head SHB (Fl(3)G.10s) to starboard. The Bench Head buoy is generally thought of as the beginning of the Blackwater.

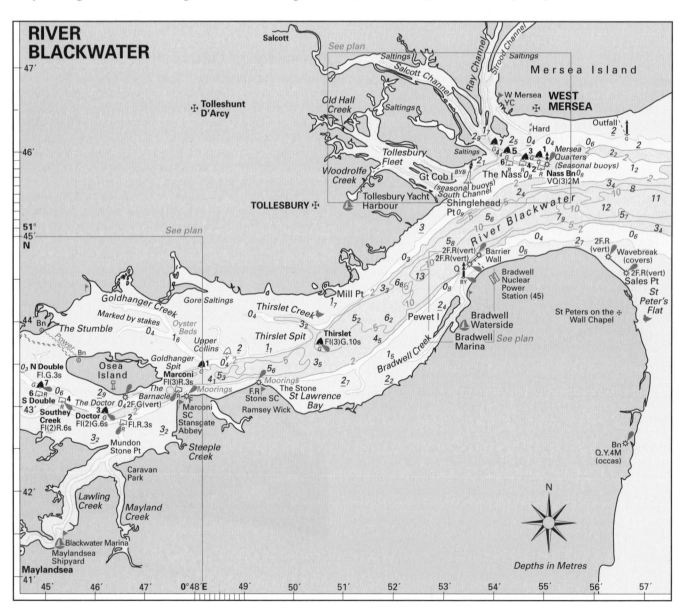

Looking WSW from the Colne past the East Cardinal beacon marking the wreck on the Cocum Hills to the Blackwater Estuary with Bradwell power station at left

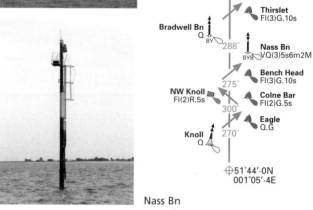

River Blackwater
Blackwater SC
-Iso.G.5s bearing 300°

Hillypool Pt-No.8 Fl(2)R.3s

N Doubles-No.7 Fl.G.3s

S Doubles-No.6

Southey No.4 Fl(2)R.6s

Doctor-No.3 Fl(2)G.6s

No.2 Fl.R.3s

Marconi Fl(2)R.3s

Goldhanger-No.1

Thirslet Fl(3)G.10s

Bradwell Bn Q BY 288°

Nass Bn VQ(3)5s6m2M BYB

Bench Head Fl(3)G.10s 275°

NW Knoll Fl(2)R.5s

Colne Bar Fl(2)G.5s 300°

Eagle Q.G

Knoll Q 270°

⊕51°44'·0N 001°05'·4E

Nass Bn

If crossing from the River Colne to the Blackwater, sea conditions, draught and state of tide will dictate your course. It may be necessary to go right out to the Bench Head buoy near to low tide on a rough day, but a more likely course is out round the Inner Bench Head, then on a course made good of about 250° into the deep water channel with the Bench Head buoy bearing about 110°. Shallow draught boats may be able to leave the Colne S of No.8 PHB and make a course of about 220° to stay S of the ECM (1M distant) marking the wreck of the *Molliette* on the Cocum Hills. From there they can turn onto about 250° with Bradwell Power Station fine on the port bow until again finding the deep water of the Blackwater itself.

Entry

Once past the Bench Head it is often difficult to identify any marks other than the two massive lumps of Bradwell Power Station on the S shore and a general view of 'that's W Mersea' on the starboard bow. So, from the Bench Head, making good a course of about 290° will take you clear of Sales Point - but keep checking your position as you will have tide running athwart your course for the full 4M distance - towards the Nass Beacon ECM (VQ(3)5s6m2M) marking the entrance to Mersea Quarters and Tollesbury, with the option of leaving it to the N and going on up the Blackwater.

West Mersea church from the Quarters

WEST MERSEA

First port of call on the Blackwater is West Mersea. Enter the Quarters from close E of the Nass Bn ECM (VQ(3)5s6m2M), following the line of unlit port and starboard buoys towards the mass of moorings.

The starboard hand buoys are often harder to spot than the port hand ones, but be aware that from the third PHB, No.6, you must look for SHBs or follow the lines of

WEST MERSEA

Contact
Moorings WMYC boatman, call sign *YC1* (*Yankee Charlie One*) on Ch 37
Access 24hr
West Mersea YC ☎ 01206 382947
Email wmersea.yc@rya-online.net
www.wmyc.org.uk

Fuel In town

Water On pontoon

Gas Calor and Gaz from chandlers

Chandler MarineStore Wyatts ☎ 01206 384745
Peter Clarke's Boatyard ☎ 01206 385905

Scrubbing posts Contact WMYC

Provisions In town

Post office In town

Boat repairs Peter Clarke's Boatyard ☎ 01206 385905

Sailmakers Gowen Ocean ☎ 01206 382922

Pub/restaurant Many along front, including WMYC and the Company Shed ☎01206 382700 (for shellfish and oysters), and in town

Clubs West Mersea YC ☎ 01206 382947
Dabchicks SC ☎ 01206 38378.

Transport Buses to Colchester.

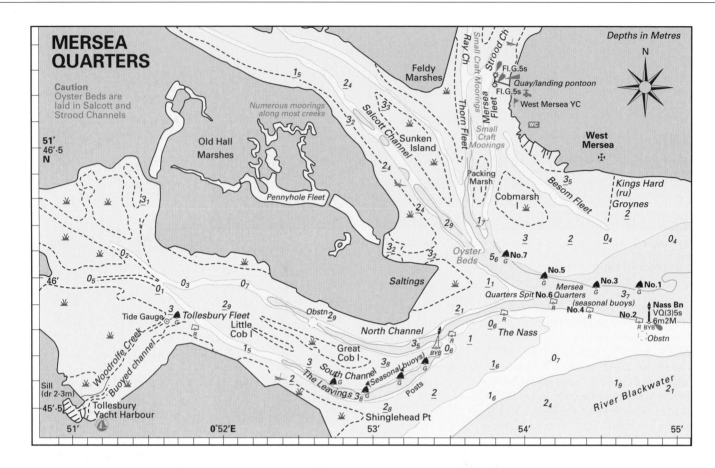

moorings, otherwise you will steer W towards Tollesbury.

There are boats moored well out in Mersea Quarters, but there is still room to anchor there. However, it can be rather exposed at HW with a heavy swell.

Once among the moorings there is nowhere to anchor (partly to avoid fouling ground chains and partly to avoid the extensive oyster beds, which even cover the banks outside the lines of moorings in Salcott Channel and the areas between Cobmarsh and Packing Marsh Islands) and you

must seek a mooring. This is best done by calling the West Mersea YC boatman, call sign *YC1* or *YC2* on VHF Ch 37, when passing the Nass Bn. He will do his best to find you a berth and he also provides an excellent launch service to get you to and from the landing at Mersea Hard and has, of course, a wealth of local knowledge if you need repairs or services.

Once inside the Quarters, the channel divides into several separate arms. Each branch generally has a clear line between the moorings and it is best to follow these.

Approaching the landing at West Mersea aboard the West Mersea YC launch

West Mersea YC boatman going to pick up from the moorings

The oyster packing shed on Packing Marsh Island, West Mersea, a prominent landmark

Keeping to port will take you up the Salcott Channel to the W of Sunken Island. Heading a little to starboard leads into the Thornfleet on the W side of Packing Marsh Island with its distinctive oyster shed. On the E side of Packing Marsh is Mersea Fleet, while way over to the E of Cobmarsh Island is Besom Fleet, which runs right along the West Mersea foreshore. A channel, The Gut, cuts through from the Thornfleet to the Mersea Fleet and Strood Channel opposite the hard and landing pontoon. The Strood Channel runs on inland round the back of Mersea Island towards the Strood causeway between Mersea and the mainland. (Beyond this causeway is the head of the Pyefleet, which runs E into the Colne.)

All of these channels are thick with moorings and their headwaters are really only suitable for exploration by dinghy.

If you choose to seek a mooring without contacting YC1 or 2, do not use the piles that stand in the Strood Channel to the W of Ray Island unless they are clearly in a good state of repair. They have been derelict for some years but the WMYC is planning to renovate them for additional mooring space.

Looking in towards the Tollesbury channels from Mersea Quarters. Two port hand buoys, the East cardinal on the spit from Great Cob Island, marking division between North Channel and more often used South Channel, where the green starboard hand buoys go on round to the Leavings, where the white boat is moored

TOLLESBURY

Tollesbury shares a common entrance with Mersea from the Nass Bn ECM (VQ(3)5s6m2M), its creeks running W from Mersea Quarters. Follow the line of PHBs in from the beacon and turn to port at the third (No.6) along another line heading W.

A word of warning is needed here. In common with many East Coast ports, when entering Tollesbury in the late afternoon, the sun will be low and directly ahead. This makes spotting buoys and/or identifying them extremely difficult, so proceed with caution.

Two PHBs are placed along the N edge of the Nass sand bank and, depending upon wind and tide conditions, at anything less than HW these can drift over the bank, so watch the depth and be prepared to stand a little off them. The second PHB is paired to the N with a small ECB at the seaward end of the long spit out from Great Cob Island. The South Channel, the main Tollesbury channel, carries on, leaving this buoy to the N, but a few local boats enter the North Channel, leaving the ECB to port, and find a shallow secluded anchorage.

The South Channel is now marked with SHBs. With a low sun these appear as black shapes, no more, but they should still be left to starboard. In the season there should be four to pass, each with a green topmark.

At the third SHB the channel turns sharply to starboard in a NWly direction. This reach is known as The Leavings, which used to be an anchorage for local fishing smacks, but

Leavings

ECB on Cob Island spit

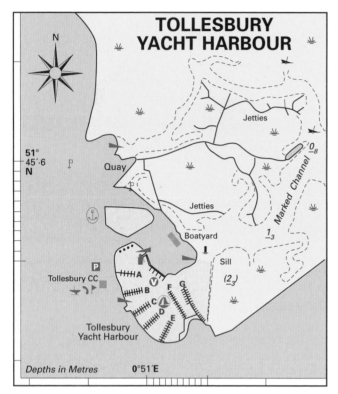

TOLLESBURY YACHT HARBOUR

51° 45'.6 N

Quay

Jetties

Marked Channel

0⸱8

Jetties

Boatyard

1⸱3

Sill

(2⸱3)

Tollesbury CC

A
V
B   C   F G
D
E

Tollesbury Yacht Harbour

Depths in Metres   0°51'E

TOLLESBURY MARINA

Contact
VHF Ch 80 & 37
Call sign *Tollesbury Marina*
Harbourmaster ☎ 01621 869202
Email marina@woodrolfe.demon.co.uk
www.woodrolfe.com
Access ±1½hr

Fuel Diesel at berth below yard crane

Facilities WC. Showers. Launderette

Water On pontoons

Electricity On pontoons

Gas Calor and Gaz

Chandler On site

Provisions In town (10 mins)

Post office In town

Boat repairs 20-ton boat-lift and cranes, 3 slipways up to 30 ton

Scrubbing posts In marina

Telephone At Tollesbury CC

Pub/restaurant Tollesbury CC on site and in town

Pharmacy In High St

Clubs Tollesbury Cruising Club ☎ 01621 869561
Tollesbury SC ☎ 01621 868218
Email tsc@tollesburysc.co.uk
www.tollesburysc.co.uk

Taxi ☎ 01621 819225.

The former light vessel *Trinity* now used by the Fellowship Afloat Charitable Trust for teaching youngsters to sail. She is berthed in Woodrolfe Creek

now sees the beginning of the Tollesbury moorings. Follow the line of these moorings, being very careful of depth if tacking outside the line of starboard hand withies, and Woodrolfe Creek will open up to port with the landmark white blocks of flats easily visibly over the saltings, together with the masts in the marina and the red light vessel, HQ for the Fellowship Afloat Charitable Trust.

Off the mouth of Woodrolfe Creek there are one or two orange mooring buoys labelled 'Marina', which are waiting buoys to be used when there is not enough water to get up the creek.

Woodrolfe Creek dries and has a narrow, winding channel, but is well marked initially with port and starboard buoys. The line of moorings then gives guidance as to the

A Dutch yacht sailing in up the Tollesbury South Channel with the red yacht astern entering Mersea Quarters

ECB on Cob Island spit

Scrubbing posts and slipway in Tollesbury Marina. Fuelling berth is alongside the steel piling below the crane

best water. There's a tide gauge on the N bank at the mouth, but it's not always easy to read. Another will be seen outside the marina, again showing depth over the cill, which is about 2m at HWS and 1.5m on neaps.

As you pass the light vessel to starboard and approach Tollesbury Marina the entrance is clearly seen to the left of an old black weatherboard shed beside the Woodrolfe Boatyard slipway. An arm of water also turns sharply to starboard along Tollesbury waterfront but should not be followed unless previously inspected at LW.

On entering the marina, the fuel berth is hard round to starboard under the boatyard crane, while pontoon A is furthest in to starboard and you pass G in the entrance.

BRADWELL

On entering the Blackwater the outstanding landmark is Bradwell Power Station, close to which lie Bradwell Creek and Bradwell Marina. The distance diagonally across the Blackwater deepwater channel from the Nass Bn is 1.5M to the breakwater, which has 2FR(vert) lights at either end and can often look like a ship from a distance. Sections of the breakwater are, slowly, being removed as part of the decommissioning process for the power station, but it is currently still a substantial barrier.

A short distance beyond the W end of the breakwater there's a NCM pile beacon (Q) with a depth gauge showing water in the marina entrance. To enter Bradwell Creek and the marina, leave this Bn to starboard and head in between the orange buoys to port and withies to starboard. The tide can flow quite strongly across this approach with the buoys being pushed across the bank or into the channel, making it narrower than ever. The depth will vary frequently.

At the last, fourth, orange buoy, bear to port and head for a green conical SHB. (Ignore the dilapidated leading marks on the seawall beyond the SHB, if they are even identified, because they are well out of line with the current channel.) Leaving the SHB very close to starboard, turn hard to starboard and follow the lines of moorings into Bradwell Creek. Here the tide runs very strongly, either from ahead or astern.

To port will be seen the remains of Bradwell Quay and some scrubbing posts (belonging to the nearby Bradwell Quay YC) beside a public slipway. Off the end is a large red beacon to be left to port on entering and shortly beyond is a single orange buoy marked 'Bradwell'. Turn to port around this and the marina entrance is open ahead, but remember the tide runs swiftly across the approach.

When entering Bradwell Creek, keep between orange buoys and the withies. At last orange buoy make for the green starboard hand conical buoy under the shore. Round it close to and then follow lines of boats

Bradwell Beacon. North cardinal showing clear water out in Blackwater. Leave to starboard on entry to Creek. Depth gauge for water in marina entrance

Bradwell Marina entrance. Turn in from the Creek past the orange buoy (to port) and run in between the port and starboard posts. Visitors' berths on the hammerheads straight ahead and to the right

Pass between the red and green piles and the hammerhead berth dead ahead (row A) is the main visitors' berth with a secondary berth on the hammerhead next to it to starboard (row B). The fuelling berth is ahead to port beneath the black and white marina tower.

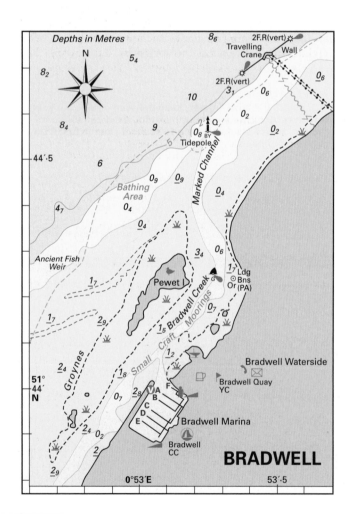

BRADWELL MARINA

Contact
 VHF Ch 80
 Call sign *Bradwell Marina*
 Harbourmaster ☎ 01621 776235
 Email roy@bradwellmarina.com
 www.bradwellmarina.com
 Access ±4½hr

Fuel Diesel, petrol and LPG berth at base of tower. Tight turning space

Facilities WC. Showers. Launderette

Water Taps and hoses on pontoons

Electricity On pontoons

Gas Calor and Gaz

Provisions In village (turn right out of marina, 15 mins)

Post office At Bradwell Waterside (turn left out of marina, 5 mins)

Boat repairs 30-ton boat-lift, self-launch slipway

Telephone Pay phone beside clubhouse

Pub/restaurant Bradwell CC on site.
 Green Man ☎ 01621 776226 at Waterside.
 King's Head ☎ 01621 776224 in village

Clubs Bradwell CC.
 Bradwell Quay YC
 www.bradwellquay.fsnet.co.uk

Transport Bus to Southminster train station

Taxi ☎ 01621 773773

It is sometimes possible to borrow a mooring in Bradwell Creek, but anchoring is not advisable. When picking up a mooring, be aware of the strong run of tide.

If holidaying and staying at Bradwell, it is worth the walk, either by way of the sea wall or the village, to visit St Peter's on the Wall (www.bradwellchapel.org). Established by St Cedd in 654AD, it is an extremely simple but calm place of worship, perhaps the oldest site of Christian teaching in England.

Bradwell to Thirslet

On departing Bradwell Creek, be sure to round the beacon to port before turning up river. It is tempting to make directly towards Osea Island, which appears dead ahead, but between Bradwell and the island lies Thirslet spit on the N side of the main channel. It is marked by a SHB (Fl(3)G10s), which, when finally located, is quite obvious, but spotting it can be difficult. Thirslet spit is made of very hard sand and is steep to on its river side. Many, many vessels have grounded on it as they make their way straight up or down the Blackwater. A dogleg around it is essential, so steer for the moorings at Stone rather than directly towards Osea. (When returning down river, from Osea, steer on Bradwell, after passing close outside the Stone moorings, until past Thirslet.)

Thirslet Creek runs NW from the spit buoy and can provide a sheltered anchorage when the sand banks are uncovered. However, once the banks are awash it becomes rather exposed.

Opposite Thirslet, on the S shore, St Lawrence Bay provides an area popular with PWCs and water-skiers.

STONE

On the S shore ½M above Thirslet is Stone with a long shingle beach, many moorings and several large, highly active fleets of racing dinghies that criss-cross the entire river. For information about possible use of moorings, phone Stone SC ☎ 01621 779344, which also has details of its racing events on the website www.stonesc.co.uk.

Tides run fast through the moorings and it is best to shape a course to pass outside them all.

Stone to Osea

A further ½M up river, but across on the N side, the No.1 SHB marks the end of Goldhanger Spit and the entrance to Goldhanger Creek. The spit extends from the E end of Osea Island and the Creek cuts NW towards the village of Goldhanger with an arm breaking away to run behind Osea Island towards The Stumbles, eventually rejoining the main river and actually making Osea an island.

There are oyster layings in Goldhanger Creek making it difficult to find an anchorage. Like Thirslet, it only offers shelter once the banks are dry. One or two small craft do lie at the head of the creek where there is also the Goldhanger SC. If your boat can take the ground comfortably then there is a landing, and Goldhanger village with its pubs, The Chequers Inn and The Cricketers, is a short walk away.

Thirslet Spit buoy

Marconi port hand channel buoy off Stansgate

The anchorage east of the pier at Osea Island

Across on the S shore at Stansgate there are more moorings and the Marconi SC (☎ 01621 772164 *Email* info@marconi-sc.org.uk   www.marconi-sc.org.uk).   The clubhouse boasts two bars plus showers and catering. The club also has useful scrubbing posts on the sand shore.

Barbican 33 *Blue Nereid* entering Lawling Creek, River Blackwater, with Mundon Stone Point at left, Osea Island in distant background and red No.2 Blackwater channel buoy in between. Some green Lawling channel buoys also astern

Mundon Pt   No.2 buoy and   Osea Island
                 green Lawling
                 Channel marks

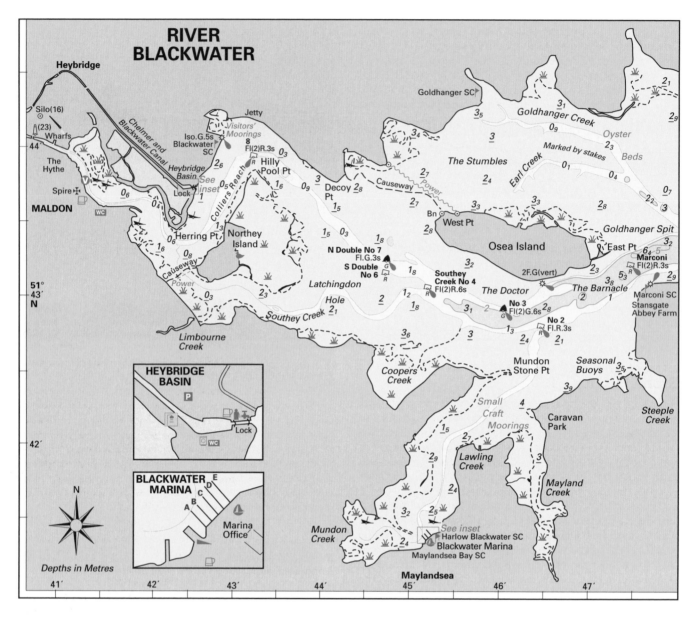

RIVER BLACKWATER

Depths in Metres

HEYBRIDGE BASIN

BLACKWATER MARINA

NW of Stansgate, at the W end of the Marconi club moorings, there is a PHB (Fl(2)R.3s) that doesn't always stand out too well, being constructed with a wide, flat float and only a thin pillar to see from a distance. It is placed in good water, but at a point where the river channel narrows and it should be left to port for safety. The area between this Marconi buoy and the anchorage E of Osea pier is always choppy and can be disturbingly rough with wind against tide.

The pier at Osea is now a shadow of its former self, but still carries 2F.G(vert) lights that act as a useful guide. There's good depth and holding E of the pier with the shell beach of Osea a popular place for walking and picnicking. At LW, deep draught boats must beware The Barnacle shoal patch a cable E from the pier.

The Osea anchorage has been used by many different types of craft down the centuries, from raiding Vikings to barges, coasters off-loading into lighters for Maldon and Heybridge and from gentlemen's yachts through to modern cruisers. There's good holding if you set the anchor properly and shelter from N winds, in addition to offering a pleasant place to stretch your legs ashore or swim off the beach – and

Boats entering Lawling Creek around Mundon Stone Point. SWB carries welcome notice and contact channel (Ch 37) for Blackwater Marina

Blackwater Marina, Lawling Creek, seen from off the Harlow Blackwater SC. Approach channel is not direct and must be followed. Marina berths dry out

children can paddle about the anchorage in dinghies, practising their boat handling skills.

Lawling Creek

South from Osea is the No.2 PHB (Fl.R.3s), which marks the S side of the main river channel, but also the entrance to Lawling Creek. This creek runs SW to Maylandsea and the Blackwater Marina.

Enter leaving the No.2 buoy to starboard (it is a PHB for the river only) and follow the green and red buoys S. These lead through the best water to round Mundon Stone Point, which has a tall pole unlit beacon on its highest point, and enter Lawling Creek itself. On the way, pass a SWB with 4kn speed limit notice and details for contacting the Blackwater Marina.

There is a sheltered anchorage on the S side of Mundon Stone Point, but be warned that the mud bank inside the headland is extensive. The small knoll of sand that forms the headland is often used for barbeques by visiting club cruises and is also a frequent perch for several herons.

Opposite Mundon Pt is the entrance to the drying Mayland Creek, which has a few moorings in it.

BLACKWATER MARINA

Contact
 VHF Ch 37
 Call sign *Blackwater Marina*
 Harbourmaster ☎ 01621 740264
 Email info@blackwater-marina.co.uk
 www.blackwater-marina.co.uk
 Access HW±2hr
Fuel Diesel
Facilities WC. Showers
Water Taps and hoses on pontoons
Electricity On pontoons
Gas Calor and Gaz
Provisions In village, 5 mins' walk
Boat repairs Slipway
Pub/restaurant On site and takeaways in village
Taxi ☎ 01621 773773.

A line of moorings in Lawling Creek, which is steadily silting up, shows the course of the creek, but the recently laid port and starboard buoys follow a much straighter course and sticking to it is recommended.

About a mile in from the entrance, on the E bank, where the moorings thicken, stands the Harlow Blackwater SC (☎ 01621 740300 *Email* enquiries@harlow-blackwater-sc.org.uk www.harlow-blackwater-sc.org.uk). The club runs an area of about 40 drying moorings – the boats on them are afloat at HW±2hrs – near their launching ramp and the weatherboard clubhouse has showers, toilets, a bar and serves hot snacks when there's racing going on. The launching ramp has water at HW±2hr.

The Blackwater Marina will be seen ahead from the HBSC, but must be approached by following the winding line of moorings carefully. The marina has drying pontoons that can be reached no better than HW±2hr.

Approach the pontoons on a direct line from the moorings with the big sheds straight ahead and the slipway on the right. 'A' pontoon is beside the slipway; 'E' is at the seaward end.

Above the marina the creek narrows rapidly and dries completely, but there is an active dinghy club, the Maylandsea Bay SC ☎ 01621 740470 *Email* contact@maylandseabay-sc.org.uk www.maylandseabay-sc.org.uk just upriver. The club has a few drying moorings for its group of cruising members.

Lawling Creek to Heybridge

From Osea, leave No.2 PHB to port and No.3 SHB 'Doctor' (Fl(2)G.6s) to starboard. The water inshore looks inviting, but the Doctor flats have caught the keel of many a yacht trying to take a short cut inside the buoy.

At the Doctor the river turns NW and shortly the No.4 PHB (Fl(2)R.6s) marking the entrance to Southey Creek will be reached. This creek winds away W behind Northey Island to rejoin the main Blackwater river at Herring Point. It is a broad expanse of water at HW, but quickly narrows and dries as the tide ebbs. Passage can be made behind Northey on a good tide, but there is a hard causeway between the

Looking back down the River Blackwater, from No. 3 buoy, the Doctor, south of Osea, to Stansgate with the Marconi SC and scrubbing posts, past Stone to Bradwell power station

Lock and traffic signal

Heybridge Basin and lock with Hillypool Point No. 8 channel marker in foreground

Approach to Heybridge Basin with red traffic light showing. Leave green Lock Approach buoy to starboard and follow the withies when lock open

end of the causeway across to Osea Island, up to Heybridge. The channel off Mill Beach is narrow and there's little water at LW, although on a big tide Northey Island now largely floods.

There are moorings all along the Mill Beach foreshore, but the main marks to look ahead for are the towers of the old mill and the Blackwater SC (a long white building with a black roof set behind the seawall), which shows an Iso.G.5s light at night. The club has a large number of drying moorings, a concrete launching ramp and a floating wooden pontoon that cruisers can go alongside at HW.
☎ 01621 853923

island and the mainland at the SW corner to be aware of.

Just above Southey Creek a pair of buoys, the Doubles, mark a distinct narrowing of the fairway and shallowing to under 1m at LWS. The SHB, North Doubles, is lit (Fl.G.3s) and marks the rejoining with the main river of the arm of Goldhanger Creek that has gone round the N side of Osea Island across the Stumbles.

The river now runs between the NE shore of Northey Island to port (site of the Battle of Maldon in 991AD) and Mill Beach, which runs from Decoy Point, at the mainland

HEYBRIDGE BASIN

Contact
VHF Ch 80
Call sign *Basin Lock*
Lock Master ☎ 01621 853506
Access HWS±1hr, HWN–1hr

Facilities WC. Showers. Launderette

Water Taps

Electricity At a few shore points

Boat repairs Stebbens Boat Yard ☎ 01621 857436.

Pub/restaurant The Old Ship ☎ 01621 854150
The Jolly Sailor ☎ 01621 854210

Café On seawall (substantial breakfasts)

Taxi ☎ 01621 851150.

Boats preparing to lock out from Heybridge Basin, led by a
Fairey Atalanta 26

Email secretary@blackwatersailingclub.co.uk
www.blackwatersailingclub.co.uk

Off the BSC the channel turns SW around the No.8 PHB
(Fl(2)R.3s) Hillypool Point off the N tip of Northey Island.
As its name implies, the river bed here is indeed uneven, but
best water is found towards the mainland (W) shore.

Half way along this reach, known as Colliers Reach from
the days when colliers brought up here, lies Heybridge Basin,
the seaward end of the Chelmer & Blackwater Navigation,
a canal running inland to Chelmsford. The basin is a
traditional wintering berth for yachts, but has also become a
popular summer stop-over since the end of the timber trade
and removal of the stacks of seasoning timber from the canal
banks.

Drying moorings extend along the foreshore between the
BSC and the Basin lock, but not much further. The entrance
to the lock is readily identifiable by a large clump of trees
and white buildings with a space (the lock) between them. It
is usually difficult to tell whether the lock gates are open or
shut until directly in line with them when the red or green

Tide time at Heybridge Basin and everyone wants to lock out,
watched by onlookers

The popular Old Ship Inn alongside the lock at Heybridge

River Bailiff's office   MLSC   Visitors' pontoon

Maldon waterfront at Hythe Quay. Church at left and barges symbolise Maldon. Black shed at left Walter Cook's barge yard. Leave yellow drying mooring buoys to starboard when approaching town

traffic light on the left hand side makes it clear.

The approach channel begins at a small SHB 'Lock Approach' and is marked by withies to be left to port. There are depth gauges on either side of the lock entrance and the lock is worked (at best) for an hour either side of HW. Visitors should berth in the basin as directed after prior booking.

Once berthed in the Basin it is a pleasant dinghy trip up the canal to land at the back of Tesco's supermarket in Maldon to re-provision. There are also some shops at Heybridge, reached by walking or cycling about 1M up the towpath and turning right along the road that crosses the canal.

Heybridge to Maldon

From Heybridge Basin, Colliers Reach continues SW to Herring Point where the river turns NW once more and winds up to Maldon. A few smacks may be anchored opposite the Point in the bight off the end of the mole, but they dry out soon after HW.

Leave Herring Point No.9 SHB to starboard and keep following the red and green buoys past the end of the Promenade. A large red PHM beacon that stands a short way along the mole marks the end of a concrete launching ramp and should be left well to port.

Lines of drying moorings outside the channel on both the Prom foreshore and the opposite bank, together with the channel buoys, give a good indication of the deep water. Beware Thames barges motoring to and from the Hythe Quay around tide time, because they need the full width of the deep water to manoeuvre in, particularly if they are to be turned to berth with their heads downstream.

Above the Hythe Quay, boat yards and mud berths line the W bank right up to the road bridge at the Fullbridge, but there are few available berths and visitors must try to go alongside the floating pontoon at the N end of the Quay and be prepared to dry out, unless their visit is to be very swift at HW.

Maldon town climbs the hillside with the spire of St Mary's church standing clear above the masts of barges lying in their permanent berths at the Hythe, while further upstream and to the right are the grey buildings of the old timber yards and flour mills. This was once a thriving port

MALDON

Contact
River Bailiff ☎ 01621 856487
Mobile 07818 013723
Email rivers@maldon.gov.uk
Access ±1hr to pontoon berth at Hythe Quay

Facilities WC. Showers. Launderette

Water Tap

Gas Calor and Gaz at MarineStore Chandlers
☎ 01621 854280 North St

Chandler MarineStore, North St

Provisions In town

Post office In town

Boat repairs Various yards along North St and Downs Road

Pub/restaurant Queens Head ☎ 01621 854112
Jolly Sailor ☎ 01621 853463
Many in town
Maldon Little Ship Club

Clubs Maldon Little Ship Club ☎ 01621 854139 *Email* info@mlsc.org.uk www.mlsc.org.uk

Taxi ☎ 01621 855111.

MYC   Hythe Quay   Promenade   Mills

Maldon waterfront from Herring Point, with Maldon YC, church, barges, Queens Head pub, boatyards and Sadds mills in distant view

with smacks lining the foreshore along the prom, barges being repaired at Walter Cook's yard (where the blocks are still used by barges), and barges and coasters coming and going to the mills, plus a number of busy boatbuilding yards above the town and a sailmaker's in between. Today the barges at the Hythe are used for corporate and private charters, and yachts and motor boats fill the mud berths that line the bank from the Hythe right up to the Fullbridge fixed road bridge by the mills. However, the commercial traffic and smacks have gone.

Maldon YC moved from its position on the Quay to a new site at the end of the Prom some years ago, but the Maldon Little Ship Club still stands behind the Quay and the 'Jolly Sailor' and 'Queens Head' still serve the needs of thirsty sailors. The River Bailiff has his office at the seaward end of the Quay close to Walter Cook's old black shed and there's now a small museum there too. The whole Quay has been 'sanitised', but there is still an East Coast air that thickens as you move up river through the various boatyards, where the charm of mud and old wooden boats still persists.

Launching slip on the Prom below Maldon

The Fullbridge above Maldon, the effective head of navigation

11. River Crouch

⊕ **Landfall waypoint**
51°41′.8N 001°08′.3E (just S of Swin Spitway Bell buoy)

Charts
Imray *2000 series*
Admiralty SC *5607, 3750*

Tides
Burnham-on-Crouch
HW Dover +0115

Crouch Harbour Authority
Harbourmaster
☎ 01621 783602
Email
ianbell@crouchharbour.org
www.crouchharbour.org

Main hazards

The Whitaker Channel, leading in towards the River Crouch, runs roughly NE-SW between Foulness Sand (on the S side) and the Buxey and Ray Sands (on the N side). Both sandbanks are extremely hard and present a serious hazard to any vessel grounding in rough weather. The buoyage in the channel is good, but navigators must take care to identify each mark carefully and to progress from one to the next, always keeping an eye on the depth.

There is shoal water between the Swin Spitway and the Whitaker Beacon, also a drying bank between the Swallow Tail SHB and the SWB to the W.

Tides are strong, but follow the lie of the channel without too much set across the sands.

Approaches

From NW, N and NE

From the Rivers Colne and Blackwater the normal route will be through the Spitway, which is the shallow channel running between the Wallet and the Swin. Identify and pass comfortably close to both the Wallet Spitway (LFl.10s Bell) and Swin Spitway (Iso.10s Bell) SWBs before turning SW into the Whitaker Channel.

As an alternative to the longer haul out to the Spitway, shoal draught boats may slip through the shallow inshore Ray Sand (Rays'n) Channel from the Blackwater or Colne. This runs between the Buxey Sand and the Dengie Flats. It is a passage recommended only on a rising tide, above about half tide, and with frequent sounding. The sole mark is the Buxey Beacon NCM until you reach the southern exit where there is often a yellow buoy. There is no clear channel across the last mile where the Buxey and Ray Sands (S end of the Dengie Flats) join together and the yellow buoy only gives an indication of where the best water may lie.

The Rays'n is like a funnel. The E arm runs from the Knoll NCB across the Swire Hole (with its rapidly changing depths) to a point where the Buxey Bn bears S. From there alter course to about SSW, leaving the Beacon ½M or so to port. While making towards the tall pylons on Foulness, enter the neck of the funnel and turn S towards the yellow buoy and Outer Crouch SCB (Q(6)+LFl.15s).

A shallow draught boat can use the western arm of the funnel when on passage from the Blackwater. From Sales Point, round the tip of St Peter's Flats then shape a course of about 185°, leaving both the outer wrecked target vessels about 1M W. After passing the Buxey Bn, which should be about 1M E, head a little more W (around 195°) and make towards the Foulness pylons, finally turning S as before towards the charted yellow buoy and the Outer Crouch SCB.

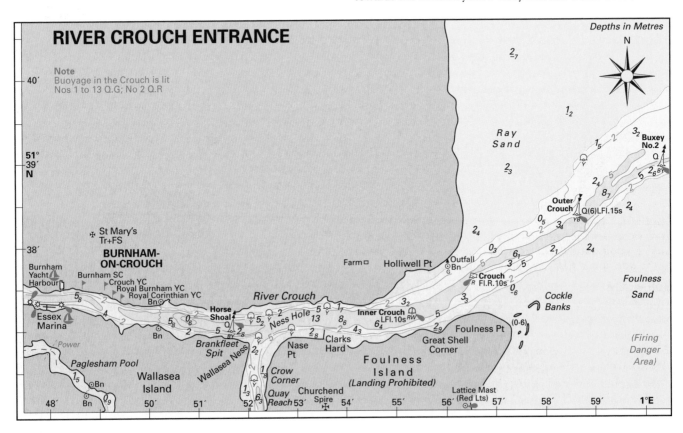

From Harwich and ports to the N, the approach may either be through the Wallet and the Spitway or the East Swin on the S side of the Gunfleet Sand. In either case make for a point between the Swin Spitway buoy and the Whitaker ECB (Q(3)10s Bell) before setting course along the Whitaker Channel.

From E, S and SE
Coming in from E means navigating through the off-lying sand banks towards the Whitaker ECB (Q(3)10s Bell) before turning SW into the Whitaker Channel.

From the River Thames or the North Kent coast, the navigator will again have to work through the sands towards the Whitaker ECB. In the right conditions a tighter turn can be made, passing midway between the Whitaker No.6 NCB (Q) and the Whitaker Bn to join the Whitaker Channel at the Ridge PHB (Fl.R.10s).

Entry
From the area of the Swin Spitway buoy and the Whitaker buoy, the Whitaker Channel runs SW for almost 9M to the Crouch PHB (Fl.R.10s) at Shore Ends. The deeper buoyed channel lies along the edge of the Foulness Sand with good water all the way, although care must be taken in the region of the Sunken Buxey as there is a kink in the channel between Buxey No.1 SCB (VQ(6)+LFl.10s) and Buxey No.2 NCB (Q).

An alternative route can be taken along the Buxey side, heading first for the SWB to the W of the Swallow Tail, thence to the Sunken Buxey NCB (Q) passing the South Buxey SHB (Fl(3)G.15s) to port on the way. From the Sunken Buxey make for the Outer Crouch SCB (Q(6)+LFl.15s) and rejoin the main channel.

Both routes arrive at the Crouch PHB (Fl.R.10s) marking the start of the River Crouch itself. There is often a sizeable seal colony hauled out on the Foulness Sand shortly before Shore Ends, which makes a fine sight.

Shore Ends to Burnham
From the Crouch buoy the river runs W past the Inner Crouch SWB (LFl.10s) for about 3M to the mouth of the River Roach, which opens S. On the W side of the Roach entrance is the spherical yellow Branklet Spit racing buoy, which must be left to port, because it marks the mud spit out from Wallasea Ness.

From the Branklet Spit a slight dog-leg around the Horse Shoal NCB (Q) - the first lit buoy since the Inner Crouch - should keep you in a dredged section up to the Fairway No.1 (Q.G), but there is some doubt about whether this is still a necessary diversion. From Fairway No.1 the deep water channel runs along the S shore of the Crouch well up beyond Burnham town, but once the lines of moorings are reached there is good water anywhere across the river - but be aware of the tide, it can easily run at up to 3kn.

BURNHAM
Approaching Burnham on Crouch from seaward, the first of the long lines of swinging moorings on the N side of the river starts at the Rice & Coles boatyard, identified by a crane on the seawall. A group of four large yellow spherical buoys, a short way downstream, marks the crossing point for high voltage power cables and no attempt should be made to anchor nearby. Anchoring is also prohibited anywhere in

Outer Crouch

Buxey Beacon

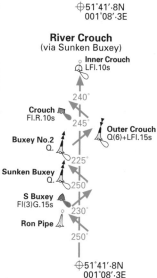

Crouch

River Crouch
(via Whitaker Channel)

Inner Crouch LFl.10s
240°
Crouch Fl.R.10s
245°
Outer Crouch Q(6)+LFl.15s
Buxey No.2 Q.
235°
260°
Buxey No.1 VQ(6)+LFl.10s
S Buxey Fl(3)G.15s
Foulness Fl(2)R.10s
245°
Ridge Fl.R.10s
Swallow Tail
235°
⊕51°41′.8N
001°08′.3E

River Crouch
(via Sunken Buxey)

Inner Crouch LFl.10s
240°
Crouch Fl.R.10s
245°
Outer Crouch Q(6)+LFl.15s
Buxey No.2 Q.
225°
Sunken Buxey Q.
250°
S Buxey Fl(3)G.15s
230°
Ron Pipe
250°
⊕51°41′.8N
001°08′.3E

the Fairway and is to be avoided anywhere within the moorings.

Outside Burnham Week (usually last week of August) there are moorings available up and down the river. These are looked after by the various boatyards and yacht clubs, which also have their own landing pontoons.

The first landmark for Burnham is the big white building of the Royal Corinthian YC. From there on through the town

Royal Corinthian YC, Burnham on Crouch

Royal Burnham YC and floating pontoon, Burnham on Crouch, with club launch approaching pontoon

BURNHAM YACHT HARBOUR

Contact
VHF Ch 80
Call sign *Burnham Yacht Harbour*
Harbourmaster ☎ 01621 782150
Email admin@burnhamyachtharbour.co.uk
www.burnhamyachtharbour.co.uk
Access 24hr

Fuel Diesel at berth on row F, landward end close to boat-lift. Tight turning space

Facilities WC. Showers. Launderette

Water Taps and hoses on pontoons

Electricity On pontoons. Charged per night

Gas Calor and Gaz

Chandler On site

Provisions At Co-Op (Fiveways), about 10 mins' walk, or in town, about 15 mins' walk

Post office At Fiveways

Boat repairs 32-ton travel-lift, 100-ton slipway

Sailmakers In town

Telephone Pay phone in Swallowtail bar

Pub/restaurant Swallowtail on site, many in town

Pharmacy At Fiveways near Co-Op

Trains Service to London via Wickford

Taxi ☎ 01621 784878, 784154.

there are the Royal Burnham YC, The White Harte, The Ship, Prior's boatyard, the Crouch YC and the little Burnham SC before reaching Burnham Yacht Harbour. It's an interesting waterfront steeped in history, but is no longer as busy, with as many active yards, as it once was. However, it is still a main centre for shopping, chandlery, sail and boat repairs or maintenance.

Burnham Yacht Harbour

Cut into the N shore of the Crouch just up river from Burnham town, there is a yellow pillar SWB with an X topmark (Fl.Y.5s) off the entrance. It is important to pass close to this buoy as the entrance channel is dredged through mud banks that dry.

From this offing buoy head in towards big blue-grey shed and pass between a pair of large piles, red (Fl.R.10s) to port and green (Fl.G.10s) to starboard.

There is no designated visitors' berth, so call ahead and, if arriving late, request codes for the gate to the pontoons and the door to the ablutions block.

From the entrance, turn to starboard for pontoon row A and to port for row H. Berth numbers are on ends of fingers

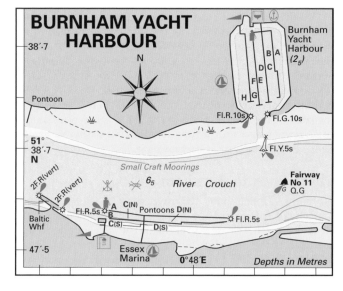

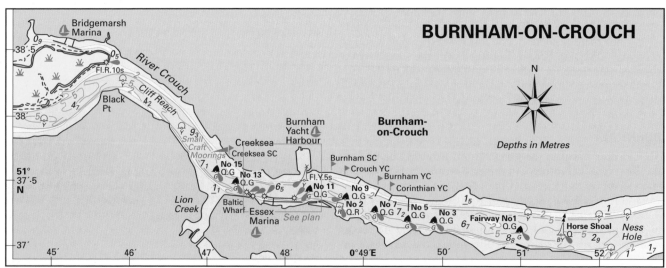

Entrance to Burnham Yacht Harbour from down river with yellow safe water mark. Pass close and then between port and starboard piles

The fuelling berth at Burnham Yacht Harbour. Foot of slipway at top of pontoon F

Wallasea and Essex Marina

On the S shore of the Crouch, slightly upstream from the Burnham Yacht Harbour, is Wallasea Bay with the Essex Marina, whose pontoons run parallel to the river. At the W end of the bay is the Baltic Wharf where ships bring in cargoes of timber. This trade is less than in years past, but watchkeepers must still keep an eye out for ships in the main channel.

Approaching the marina is more a case of not passing it by. A pair of outer and inner pontoons run parallel to the river with entrances at either end, there being a linking walkway between them and the shore half way along. Riverside berths (along A arm) are alongside the main pontoon, while all others are on fingers from inside the berthing arms. Contact the marina office for berthing instructions and ask whether to enter from downstream (East) or upstream (West).

Burnham Yacht Harbour with slipway and travel-hoist

with low numbers close to the shore and high numbers near the river. Some fingers, particularly in row A, are shorter than the boats occupying them, which makes finding the numbers difficult.

Approaching Essex Marina, Wallasea, River Crouch, up river from the East. Noticeboard on end of outer pontoon is about fuel barge

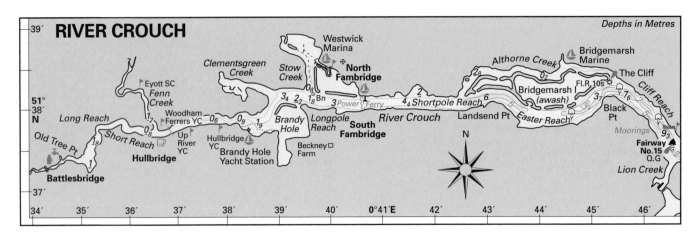

RIVER CROUCH — Depths in Metres

ESSEX MARINA

Contact
VHF Ch 80
Call sign *Essex Marina*
Harbourmaster ☎ 01702 258531
Email info@EssexMarina.co.uk
www.essexmarina.co.uk
Access 24hr

Fuel Diesel and petrol from barge at W end beside boat-lift.
Also LPG

Ferry Crossings to Burnham town in season

Facilities WC. Showers

Water On pontoons with hoses

Electricity On pontoons

Gas Calor

Chandler On site

Boat repairs 70-ton travel-lift, 100-ton slipway

Pub/restaurant Essex Marina YC on site

Hotel On site.

Wallasea to Althorne Creek

Above Wallasea and the Baltic Wharf the river turns NW with shallows along the N shore, so it's wise to leave Fairway buoys 13 and 15 to starboard (both Q.G). Here the Fairway ends, off Creeksea, and the river scenery becomes more rural and interesting compared to the reaches below Burnham.

The NW section to Althorne Creek and Bridgemarsh Marine is known as Cliff Reach, because of the 40–50ft cliffs along the N shore, and offers one of the few places in the Crouch with any shelter from SW (or NE) winds. Anchorage

BRIDGEMARSH MARINE

Contact
☎ 01621 740414 Mobile 07968 696815
Access HW±4hr

Fuel Diesel

Facilities WC. Showers

Water On pontoons

Electricity On pontoons

Gas Calor

Boat repairs Slipway and 8-ton crane

Pubs In Althorne village

Post office In Althorne village

Transport Railway station, 1hr to London, 10 mins Burnham

Taxi ☎ 01621 784878, 784154.

can be found under the cliffs, but there are some foul patches along the low water line.

Throughout Cliff Reach and indeed most of the succeeding reaches, the best water lies about midway between the banks. Keep towards the outsides of bends as there are often spits and shoals off points and headlands.

To port at the top of Cliff Reach is Black Point where the main river bends back SW and Althorne Creek runs off to the N behind Bridgemarsh Island (no landing allowed). Althorne Creek is the location for Bridgemarsh Marine.

Looking into Bridgemarsh Marina, Althorne Creek, River Crouch. Red can buoy marks channel and board on end of pontoon indicates channel to port if going further into creek

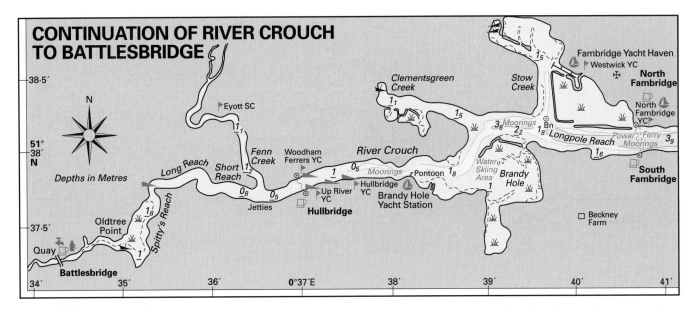

Bridgemarsh Marine

A large red beacon (Fl.R.10s) labelled Ada Point, off the E tip of Bridgemarsh Island, is the first sign of Althorne Creek. If entering the creek, leave this beacon to port and as the entrance opens up, follow the line of red can buoys leading in around the bend W to the marina hidden behind the island. Approaching the marina (Bridgemarsh Marine) the end of the main pontoon is directly ahead. A sign indicates that the fairway continues to port along the S side of this pontoon.

Althorne to Fambridge

From Cliff Reach the main river takes a dive SW past the Canewdon yellow racing mark (summer), then W along the S shore of Bridgemarsh Island, which floods on spring tides, through Easter Reach, NW through Raypits Reach before returning to a Wly course with Shortpole Reach passing the W end of Bridgemarsh Island. (Circumnavigating Bridgemarsh Island by way of Althorne and Bridgemarsh

Creeks is possible with a shoal draught boat and a fair wind, but the channel is tortuous and it's not recommended.)

A little over 1M above Bridgemarsh there are lines of moorings at Fambridge with the North Fambridge YC and North Fambridge Yacht Station on the N shore. There is a floating landing pontoon outside the clubhouse and the moorings belong to the Yacht Station. Anchoring is only advisable above or below the moorings, but there is good depth. A launch service runs to the moorings at busy times and can be hailed.

West Wick (Stow Creek)

A little over ½M upstream from Fambridge, Stow Creek branches off to the N with Fambridge Yacht Haven and West Wick YC at the top. In the mouth of the creek there's an unlit beacon with an 8kn limit sign on it. This should be passed close to starboard when making for the marina.

Approaching the North Fambridge YC and pontoon on the River Crouch

Boatman at North Fambridge YC

FAMBRIDGE YACHT HAVEN

Contact
  VHF Ch 80
  Call sign *Fambridge Yacht Haven*
  Harbourmaster ☎ 01621 740370
  Access HW±5hr
Fuel Diesel
Facilities WC
Water On pontoon
Electricity On pontoons
Gas Calor and Gaz
Chandler On site
Provisions At N Fambridge
Post office N Fambridge
Boat repairs Slip and 5-ton crane
Pub/restaurant Ferry Boat Inn, N Fambridge
Taxi ☎ 01622 322262.

Stow Creek to Brandy Hole

Just W of Stow Creek the main river veers off to the SW while an arm, Clementsgreen Creek, carries on W, but is not navigable for cruisers. The SW stretch of the river, called Brandy Hole Reach, sees the Crouch becoming much narrower and shallower with moorings mostly drying at LW, although some remain afloat in Brandy Hole Bay, a designated waterskiing area, and near the Brandy Hole Yacht

Motor cruiser coming out of Stow Creek after leaving Fambridge Yacht Haven (in background). The beacon should be left close to starboard on entry (port on exit)

NORTH FAMBRIDGE YACHT STATION

Contact
  ☎ 01621 740370
  Access 24hr to moorings
Fuel Diesel from yard
Facilities WC. Showers
Water At landing
Gas Calor and Gaz
Chandler On site
Provisions In village, short walk
Post office In village
Boat repairs Slip and 5-ton crane
Pub/restaurant Ferry Boat Inn at top of yard
Transport Railway station in village, trains to London or Burnham
Taxi ☎ 01245 322262.

The ¼M channel has occasionally been marked with starboard hand withies, but is straightforward and can be negotiated by keeping an eye on the depth sounder. As soon as the marina opens up to starboard you can turn sharply in along the long pontoon, the fairway being on the S side.

Entrance to Fambridge Yacht Haven from Stow Creek off the River Crouch

BHYC   BHYC pontoon

Coming up river and looking across the corner of the channel
from Brandy Hole Reach to Brandy Hole YC and pontoon

Station and the Brandy Hole YC. Both of these stand on the S shore where the river once more turns W. The lines of moorings extend for over a mile, past Hullbridge YC, Hullbridge and the Up River YC to Fenn Creek.

Brandy Hole to Battlesbridge

So far up river - HW here is half an hour after Burnham - it's surprising to find several very active clubs and large numbers of moorings. The first club is Hullbridge YC, just ½M up river. It is well provided with a slip, a jetty and scrubbing posts. The jetty has tide gauges to show depth alongside and there are showers and toilets at the clubhouse where water can also be obtained. Call the club ☎ 01702 753311 to arrange use of the scrubbing posts.

Next club is the Up River YC ☎ 01702 231654 *Email* info@upriver.org www.upriver.org, which has a private slipway and a clubhouse with bar, kitchen and changing rooms, plus moorings in the river. Both the dinghy and cruiser fleets are very active right through the season.

The South Woodham Ferrers YC and Water Ski Club ☎ 01245 325391 stands on the N shore near the ford.

From Fenn Creek up to Battlesbridge the river follows a winding, narrow route with enough water on a high tide for a boat drawing about 2m to reach the old mill buildings and antiques centre for a swift pint in The Barge, but do not linger when the tide turns. Should the antiques (or the pints) prove too much of a temptation, it is possible to stay over a tide alongside the concrete hard on the N shore or a pontoon on the S bank. Call Battlesbridge Harbour ☎ 01268 768282 (or Crouch Harbour Authority ☎ 01621 783602) for more information.

The Brandy Hole YC and pontoon shared with Brandy Hole Yacht Station.

BRANDY HOLE YACHT STATION & YACHT CLUB

Contact
    VHF BHYC Ch 37
    Yacht Station ☎ 01702 230248
    Yacht club ☎ 01702 230320 *Email* mail@brandyhole.com
    www.brandyhole.com
    Access HW±4hr

Moorings Contact Yacht Station

Landing At YC pontoon

Fuel Diesel at Yacht Station

Facilities WC in clubhouse

Water On pontoon

Gas Calor and Gaz

Provisions At Hullbridge village

Boat repairs Boatyard by BHYC

Pub/Food At BHYC.

12. River Roach

⊕ **Waypoint**
51°37′.0N 000°52′.3E (just
E of Branklet Spit buoy)

Charts
Imray *2000 series*
Admiralty SC *5607, 3750*

Tides
Paglesham
HW Dover +0110
Crouch Harbour Authority
Harbourmaster
☎ 01621 783602

Email
ianbell@crouchharbour.org
www.crouchharbour.org

Roach Sailing Association
Secretary ☎ 07836 344508
Email
admin@paglesham.org.uk
www.paglesham.org.uk/rsa

When approaching from the Crouch, make for the yellow spherical Branklet Spit racing buoy ½M E of the Horse Shoal NCB (Q), but remember to pass it to starboard, because the Branklet Spit is extensive.

The main barrier to entering from seaward is the depth on the Maplins, particularly over the Broomway, which is an ancient raised track with a maximum of 2m over it at HWS and often as little as 0.5m at neaps.

Approaching from seaward requires navigation, rather than pilotage, because shore marks are almost impossible to detect over the distance from the Warp or West Swin. Make for the S Shoebury SHB (Fl.G.5s) before turning across the sands on a course made good of about 355° to leave the wreck (about 1M from entrance) to port. Once abeam the wreck make good about 330° to open the entrance channel towards the bridge.

Many confusing marks may be seen on the sands and Broomway, but once the bridge is close and you move in between the sea walls, there is better water on the N side of the channel.

Entrance across the sand requires good weather and a high tide, and permission from the Shoeburyness Firing Range Officer is required before an approach can be made to the Havengore bridge (Ch 72 *Shoe Base* or ☎ 01702 383211). Maximum recommended draught for using this 'overland' approach (or exit) is 1.5m, even at HWS. The Shoebury ranges are used on most weekdays, so 24hr notice to the Range Officer is required, but at weekends the bridge is manned HW±2hr (daylight hours only) and may be lifted on request.

Main hazards

The main hazard is entering via the Havengore Bridge, which requires good weather and shallow draught, plus permission from the live firing range officials. Otherwise, there are no real hazards within the Roach, provided you follow the channel and avoid spits extending from offshoot creeks.

There is freighter traffic in the river, so anchorages need to be chosen with care to avoid obstructing fairways.

Approaches

There are two ways of entering the Roach; either from the Crouch or directly from the sea across the Maplin Sands via the Havengore lifting bridge.

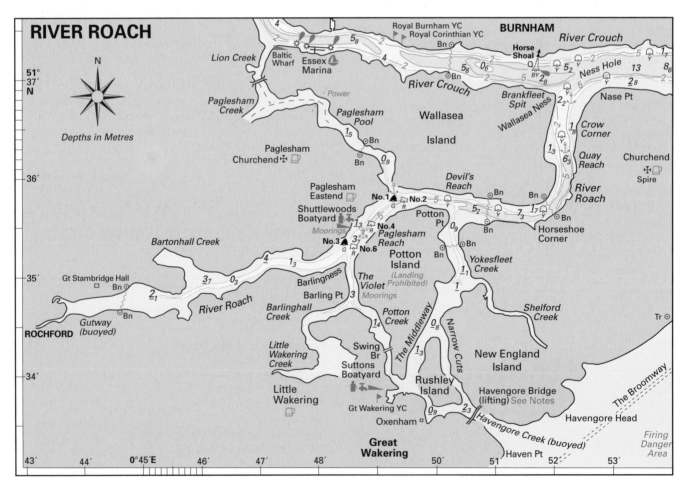

The labels visible on the image: Sutton's Yard, The Middleway, Roach, Rushley Island, Narrow Cuts, Potton Creek

The Havengore from seaward with the channel beyond the bridge dividing around Rushley Island. The right hand arm is Narrow Cuts; the left becomes Potton Creek towards Sutton's Yard. At the top of the picture is the Roach

Entry from Crouch
Leave the Branklet Spit spherical yellow racing buoy close to starboard at the entrance in order to keep off the mud bank spreading out from Nase Point on the E shore. Then keep to the middle of the channel, favouring the outside of bends. There are racing buoys, but channel marks do not start until approaching Paglesham.

Branklet to Paglesham
Unlike the Crouch, there is shelter to be found within the Roach from all wind directions. The first useful spot is in

Brankfleet at the N end of Quay Reach, just within the mouth of the river, under the W shore where there is fair depth close in under the sea wall and good holding. Be sure to remain N of the yellow racing buoy Jubilee, because this is positioned off a bay that dries out.

A few boats are moored on the E side of Quay Reach near a landing on Foulness Island. The landing is none too clean and somewhat slippery, but does give access to Church End and the 'George and Dragon' pub. As this is all MOD land, you must keep to the path and the walk will take almost three-quarters of an hour.

Power cables cross the river at the S end of Quay Reach where the channel bends sharply W. Keep well to the outside of this bend where a yellow racing buoy 'Roach' indicates the deepest water. A short way on, in Devil's Reach, more cables

Morning at Paglesham with Shuttlewood's old black shed at the top of the hard and the Essex Boatyards' pontoon

Pontoon berths at the boatyard at Wakering, often referred to as Sutton's Yard, in Potton Creek at SW corner of Potton Island

cross and immediately afterwards Yokesfleet Creek opens off to the S to run down the E side of Potton Island. Another sheltered anchorage can be found just inside the entrance under Potton Point, but beware the mud banks on either side of the entrance.

On the N side of the main channel in the area of the Yokesfleet Creek mouth there are often oyster crates marked by small green buoys, which must be avoided. Similarly, beware some oyster layings on the Potton side a little further on.

It's at this point that the river turns SW into Paglesham Reach. On the corner a narrow creek branches off NW, confusingly known as both Paglesham Creek and Paglesham Pool. There's a sheltered anchorage just inside the mouth, protected by the mud spit off the point, but it's best found below half tide. There is a landing just above the pill box on the point, making it possible to walk from there to the 'Punchbowl' at Church End or along the seawall to the nearer 'Plough and Sail' at the top of the lane above the boatyard.

Also on the corner are fairway buoys Nos.1 and 2, the start of a buoyed channel through the moorings at Paglesham. This fairway is used by coasters going up to the Stambridge Mills at Rochford, so boats must anchor outside it, either above or below the lines of moorings, and set a riding light.

Immediately the Reach opens up, the old black, timber shed of Shuttlewood's yard will be seen on the N side, together with a pontoon landing and hard. The pontoon is used by a local builder of motor boats for demonstrations and landing is not allowed. If going ashore, use the hard on the upstream side of the pontoon.

The Roach Sailing Association has a few buoys downstream from the hard that visitors may use.

It is under the mud of the Paglesham foreshore that the remains of HMS *Beagle* are believed to have been found. Darwin's famous ship was pensioned off after her third voyage, a survey of Australia, and used for some years as a watch vessel in the Roach. Then she was sold for scrap in 1870 and what are believed to be her remains were discovered recently in the Paglesham mud, together with possible parts incorporated in the structure of the Shuttlewood's old black shed.

Paglesham to Rochford

A short way above the last of the Paglesham moorings, at fairway buoys Nos.3 and 6, off Barlinghall Ness, a creek forks off to the S while the main river runs on to the W. This creek runs a short way S and then divides with Barlinghall Creek to the W meandering narrowly and muddily up towards Little Wakering, and Potton Creek winding on S to Sutton's Boatyard near Great Wakering. On the way S it crosses a ford, which should only be approached above half tide by shoal draught cruisers and even then only very cautiously, before passing through the Potton Island swing bridge (VHF Ch 72, ☎ 01702 219491 or 3 horn blasts for opening in daylight, HW±2hr). Beyond Sutton's yard the channel rejoins the Middleway, W of Rushley Island, and carries on towards Havengore Bridge.

These are both creeks for exploration on the last of a rising tide with plenty of time to retreat before being stranded, but they do have an air of muddy secrecy that can be appealing.

The main channel of the Roach continues W above Barling Ness. There is good water with up to 1.5m at LW as far as the old Barling Quay on the S shore, but then it shallows considerably and, sensibly, can only be explored close to HW. That said, boats of up to 1.5m draught do make it up the next 1.5M towards Stambridge Mills on the top of the tide and include grain ships for the Mills.

Surprisingly, there is an active yard right at the head of the river where the Wakering YC ☎ 01702 335325 is based.

Yokesfleet Creek

Yokesfleet Creek branches S from the Roach in Devil's Reach at Potton Point between a long spit of mud from the Point and another broad flat around the Foulness headland.

A good anchorage can be found close under Potton Point or further up the first reach with shelter from all but N or S winds.

Slightly under a mile into the Creek two others branch off SE. The first is the narrow and drying Shelford Creek; the second is the dammed New England Creek. A distance of perhaps 2 cables further on along what is now called the Middleway, another creek branches off S called Narrow Cuts, which runs down the E side of Rushley Island and is the main route to and from the Havengore Bridge.

Approaching the Havengore Bridge from the West (Wakering side) of Rushley Island

Continuing along the Middleway down the W side of Rushley Island, the creek is narrow and tortuous but pleasingly full of muddy mystery. Potton Creek appears to starboard around the Southern tip of Potton Island and some drying pontoon moorings as well as the slipway and cranes of Suttons Boatyard come into view. Great Wakering village is a good mile's walk from the yard.

From there, the creek, whether it is Potton or the Middleway is hard to tell, turns SE and then E to join the S end of Narrow Cuts at the Havengore Bridge. There are one or two moorings in the creek to give some guide as to where the channel is.

Central bascule of Havengore Bridge with light signals and control tower

Narrow Cuts

Though drying, Narrow Cuts, as its name implies, is a narrow dug channel that gives the best approach to (or return from) the Havengore Bridge. It is well marked with poles, but do follow them carefully, right through to the pool by the grey concrete piers of the bridge. It must be realized that the channel through Narrow Cuts is marked from seaward, with the last of the flood tide, so they are green to starboard going N and the reverse heading S.

Havengore Bridge

The bridge is much larger than might be expected and is heavily used by MoD traffic, but the Keeper will do his best to accommodate yachts wishing to pass through, after consultation with the Range Officer and Bridge Keeper. Traffic lights clearly show when to proceed through the open bridge.

HAVENGORE

Havengore Bridge ☎ 01702 383436
Range Officer ☎ 01702 383211
VHF Ch 72 *Shoe Base* (Range Officer); Ch 16 to call and Ch 72 to work *Shoe Bridge* (Havengore Bridgekeeper).

13. River Thames

⊕ **Landfall Waypoint**
51°29′.56N 000°52′.61E
(close N of Sea Reach No.1 buoy)

Charts
Imray *2100 Series, C1, C2*
Admiralty SC *5606, 1185, 1186, 2151, 2484*

Tides
(London Bridge)
Dover HW+0252

Port of London
Most information available from www.portoflondon.co.uk

London VTS
VHF Ch 69 (PLA seaward limit to Sea Reach No.4)
Ch 68 (Sea Reach No.4 to Crayfordness)
Ch 14 above Crayfordness including the Thames Barrier Control Zone
Call sign *London VTS*

Coastguard
London Coastguard
Ch 16 (Shell Haven to Teddington)

Thames Barrier Control
VHF Ch 14
Call sign *London VTS*
☎ 020 8855 0315.

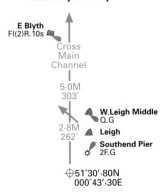

Southend Pier to East Blyth Buoy

E Blyth
Fl(2)R.10s
Cross Main Channel
5·0M 303°
2·8M 262°
W.Leigh Middle Q.G
Leigh
Southend Pier 2F.G
⊕51°30′·80N 000°43′·30E

Main hazards

Large ships, floating debris, some shallows on the bends.

Approaches

Sea Reach No.1 buoy marks the seaward end of the dredged channel into the River Thames and lies in the centre of the deep water shipping channel.

Small craft should stay outside this main channel and make their approach to the Thames following the navigation buoys that lie at the edges of the drying shallows, staying well out of the way of commercial shipping.

Sea Reach to Tower Bridge general information

A first trip up the Thames, or the London River as it's commonly known, from out in the Estuary may seem daunting, but will be an experience to be enjoyed and remembered.

Traditionally, the river passage begins at Sea Reach No.1 buoy, but the PLA's Lower River Sector actually starts at Sea Reach No.4 buoy (Fl.Y.2.5s), N of Medway entrance, and finishes at Tower Bridge. The tides run strongly in the river, reaching 4kn in places at Springs, and the 40M to the Pool of London is readily accomplished on one tide by a small boat, because there are 7hrs of flood to help.

Conversely, the trip downriver gives only 5hr of fair tide. However, the combination of the tide plus 5–6kn of boat speed should still see you off the Medway by LW.

The Thames Barrier is closed regularly for testing, as well as in times of flood risk, and the Barrier Duty Officer should be contacted when planning the river passage to ensure closure is not planned on the day of your trip.

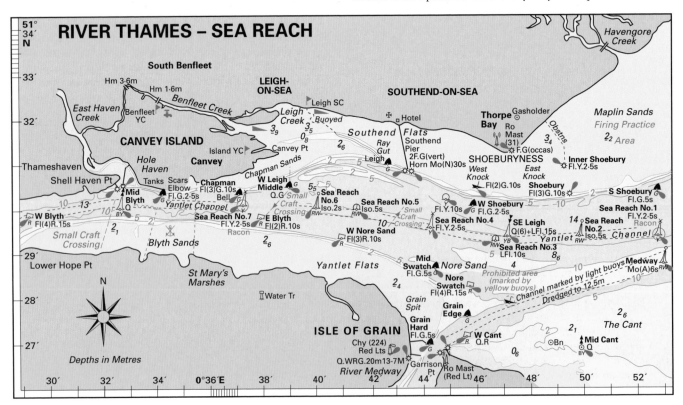

RIVER THAMES – SEA REACH

Depths in Metres

With the need to set off upstream at LW, Queenborough is an ideal anchorage to wait for the tide. It is just over 3M to the Nore Swatch buoy and a good time to leave is 1-1½hr before LW.

An alternative port of departure is Holehaven on Canvey Island. It's 8M up river from the Nore Swatch and that allows a later start, which ensures sufficient water to cross the shallows in the creek entrance.

The first part of the upstream journey needs to be made along the S shore to stay clear of the oil installations at Canvey, Shellhaven and Coryton. If leaving from Holehaven, cross immediately to the S side when safe to do so. If inbound from NE, cross to S side of the estuary from W Leigh Middle SHB (Q.G) heading SW towards E Blyth PHB (Fl(2)R.10s).

Further up, in Lower Hope Reach, resume the starboard side of the river.

Outbound, stay on the S shore throughout, heading NE, if necessary, only between Sea Reach Nos.4 and 5 buoys. These routing instructions are all clearly charted.

It should be noted that there is nowhere on the Thames from Tower Bridge to the Estuary, where you can take on fuel alongside through a hose, other than at the fuel barge outside St Katharine Haven. Nor is there fuel available at Queenborough. The nearest in the Medway is at Gillingham.

Queenborough to Gravesend

For the passage to London, leave Queenborough 1-1½hr before LW and sail by way of Grain Hard SHB (Fl.G.5s) and Grain Edge SHB (unlit) to the Nore Swatch PHB (Fl(4)R.15s).

From Nore Swatch, make good about 295° through the Swatchway S of Nore Sand, past the Mid Swatch SHB (Fl.G.5s) then 290° to the W Nore Sand PHB (Fl(3)R.10s). Between these buoys, inshore, there is an arc of yellow buoys marking a firing range off the shore of Grain. Just W is the wandering gutway that leads in to Yantlet Creek. Yantlet is a possible stopover for shoal draught boats able to take the ground, but is not an appealing place.

Continuing past the Yantlet Flats, towards the E Blyth PHB (Fl(2)R.10s), the small town of Allhallows is prominent on Grain. From there the N and S shores close in and it feels more like a river than an estuary.

There are various oil refinery works on the starboard bow and the entrance to Holehaven opens on the N shore just before Mid Blyth NCB (Q), which can safely be left some distance to starboard.

About 2M on, the river turns S into Lower Hope Reach (The Lower Hope). The shore to port is less steep to around the bend, so do not cut across it.

The deep water channel here is much narrower and it's time to change sides. Look for a gap in the traffic, watching astern for small, deep-laden coasters using the same inshore course, and plan to reach the W side before Mucking No.7 SHB (Fl.G.5s).

The river now bends to starboard round Coalhouse Point, with its curious tower that looks exactly like a giant box-kite, into Gravesend Reach. Rounding the bend just inside the Ovens SHB (QG, bell), a line of groynes appears on the starboard bow. These are all lit Fl.G.2.5s and must be left to starboard. Pass close N of Tilbury SCB (Q(6)+LFl.15s) to keep clear.

Once in Gravesend Reach, Gravesend town is clear on the S shore. Large tugs moor along the shore off the Gravesend SC and Gravesham Marina. The sailing club, about 500m before the town proper, can be hard to locate and is a low building with a white flagpole. The gated entrance to the marina is a few metres downstream and only opens near HW on free-flow because there is only one gate.

Gravesend to Erith

Beyond the sailing club, the town looms large on the S shore and the Tilbury cruise-ship and ferry terminal follows soon after on the N side. A small ferry runs across the river here, but is not so frequent as to be a problem.

The shipping activity continues, especially on the N shore, as you leave Gravesend Reach and turn gently to starboard into Northfleet Hope. (Incidentally, a 'fleet' is an area of shallow water and 'hope' means a small bay and the anchorage off it.) There is a container-ship terminal to starboard, outside the entrance to Tilbury Docks, followed by a large grain terminal, which is an unpleasant source of dust in a N wind.

Up ahead to starboard, as development thins out on both shores, is Thurrock YC,

Nore Swatch buoy to Gravesend via East Blyth buoy

Gravesend Town

Tilbury Jetty

Several groynes All Fl.G.2·5s

1·7M
260°

Tilbury
Q(6)+LFl.15s

238°

'Boxkite' Tower

Ovens
Fl.G

207°

Mucking No.7

200°

Mucking No.5
Fl(3)G.10s

Cross main channel

225°

Lower Hope
Fl.R.5s

230°

W.Blyth
Fl(4)R.15s

2·2M
262°

Mid Blyth
Q

Holehaven entrance

3·4M
275°

E.Blyth
Fl(2)R.10s

Shallows close to port

1·9M
280°

W.Nore Sand
Fl(3)R.10s

2·2M
290°

Mid Swatch
Fl.G.5s

295°

Nore Swatch
Fl(4)R.15s

⊕51°28'·30N
000°45'·70E

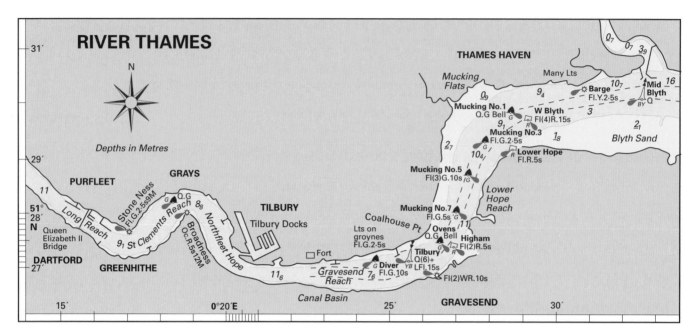

Gravesend Sailing Club (centre right) with the gate into
Gravesham Marina below the crane to the left

GRAVESEND

Tides HW Dover +0140

Yacht club Gravesend Sailing Club ☎ 01474 533974
  Email secretary@gravesendsc.org.uk
  www.gravesendsc.org.uk

Moorings Visitor moorings, but check whether dry at LW

Landing Steps at HW or PLA upstream

Gravesham Marina
  Harbourmaster ☎ 01474 352392
  Email Dredger3@aol.com
  Access HW–1hr to HW, via locked basin

Facilities WC. Showers

Water On site

Boat repairs Crane, slipway.

identifiable by three large grey and white tower blocks close
by and yachts moored in the river at the end of the club's
landing stage. Visitors' moorings may be available and diesel
may be available in cans from the Bosun on weekdays. The
club is now in a building ashore, but was once in the old
light vessel nearby. Contact Thurrock YC ☎ 01375 373720.
Open weekends and Thursday evenings.
Email publicity@thurrockyachtclub.org.uk
www.thurrockyachtclub.org.uk

After Thurrock, the river turns SW for a mile or so in
Fiddler's Reach and a modern housing development at
Greenhithe covers the S bank with woods behind. There are
a few moorings here and a causeway where it may be
possible to land.

The huge QEII road bridge (54m) dominates the view W
as the river turns NW into Long Reach. Here the tide runs
in excess of 3kn under the bridge and there are 17M to go
to Tower Bridge.

Watch for ships manoeuvring at berths on both shores
just above the QEII bridge. There is an oil terminal to port
and docks are strung along the starboard shore. Once past,
however, the view ahead is almost rural. In the far distance,
two large wind turbines can be seen at Dagenham and to
port is the imposing concrete blockhouse of the Dartford
Creek Tidal Barrier.

Rounding Crayford Ness to port, Erith YC is visible on
the S shore housed in the old Norwegian car ferry
Folgefonn, with many yacht moorings close by. The club
offers a useful stop (with toilets, showers and water
available) if you are running out of tide and there is normally
a vacant mooring for yachts up to 35ft. Larger boats can
anchor just upstream, where holding is good in mud.

Thurrock Yacht Club

Erith Yacht Club

QE2 bridge

Contact Erith YC ☎ 01322 332943
Email secretary@erithyachtclub.org.uk
www.erithyachtclub.org.uk

Erith to Thames Barrier

Continuing upriver, the environment once again becomes industrial, with an enormous landfill site on the N shore at Rainham Marshes and the Ford motor works at Dagenham beyond. On the S shore a structure like a beached whale is actually a sewage works.

Rounding Cross Ness point into Barking Reach and passing the modern sprawl of Thamesmead to port, a huge illuminated sign-board stands on the N shore. This is the downstream signal station for the Thames Barrier. Normally it shows instructions to call *London VTS* on Ch 14. It can also display amber lights, meaning 'proceed with extreme caution', or red lights, meaning 'navigation within zone prohibited'. In some circumstances, audio instructions may boom out as well.

The sign is 3M from the barrier, but call the Barrier Duty Officer and announce your position and your intentions. He will usually give the all clear and say which span to pass through.

In Gallions Reach, London City Airport stands amid the docks to starboard, beyond the gated entrance to Gallions Point Marina.

Vessels on passage downstream from the non-tidal Thames often use Gallions Point Marina as a stopover to wait for the tide. Equally, if heading up to London, but held

up by a closure of the barrier, this marina would be a useful place to stop. It is also handy for visiting the Excel Exhibition Centre. However, it can be noisy, being a few hundred metres from the end of the City airport runway.

Unfortunately there is no fuel available (the nearest is upstream at Wapping).

The river sweeps past Gallions Point, turning W into Woolwich Reach and, just ahead are the Woolwich Ferry terminals, large grey rectangular buildings standing on each shore. The pair of ferries swap sides of the river frequently, but they use Ch 14 to give warning and will respond to a call on the radio if confirmation is needed.

GALLIONS POINT MARINA

Contact
VHF Ch 80
Call sign *Gallions Point Marina*
Harbourmaster ☎ 020 7476 7054
Email info@gallionspointmarina.co.uk
www.gallionspointmarina.co.uk
Access HW±5hr

Facilities WC. Showers. Pump-out

Water On pontoons and quay

Electricity On pontoons

Gas Calor

Engineer On site

Sailmaker M Putt ☎ 020 8599 1413

Transport Docklands Light Railway, North Woolwich. London City Airport.

The lock-gate entrance to Gallions Point Marina

The Thames Barrier

The Thames Barrier, less than a mile from Woolwich Ferry, displays clear lights on each bascule to indicate which span (gap) to use. Green arrows point in from each side of the span in use. The closed spans are marked by a large red 'X' on each side and no attempt must be made to use them. Information is broadcast by Woolwich Radio on Ch 14 at H+15 and H+45.

Do not approach within ¼M of the barrier unless you are on passage through it and use your engine, do not sail through.

Charts show the designation of the spans (B to G, with C, D, E and F most frequently used).

Under 1M above the barrier, the Greenwich YC's grey building stands on stilts against the S bank. A call to their Harbourmaster may result in permission for an overnight stop, possibly against their pontoon in front of the clubhouse. The pontoon has water and electricity, and there are many shops nearby.

GREENWICH YACHT CLUB

Contact
Harbourmaster ☎ 07958 993852
Club ☎ 020 8858 7339
Facilities (when club open) WC. Showers. Water On pontoon
Electricity On pontoon
Provisions Shops nearby.

Thames Barrier by night. The control lights can clearly be seen

Looking astern through the Thames Barrier. The Woolwich Ferry can be seen in the distance

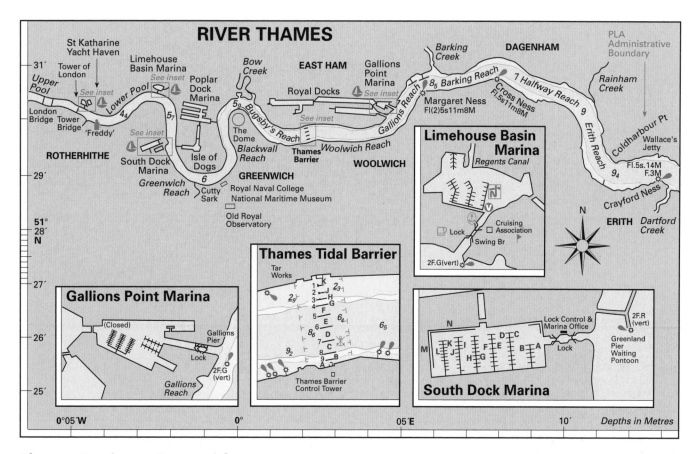

Thames Barrier to Greenwich

The Millenium Dome dominates the scene above the barrier, virtually filling Blackwall Point at the end of Bugsby's Reach.

Beside the Dome, on the port bank, is the upstream-facing signal station for the Thames Barrier, identical to the one downstream at Barking and serving the same function.

Once past the Dome and into Blackwall Reach, the Greenwich Meridian is crossed and the massive office blocks of Canary Wharf stand out to starboard. Suddenly London itself seems to be all around, and ahead are the glorious buildings of the Royal Naval College at Greenwich with the National Maritime Museum and the *Cutty Sark*.

Over on the starboard side of Blackwall Reach, through an impressive blue-painted lifting bridge, lies another modern marina in the old docklands, the Poplar Dock Marina. Booking at least 24hr in advance is essential to gain access to this marina, which involves passage through five more bridges after the blue one. Don't be put off by this

Canary Wharf and the lifting bridge access to Poplar Dock Marina

Royal Naval College, Greenwich

Thames Barrier, looking upstream. Greenwich Yacht Club is just before the Millenium Dome

POPLAR DOCK MARINA

VHF Ch 13
Call sign *West India*
Contact for bookings ☎ 020 7517 5550
Marina control ☎ 020 7987 7260
Access 0600–2200 and HW±1hr

Facilities WC at dock and in marina. Showers. Launderette. Pump out

Water At dock and in marina

Electricity At dock and in marina

Pub/restaurant At marina

Transport Blackwall (Docklands Light Railway), Canary Wharf (Tube).

complex access, but, for a one night stay, admission to the marina itself is unlikely. Instead, a berth will be offered against the dock wall, through the first bridge and beyond the lock. This dock has water, power and toilets, but is in a public area, without the security offered by the marina. The wall may be difficult for crews of boats less than 30ft with low freeboard, and is best suited to nimble crew members.

On approach, having booked in advance, contact the marina office when about 10 mins away.

Greenwich to Tower Bridge

After Greenwich the river turns N into Limehouse Reach and, half way up on the W side is another marina, South Dock Marina, at Rotherhithe.

The entrance is just downstream from Greenland Pier, a pontoon with a white-painted ramp to the shore. This pier is used by the river bus services and the area is often very choppy, especially in a breeze. The marina advises that the upstream end of the pier serves as a waiting pontoon, but a lot of fenders would be needed and do not leave the boat there unattended.

SOUTH DOCK MARINA

Contact
VHF Ch 37
Call sign *South Dock Marina*
Lock office ☎ 020 7252 2244
www.sdockmarina.co.uk
Access HW±3hr (1m draught); ±2hr (2m draught)

Facilities WC. Showers. Launderette. Pump out

Water On pontoons

Electricity On pontoons

Boat repairs 17.5-ton crane

Transport Surrey Quays and Canada Waters Tube stations (15min walk). River bus to central London. Local bus to Greenwich.

From South Dock Marina, the river runs ½ M N before another turn to port. On the N side of the bend is one of the most popular and convenient destinations for cruising yachtsmen, Limehouse Marina.

The entrance actually faces SW and can be hard to identify from downstream. It comes after a taller apartment block than others along this stretch and there is a white flagpole by the pub just W of the entrance.

Access is through a swinging road-bridge and then a lock. Advance booking is required.

There is a waiting pontoon outside the lock, accessible HW±1½hr, but it has little to commend it, because waves funnel into the entrance and cause the pontoon to heave around quite violently. Once through the bridge and on the pontoon, a vessel is effectively trapped, so it may be better to jill about in the river while waiting to enter Limehouse Basin.

The lock has mooring lines hanging vertically against the walls and the office is in the building to port by the basin entrance. To starboard is the headquarters of the Cruising Association.

Limehouse Marina is a very convenient base for visiting London, with friendly and helpful staff, excellent facilities, and supplies available nearby, plus good transport links.

Beyond Cuckolds Point, opposite Limehouse, the river

South Dock Marina and Greenwich Pier

Beware of strong cross-tides when entering the lock. Inside, there are permanent lines hanging down on each side of the lock and, if you can moor starboard-side to, the lock keeper may be able to pass lines too.

Although the marina does take visitors, it is often full and has less to commend it than other venues, beyond its security and its proximity to the attractions of Greenwich.

Limehouse Marina. The swinging road bridge and lock can clearly be seen

Limehouse Marina lock

LIMEHOUSE

Contact
VHF Ch 80
Call sign *Limehouse Marina*
Lock Office ☎ 020 7308 9930
Berth bookings ☎ 020 7480 9022
Access 0800–1800 April–October,
0800–1630 November–March, booking essential.

Facilities WC. Showers. Launderette. Pump out

Gas Calor and Gaz from garden centre by Limehouse DLR station

Repairs Peter Lewis Marine – ask in lock office

Provisions Shops nearby

Pubs/restaurants Short walk

Transport Docklands Light Railway from Limehouse Station, just NW of the marina.

Limehouse Marina entrance. Prominent flagpole on left, tall building on right

turns SW into the Lower Pool, passing the famous 'Prospect of Whitby' pub to starboard. The next bend to starboard has the headquarters of the River Police on the N shore and brings Tower Bridge into sight ahead in the Upper Pool.

By this time the river is usually made uncomfortably choppy by the wash from barges and coasters, as well as the many pleasure boats that ply the river. Great care will be needed when working on deck.

The entrance to St Katharine Haven (widely known as St Kat's) is on the N shore just short of Tower Bridge, and about 400m before it, on the same side, is the fuel barge *Burgan*. The advertised operating times show fuel available

until 1600, but it sometimes closes earlier and does not operate at all on Saturdays. Vessels other than very large yachts and motor cruisers need to turn round behind the upstream end of the barge and secure to its N side.

St Kat's enjoys a splendid position, almost in Central London, and within walking distance of many of the attractions. It is very popular and advance booking (a week ahead in mid season) is required. Access is through a lock, securing in the lock to a floating pontoon, and is available

St Katharine Haven, by Tower Bridge

Yachts of all sizes use St Katharine's

ST KATHARINE HAVEN

Contact
VHF Ch 80 (during locking times)
Call sign *St Katharine's*
Office ☎ 020 7264 5312
Email haven.reception@skdocks.co.uk
www.skdocks.co.uk
Access HW–2hr to HW+1½hr
Apr–Oct 0600–2030, Nov–Mar 0800–1800 (but lock closed Tues and Weds)

Facilities WC. Showers. Launderette. Pump out

Water On pontoons

Electricity On pontoons

Sailmaker M Putt ☎ 020 8599 1413

Fuel At barge in river

Gas Calor and Gaz from fuel barge in river

Contact fuel barge VHF Ch 14, call sign *Burgan*, ☎ 020 7481 1774. Opening times Mon–Fri 0600–1600, Sat closed, Sun at locking times only

Pub/restaurant Tradewinds Club beside lock

Provisions Safeway nearby.

Tied up on the N side of the fuel barge *Burgan*. St Katharine's entrance is behind the jetty to the right

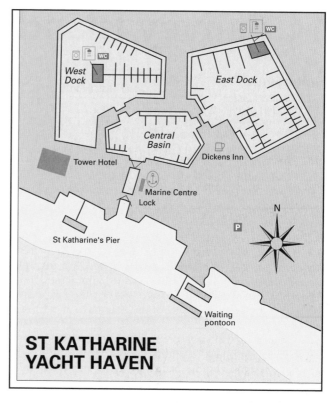

ST KATHARINE YACHT HAVEN

from about HW–2hr to about HW+1½hr, although this depends on the height of tide.

There are waiting buoys close SW of the entrance, although the inshore row of these seems perilously close to the mud at LWS. Shoal draught boats may also wait on the inside of St Katharine's Pier, just upstream.

The lock leads into the Centre Basin, with two more basins, East Dock and West Dock, leading off from it.

The marina is beautifully kept and surrounded by trees, flower beds and hanging baskets. It's busy – there are many shops, cafes and restaurants – and there are always plenty of people walking through on their way to and from work. Berths are behind locked gates.

Locking out on departure must be booked in advance.

14. Canvey Island

Holehaven

⊕ **Landfall waypoint**
51°30′.50N 000°33′.19E
(close S of creek entrance)

Tides
Dover HW+0140

Approach

Small boat traffic should stay close to the S shore of the Thames whether travelling up or downstream in this area, so the approach to Holehaven will need to be made from a point on the opposite shore when traffic permits.

Entry

The entrance is not obvious until close to and the access channel is narrow, with little water at LWS. Once over the bar and about 200m inside, it deepens to 2–3m least depth. Follow the line of moored fishing boats for the best water and anchor towards the W side of the channel to avoid stone groynes.

Two cables in, there is a steep slipway to starboard where dinghies can land. Just beyond is the old HM's office on a pier, now occupied by the National Coastwatch Institution ☎ 01268 696971.

Behind the wall here is the Lobster Smack pub ☎ 01268 660021 where the restaurant is so popular that bookings must be made. The pub is mentioned in *Great Expectations*, by Charles Dickens, and Brunel once stayed there after being burned aboard the *Great Eastern* when she blew a boiler nearby.

The deep water runs on for another ½M before reaching the disused Chainrock Jetty, which has 11m clearance. If access N is required by boats that can't pass beneath the jetty, it is possible to cross the mudflats W of its seaward end by following a drying gutway to join the deeper water again behind Coryton.

The channel meanders on inland to a junction where the drying East Haven Creek wanders away NE towards Benfleet, eventually passing beneath a fixed road bridge (3.6m), and the equally shallow Vange Creek can be followed NW through the small boat moorings up to Pitsea Hall, where the National Motorboat Museum ☎ 01268 550077 may be found.

Ray Gut, Hadleigh Ray, Benfleet Creek, Leigh-on-Sea

⊕ **Landfall waypoint**
51°31′.00N 000°42′.57E
(close S of Leigh SHB)

Tides
Dover HW+0125

Hazards

Apart from Ray Gut itself and parts of Hadleigh Ray, this entire area, including many moorings, dries soon after half-ebb. Only attempt entry on a rising tide and only in a shoal-draught boat.

Ray Gut Entry

The unlit Leigh SHB marks the entrance to Ray Gut, which gives access to Benfleet, Smallgains and Leigh Creeks, and lies ½M 290° from the end of Southend Pier (2F.G.13m8M). Apart from the pierhead, there are no lit marks at all in this area.

Benfleet YC's members' rule of thumb for getting right up Benfleet Creek from here is that the Marsh End Sand should already be covered and the tide rising.

Note there is more water NE of the Leigh buoy than SW of it, so you should actually leave it close to port. From the Leigh buoy, head NW and pass through two pairs of R and

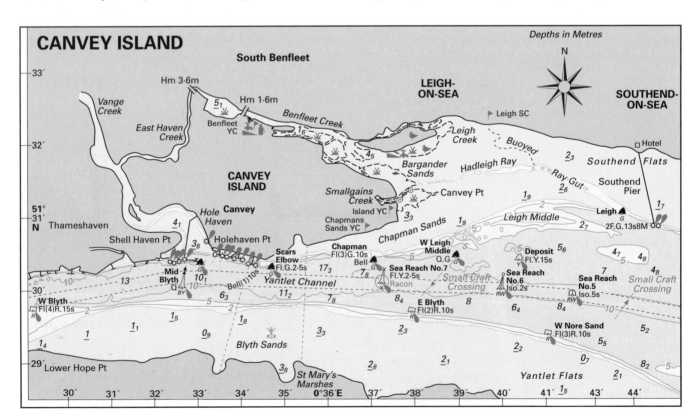

Canvey Island from the east with Benfleet creek to the North and Smallgains Creek to the South

G buoys during the first ½M. Then turn onto about 287°, heading for the large fishing boat moorings in Hadleigh Ray. About 0.9M further on, small buoys leading off generally NW show the line of Leigh Creek.

LEIGH-ON-SEA

Leigh Creek is buoyed, but for a trip ashore, consider staying in Hadleigh Ray and taking the dinghy into the creek. Otherwise, request a spare mooring from one of the clubs

Smallgains Creek entrance. Southend is in the distance

(Leigh SC ☎ 01702 476788 or the Essex YC ☎ 01702 478404) or dry out alongside at Bell Wharf or Victoria Wharf.

ISLAND YACHT CLUB

Contact
 ☎ 01268 510360
 Access HW±1hr
 Visitor pontoon, slipway
Fuel Diesel
Facilities WC. Showers
Taxi ☎ 01268 682222, 566677

Smallgains Creek

The Island YC stands on the S shore of Smallgains Creek, which runs into an inlet in the E end of Canvey Island, and looks out SE across the Estuary. It has a forest of wooden staging moorings along the S shore of the creek, with some on the N side near the entrance.

To reach the club, head W from the S end of Leigh Creek, following the large fishing boat moorings along the S side of the deeper water in Hadleigh Ray. Monitor the depth constantly. From the end of a line of four R can buoys follow a set of posts to the entrance to Smallgains and enter between the wooden piers. Just inside the entrance there is a short steep slip up onto the S staging, which is suitable for tenders.

The deeper water follows the N shore once inside, then crosses to the S after the creek bends to port. From there, follow the S shore one boat's length off the sterns of moored boats.

There's a broad slipway on the S shore and immediately before it is a visitor pontoon, although some visitors choose to pick up a mooring out in the Ray (anchoring is not advised because of clutter on the bottom) and land by dinghy. Diesel is available just beyond the slipway, but shops are a fair walk away.

Benfleet Creek

At the W end of Hadleigh Ray, a narrow buoyed channel heads off NW towards Two Tree Island and becomes Benfleet Creek. The Benfleet YC stands on the N shore of Canvey Island, E of the tidal barrier across Benfleet Creek, and has moorings in the creek. The creek and its approaches dry soon after the ebb starts, so a rising tide is essential, as is shoal draught, if trying to reach the club. Phone ahead for advice about a mooring or a place alongside the slipway.

From the Hadleigh Ray, follow some small SHBs towards the starboard-hand pole on the end of a causeway extending S from Two Tree Island from where there is water available. The island is a nature reserve and is 20 minutes walk from Leigh Station.

Turn W at the causeway and leave more moorings close to starboard before reaching the first Benfleet YC large SHB. Follow the R and G marks towards the NW again, then close with the N bank until reaching the start of the club's moorings. These consist of trots to starboard and bank-side berths to port. Continue through these moorings until the clubhouse and slipway show on the port bow.

On the N shore opposite BYC are the moorings of Benfleet Motor Boat and YC ☎ 01268 753311 which may also be able to help out with a mooring.

BENFLEET YACHT CLUB

Contact
 ☎ 01268 792278
 www.benfleetyachtclub.org
 Open lunchtimes (bar snacks) and evenings (meals) all week
Fuel Diesel
Water From club
Chandler Dauntless Yacht Centre (outside club gate)
 ☎ 01268 795554
Gas Calor and Gaz from chandler
Taxi ☎ 01268 566677.

Holehaven Creek with NCI watch station and Chainrock Jetty

IMRAY 2000 SERIES CHARTS

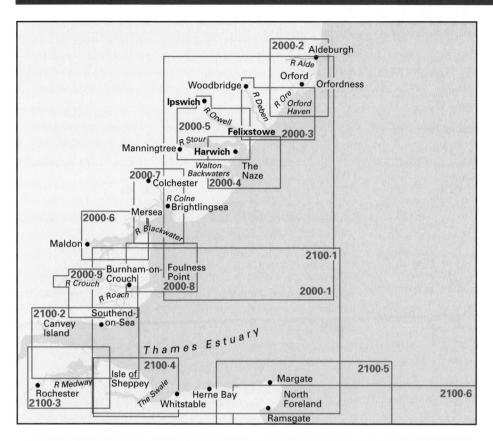

The Imray 2000 chart series is a growing range of handy-sized charts published as folios or individual sheets for use on small chart tables and in open cockpits. Designed especially for yachtsmen, these charts are clearly edited to exclude any unnecessary data that is included on other series. They are printed in colour on waterproof paper and are correctable.

- Folios of charts in a plastic wallet
- Also available as single sheets published either as flat sheets or folded to A4 in a plastic wallet
- Small format A2 size sheets – 594 mm x 420mm
- Waterproof paper

2000 THE SUFFOLK AND ESSEX COASTS

2000.1	**Suffolk and Essex Coast** 1:120,000
2000.2	**Rivers Ore and Alde** 1:35, 000
2000.3	**River Deben and Orford Haven** 1:35,000 *Plans* Woodbridge, Tide Mill Yacht Harbour
2000.4	**Harwich Approaches and Walton Backwaters** 1:35,000 *Plans* Titchmarsh Marina, Walton Yacht Basin
2000.5	**Rivers Stour and Orwell** 1:35,000 *Plans* Shotley Point Marina, Suffolk Yacht Habour, Woolverstone Marina, Fox's Marina (Ipswich), Upper Orwell to Ipswich
2000.6	**River Blackwater** 1:35,000 *Plans* Tollesbury Yacht Harbour, Bradwell Marina, Maldon
2000.7	**River Colne** 1:35,000 *Plans* Brightlingsea, Wivenhoe
2000.8	**River Crouch Entrance** 1:35,000
2000.9	**Rivers Crouch and Roach** 1:35,000 *Plans* Burnham Yacht Harbour, Bridgemarsh Marina, West Wick Marina, Continuation of River Crouch

2100 THE KENT COAST

2100.1	**Thames Estuary South** 1:120,000
2100.2	**River Thames Sea Reach** 1:50,000
2100.3	**River Medway** 1:40,000 *Inset* Continuation to Allington *Plans* Whitton, Hoo, Gillingham Marina
2100.4	**The Swale** 1:40,000 *Plan* Whitstable Harbour
2100.5	**North Foreland to Dover** 1:120,000 *Plan* Ramsgate and approaches
2100.6	**Dover Strait** 1:200,000 *Plan* Rade de Dunkerque

IMRAY C AND Y CHARTS

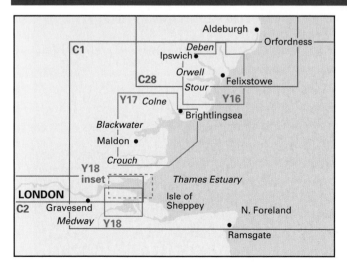

IMRAY C AND Y CHARTS

C1	**Thames Estuary – Tilbury to North Foreland and Orfordness** 1:120,000 WGS 84
C2	**The River Thames – Teddington to Southend** WGS 84 Teddington to Vauxhall 1:13,600 Vauxhall to Barking 1:15,200 Barking to Southend 1:40,400
C28	**The East Coast – Harwich to Wells-next-the-Sea** *Plans* River Deben, Rivers Ore and Alde, Southwold, Lowestoft, Great Yarmouth, Blakeney, Wells-next-the-Sea 1:125,000 WGS 84
Y16	**Walton Backwaters to Ipswich and Woodbridge** *Plans* Fox's Marina (Ipswich), Shotley Point Marina, Suffolk Yacht Harbour, Woolverstone Marina, Titchmarsh Marina, Woodbridge 1:35,000
Y17	**The River Colne to Blackwater and Crouch** *Plans* Colchester, Brightlingsea, Bradwell Marina, Tollesbury Yacht Harbour, River Roach to Havengore 1:49,000
Y18	**River Medway** **Sheerness to Rochester with River Thames, Sea Reach** 1:20,000 WGS 84

15. River Medway

⊕ **Landfall waypoints**
From E 51°27'.20N
000°45'.60E (close E of
West Cant PHB Q.R)
From W (Thames) and N
51°28'.36N 000°45'.55E
(close N of Nore Swatch
PHB Fl(4)R.15s)

Charts
Imray Folio *2100*
Admiralty SC *5606*

Tides
HW Dover +0130
(Sheerness)
HW Dover +0140
(Chatham)

Harbour Authority (Medway Ports)
Contact VHF Ch 74
Call sign *Medway Radio*
Harbourmaster
☎ 01795 596596

THE MEDWAY

The tidal Medway runs 25M inland to Allington Lock, but most yachts are prevented from reaching this point by the fixed bridge at Rochester, leaving exploration of the rural upper reaches beyond the industrial areas to motor cruisers and small craft.

As a tourist destination the Medway has much to offer with the Historic Dockyard Museum, modern shopping centres, Rochester Castle and Cathedral, and Dickensian festivals.

Main hazards

The lower part of the Medway is busy with commercial traffic, some of it large, and close attention should be paid to shipping movements. Listen on Ch 74 to Medway Radio.

This traffic not only uses Sheerness Dock, but also an LNG Terminal on the W bank close to the Victoria buoy, Thamesport Container Terminal in Saltpan Reach, Kingsnorth Power Station in Long Reach, and other ships travel right upriver close to the fixed bridge at Rochester.

There is a dangerous wreck (the *Richard Montgomery*) immediately N of the approach channel, 2M NE of

Sheerness, in a total exclusion zone marked by yellow light buoys.

There can be overfalls by Garrison Point on the first of the ebb and there are many drying areas on both shores along the river.

Approaches

On the W side of the river entrance stands the huge chimney of Grain Power Station, one of the most prominent landmarks in the Thames Estuary, 244m high and visible for tens of miles in clear weather

From E

Approach across the Cant shallows from the Spile buoy or along the S edge of the main shipping channel. Avoid the shallows S of the West Cant buoy (Q.R) and a nearby outfall marked by a small NCB (VQ).

From the Thames or from N

The Nore Swatch (Fl(4)R.15s) marks a convenient point from which to head S to the unlit Grain Edge buoy on N side of the main channel opposite the West Cant, avoiding the shallows of Grain Spit.

SHEERNESS

Contact VHF Ch 74
Call sign *Medway Radio*
Harbourmaster ☎ 01795 596596

Sheerness is not a place for leisure craft to visit, being a busy commercial port. However, one small part of the original Royal Naval Dockyard remains, a small dock called the Camber, just S of the old fort and Port Office at Garrison Point. In Nelson's time, naval ships came down river from Chatham Dockyard and were loaded with their cannons at the gun wharf in the Camber.

Sheerness RNLI lifeboats are now based there and the dock could be a place of refuge in an emergency with the consent of the Harbourmaster.

Looking South into the River Medway with Grain power station on the right and Sheerness on the left

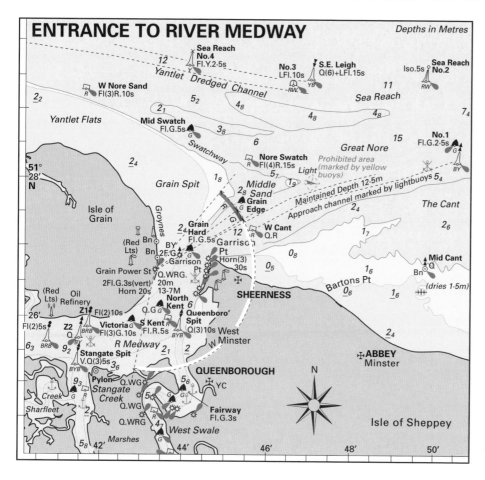

ENTRANCE TO RIVER MEDWAY

Depths in Metres

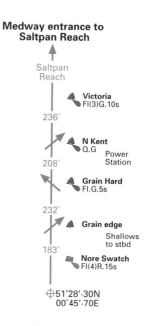

Medway entrance to Saltpan Reach

Saltpan Reach

236°

Victoria
Fl(3)G.10s

W Swale entrance

208°

N Kent
Q.G

Power Station

Garrison Point

232°

Grain Hard
Fl.G.5s

183°

Grain edge

Shallows to stbd

Nore Swatch
Fl(4)R.15s

⊕ 51°28'·30N
00°45'·70E

Entry to River Medway

Beware a disused ferry terminal jetty protruding N from Garrison Point, because the ebb sets quickly E beneath it.

The Port Control building stands on top of the large fort on Garrison Point and displays a bright light (Fl.7s) warning of shipping movements. The light is directed upstream if traffic is inbound and to seaward if traffic is outbound.

Unless certain that there is no traffic, it is best to enter the Medway along the W shore, passing close to Grain Hard SHB (Fl.G.5s) and heading on towards the N Kent SHB (Q.G), taking care not to stray onto the steeply shelving bank to starboard. The ebb is also less on this route.

Heavy shipping leaving the Medway is usually escorted in this section by large tugs, which are unsympathetic to leisure craft close to the main channel.

Medway entrance to Stangate

From the N Kent SHB, the entrance to the West Swale can be seen on the S side of the channel, marked by the Queenborough Spit ECB (Q(3)10s).

Once through the relative narrows of the entrance and into Saltpan Reach, which runs E-W, there is more scope for using the width of the river, shipping permitting. Off to starboard, on Horseshoe Point, a new LNG terminal receives large ships and, further W, stand the cranes at Thamesport container terminal.

Bearing 236° from the Victoria SHB (Fl(3)G.10s), the Stangate Spit ECB (VQ(3)5s) marks the W side of the entrance to Stangate Creek, the first anchorage in the Medway. An electricity pylon E of the entrance is prominent. There are heavy mooring buoys along the S side of the main channel, E of Stangate entrance, which are black and almost invisible at night.

Medway entrance from the NE. The jetty on Garrison Point is in the left foreground. Behind it, on the W shore, is Grain Power Station. Many car-carrying ships visit Sheerness

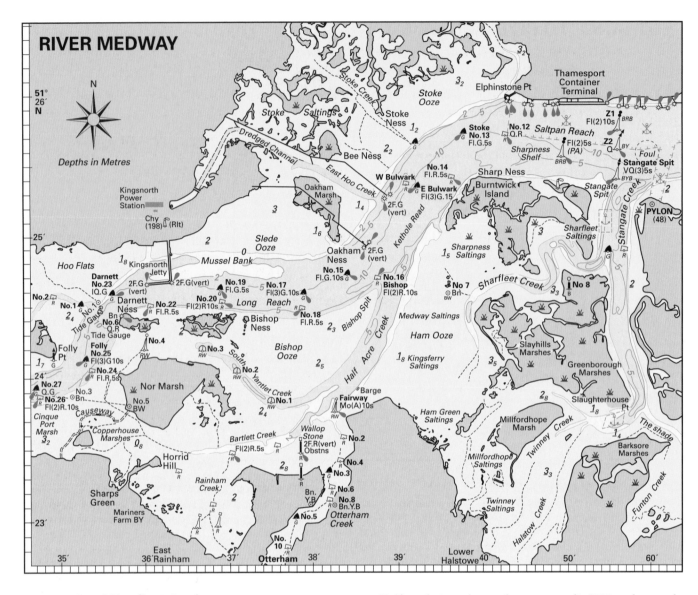

RIVER MEDWAY

51° 26' N

Depths in Metres

Stangate and Sharfleet Creeks

Stangate Creek runs due S from the Medway 1.6M from the Spit buoy and is a popular and peaceful anchorage. The bottom is mud and clay and holding is generally excellent.

The ruined building on Burntwick Island (to starboard at entrance) once housed a steam engine to pull a defensive boom across the Medway. Evidence of much older settlements are the Roman pottery fragments still to be found there.

Half-a-mile into the creek, past an unlit SHB and a wreck still showing a mast, the entrance to Sharfleet Creek turns off to the W and then NW into a horseshoe curve. This creek too is popular, although you need to choose your spot so as not to take the ground at LW and to avoid blocking the channel. There are no marks or withies. Parts of Sharfleet, once the best oyster grounds in the Medway, are very deep, and most of it has more than 2m at LWS. In a N

Entrance to Stangate Creek. Note the prominent pylon on the E side

Stangate Creek

breeze, machinery noise can carry across from Thamesport, which operates round the clock. The adventurous can take a shortcut W across the Ham Ooze from Sharfleet back to the Medway in Kethole Reach.

Stangate Creek continues S from the wreck at its junction with Sharfleet Creek and, at its S end, divides with the Shade and Funton Reach to port offering another possible anchorage. However, it soon peters out into the drying areas of Funton Creek and Bedlams Bottom, graveyard of the famous racing Thames Barges *Sirdar* and *Veronica*.

To starboard at the bottom of Stangate, immediately S of Slaughterhouse Point there is a pool affording better shelter in a N wind.

SW from this pool, the drying Halstow Creek will take shoal draught boats right up to Lower Halstow, but the whole area dries.

LOWER HALSTOW

Lower Halstow is a delightful village, with an ancient church, a pub, village shop and Post office. The old Eastwood's Wharf W of the church, once used to load bricks onto barges, has access limited to about HW±1hr and there is a fair amount of junk in the water. Anchoring off and going ashore by dinghy is possible.

In the SE corner of the inlet is Lower Halstow YC, access HW±1½hr, where there is a short jetty and a slipway with water available.

Stangate Creek to Half Acre Creek

N of entrance to Stangate Creek there is a NCB(Q) and, further N, an Isolated Danger mark (Fl(2)10s).

Pilotage W is straightforward, noting a second Isolated Danger (Fl(2)5s) on the S side of the main channel opposite Thamesport. Large ships turn in this area of Saltpan Reach.

Passing the No.12 PHB (Q.R), the river turns SW into Kethole Reach. Over to starboard, the drying Stoke Saltings was one of the areas in the Medway used by 19th century gangs of 'muddies', who, between tides, could fully load a Thames barge with the blue clay used in cement making. An unlit SHB on the edge of the flats marks the start of Stoke Creek, another drying inlet with a small boatyard and yacht moorings at its head.

Half way down Kethole Reach, the E Bulwark (Fl(G)15s) and unlit W Bulwark buoys mark the wreck of the 15,000-ton battleship HMS *Bulwark*, which blew up in November 1914 with the loss of over 700 lives.

Here the Bee Ness disused jetty juts out from the NW shore and on its SW side is the entrance to East Hoo Creek, a narrow anchorage running NW and carrying over 2.5m almost to its head. The wreck of a WWI German U-boat lies in the saltings to starboard.

Beyond the Bulwark buoys and the No.14 PHB (Fl.R.5s), a line of heavy mooring buoys stretches along the SE shore and, again, these are black and invisible at night. Just past the last one of these is the entrance to Half Acre Creek, marked on its W side by the No.16 Bishop PHB (Fl(2)R.10s), behind which lies the extensive and drying Bishop Spit.

Half Acre Creek

Running SW, Half Acre Creek is a wide, deep-water passage for a mile beyond the entrance. The tripod of the No.7 beacon is visible across the flats to port, marking the shortcut to Sharfleet Creek, and further on there is an uncharted yellow mooring, also to port, which is privately owned. High ground rises on the port bow near the Otterham Fairway buoy (Mo(A)10s). Here, Half Acre Creek divides.

South Yantlet Creek runs off to starboard, curving NW following a string of unlit SWBs. Beyond the third of these is a drying area N of Nor Marsh island, which may be crossed with 2m after half-tide towards the fourth and final red and white buoy, which carries a topmark. Continuing W for 2 cables the channel rejoins the Medway in Pinup Reach.

Back at the Otterham Fairway buoy, Otterham Creek itself continues S and is a buoyed but drying route up to the boatyard at Otterham Quay, which is to port at the end, opposite a commercial wharf.

The third, middle branch from the Otterham Fairway buoy, Bartlett Creek, heads WSW to an unlit PHB, turning W towards a lit PHB (Fl(2)R.5s) at the N end of the gutway of Rainham Creek. This was used by commercial traffic until recently to reach Bloors Wharf on the S shore via two more unlit PHBs.

Continuing W for a short distance, a gutway marked by withies leads SW to the unlit Mariners PHB, then on through a dog-leg to Mariners Farm Boatyard, a friendly DIY venue where visitors are welcomed.

An alternative route to this spot runs SE from further up the River Medway by the No.26 PHB, passing between a post and a red can to cross the causeway off the SW corner of Nor Marsh, then on SE to meet Bartlett Creek.

Mariners Farm will send a detailed chartlet on request.

Lower Halstow Hard and yacht club moorings from the old barge quay

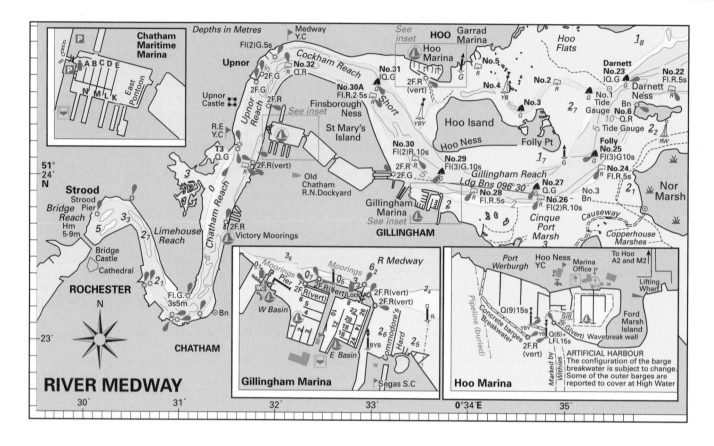

OTTERHAM CREEK

Otterham Quay Boatyard ☎ 01634 260250

Boat repairs 9-ton crane and dry dock

Engineers On site

Access HW±1hr

Pub At Upchurch (20 mins' walk)

Provisions Shops at Upchurch

Taxi ☎ 01634 233333.

MARINERS FARM BOATYARD

Contact
    ☎ 01634 233179
    Email enquiries@marinersboatyard.co.uk
    www.marinersboatyard.co.uk
    Access HW±2hr

Facilities WC. Showers

Water At yard

Provisions Short walk to Sharps Green or Lower Rainham

Taxi ☎ 01634 233333

Half Acre Creek to Gillingham and Hoo

Upstream from the entrance to Half Acre Creek, the main river runs W as Long Reach. It is safe to stay out of the main channel by skirting along its N edge, past SHBs No.15 (Fl.G.10s) and No.17 (Fl(3)G.10s), towards the huge Kingsnorth Power Station dominating the view ahead to starboard. This coal-fired station is supplied by frequent large colliers, which turn in the river opposite the jetty. The S shore shelves steeply and is a frequent trap for the unwary on a falling tide.

The final PHB opposite the power station, No.22 (Fl.R.5s), stands by Darnet Ness, a small island on another bend in the river, SW into Pinup Reach, with R beacon No.6 (Q.R) on its corner.

If visiting Hoo Marina, one of two access routes lies directly W of Darnet Ness, leading along Middle Creek (see section on Hoo Marina). Otherwise, head SW down Pinup Reach, where the shortcut through to South Yantlet Creek may be seen to port, before passing the No.25 Folly SHB (Fl(3)G.10s) and No.24 PHB (Fl.R.5s) off Folly Point. The channel is narrow here so take particular care with large traffic. An unlit G post stands on the SW corner of Folly Point to starboard, and the shallows extend a long way S of Hoo Island. Gillingham is now in clear view ahead, with a prominent gasholder, which stands close to Gillingham Marina.

Note that the speed limit upstream from here reduces to 6kn.

At SHB No.27 (Q.G) and PHB No.26 (Fl(2)R.10s) the channel turns just N of W as Gillingham Reach and yacht moorings line both shores. Beyond the next PHB, No.28 (Fl.R.5s), the walls of Gillingham Marina are prominent on the S shore.

Gas holder   Marina lock

Gillingham Marina Lock (centre). Note gasholder nearby

GILLINGHAM MARINA

Contact
  VHF Ch 80
  Call sign *Gillingham Marina*
  ☎ 01634 280022
  Email berthing@gillingham-marina.co.uk
  www.gillingham-marina.co.uk
  Access Locked basin HW±4½hr
  Tidal basin HW±1½–2hr
  (Manning hours vary, phone to check)

Facilities WC. Showers. Launderette

Fuel From pontoon outside lock gate

Boat repairs 65-ton boat hoist

Engineer On site

Sailmaker On site

Chandler Outside marina gate. ☎ 01634 283008
  Email chandlery@gillingham-marina.co.uk

Pub/restaurant At leisure centre on site.
  The Ship ☎ 01634 854570. Left out of marina, 10 mins

Taxi ☎ 01634 576666, 407408

Transport Mainline station to London Victoria.

Gillingham Marina has two basins, one behind a lock, the other tidal. Viewed from the river, the lock gate is towards the downstream end of the wall, to the left of the large pale-coloured building (a leisure centre), and the tidal basin is round behind the wall at the right hand end. The tidal basin dries to soft mud, which the marina describes as suitable for all types of boat.

Berths should be booked in advance if possible. All berths are either alongside finger pontoons or bows on to pontoons with the boat's stern secured between piles (like the Dutch 'box' system). The marina office is at the S end of the wall between the two basins.

There is a refuelling pontoon outside the lock gate. It is angled out into the stream, which can make it a little awkward to leave on the ebb.

Upstream from and next door to Gillingham Marina is the smaller Medway Pier Marine (VHF Ch 80 Call sign *Medway Pier Marine* ☎ 01634 851113) who can offer

Gillingham Marina's locked basin

drying berths with access above half-tide, with most facilities available including fuel.

At No.29 SHB (Fl(3)G.10s), which stands opposite Gillingham Marina, the river turns sharply NW round Hoo Ness into Short Reach. A ¼M past Hoo Ness, the SW corner of Hoo Island, a small unlit WCB to starboard marks the entrance to the gutway, sometimes called the Orinoco Channel, that leads ½M N across the flats to Hoo Marina.

The Orinoco Channel into Hoo Marina is marked by port-hand withies, following a dogleg course, first NE, then turning at a junction to NNW. The marina entrance is between a post lit as a SCM (Q(6)+LFl.15s) to port and 2.F.G(vert) to starboard. Once through, the dredged channel turns sharply to starboard across the cill into the marina basin, which is dredged to 2m.

The alternative and more adventurous route from the Medway starts in Pinup Reach just S of the No.1 beacon, itself close SW of the No.23 SHB opposite Darnet Ness. The channel is buoyed but the buoys are not shown on all charts. Starting with a SHB, follow WNW to a PHB marked No.2, rounding this and turning SW, using the gasholder in Gillingham as a transit to find W Hoo No.3 SHB. The route then roughly follows the shape of Hoo Island about 50m off, turning NW towards a SCB in line with a distant church steeple.

At this point you could carry on NW towards Hundred of Hoo SC and Whitton Marine ☎ 01634 250593, a basic berthing and boatyard operation with some facilities, or alternatively head W towards the R and G markers close to the Hoo Island shore that indicate a gap in the causeway between Hoo Island and the mainland.

From the R and G markers, head SW and join the Orinoco Channel leading NNW to Hoo Marina.

Hoo Marina is popular with club visits and is often full, so advance booking is wise when planning a visit. The marina has good security and the village of Port St Werburgh is a short walk away. Hoo Ness YC is a few metres W of the marina office.

Port Werburgh, immediately W of Hoo Marina and within the same breakwaters, is largely a residential moorings business.

Short reach, heading NW with St Mary's Island to port

Gillingham and Hoo to Rochester Bridge

Continuing NW along Short Reach, Cockham Woods are ahead on the N bank and, to port, lies St Mary's Island. This area was once part of the Chatham Naval Dockyard, and is now a major waterside housing development, the shore lined with modern houses. The moorings of Medway YC line the S side of the channel and are numerous, spreading to the N shore once past the 30A (Fl.R.2.5s) and No.31 (IQ.G) buoys.

As Cockham Reach bends to port, Medway YC's club house stands beneath the woods on the N shore at the apex of the bend.

HOO MARINA

Contact
 VHF Ch 80
 Call sign *Hoo Marina*
 ☎ 01634 250311
 Email info@hoomarina.com
 www.hoomarina.com
 Access Orinoco Channel route HW±2½–3hr
 Middle Creek route HW±1½hr

Facilities WC. Showers. Launderette

Boat repairs 20-ton crane

Provisions Shop near by

Pub/restaurant Café on site

Taxi ☎ 01634 253100.

Looking E across the winding Middle Creek route from Hoo Marina. Darnet Ness and its fort are in the distance

Hoo Marina at LW – dredged to 2m

River Medway looking East across Chatham Maritime Marina towards Hoo Island

Cockham Reach, heading W. Upnor is on the bow

Medway YC does not actively seek visitors, but can usually provide a mooring on request. Visitors may use the clubhouse and facilities, including the bar and restaurant. There is an all-tide floating jetty for landing by dinghy, also a weekend trot-boat service.

Upstream from Medway YC is Upnor SC, with its pontoons and its clubhouse set in a row of cottages. Close by are two large pub/restaurants, the Pier and the Ship, both popular with yachtsmen.

The river continues SW in Upnor Reach, where Upnor Castle sits on the W bank. Cannon fire from here eventually

MEDWAY YACHT CLUB

Contact
☎ 01634 718399 (0930–1630 Mon–Sat)
Email medwayyc@aol.com
www.medwayyachtclub.com
Trot Boat 0800–2000 Sat and Sun
Restaurant Weds, Fri, Sat, Sun evenings also lunch Sat and Sun.

repelled the Dutch raiders under Admiral de Ruyter in 1667 after they had sunk 16 ships of the Royal Navy.

Across the river from the Castle is the lock gate entrance to Chatham Maritime Marina, built in the old No.1 Basin of the Naval Dockyard. (Caution: the tide runs directly across the entrance, which is fairly narrow. Care needs to be taken not to end up going sideways into the lock. Check the tidal flow and apparent strength before leaving.)

This modern 300-berth marina has full facilities, including one of the best toilet/shower blocks you are likely to find anywhere. However, although the marina itself is excellent, its surroundings are still in the early stages of renaissance. There is one pub/restaurant and a small supermarket near by, plus an 'outlet shopping mall', but the area is otherwise rather desolate and it's a difficult journey into town by public transport in the evening, with buses finishing at 2000 and taxi drivers reluctant to make the journey at all.

Just upstream, a 10-minute walk away, is the magnificent World Naval Base, Chatham's Historic Dockyard Museum ☎ 01634 823807 (info line) www.chdt.org.uk which is now rated as one of Britain's major tourist attractions. Rope-making is one of the many attractions to be seen, still being

CHATHAM MARITIME MARINA

Contact
VHF Ch 80
Call sign *Chatham Marina*
Contact phone ☎ 01634 899200
Email chatham@mdlmarinas.co.uk
www.chathammaritimemarina.co.uk
Access 24hr (1.5m over cill at LWS)

Facilities WC. Showers. Launderette

Water On pontoons

Electricity On pontoons

Fuel Diesel and petrol from berth immediately to starboard after lifting bridge

Gas Calor and Gaz

Boat repairs 20-ton crane

Chandler Pirate's Cave ☎ 01634 722326 across river at Frindsbury

Trains Chatham or Rochester stations, services to London

Taxi ☎ 01634 848848, 851122.

done in the traditional way on a rope walk. Naval ships were built here from the late 1500s (including HMS *Victory*) and continued right up to the days of modern submarines, the last of which, HMS *Ocelot*, is one of the ships on display.

Above the marina, enormous sheds sit on the port shore at the beginning of the Historic Dockyard, housing slips where ships were built and maintained, one of them now displaying the national collection of RNLI lifeboats.

Towards the top of Chatham Reach, on the E shore, is a long floating pontoon, Thunderbolt Pier, running parallel to the stream and connected to the shore. There, Victory Moorings (☎ 07785 971797) runs as a berth-holders' facility that does not normally accept visitors without prior booking.

The final reaches below Rochester Bridge have little to offer the visitor in the way of shore facilities, although brief landings are possible at Sun Pier, on the port side as the river turns sharply round to NNW at Chatham Ness. A mile further on, having run up Limehouse Reach and turned SW again into Bridge Reach, the fixed Rochester Bridge spans the river with an air draught of 5.9m at HWS.

The starboard side has the most depth, but there is negligible water under the bridge at LW and easy passage is only feasible for motor cruisers or shoal-draught yachts with easily-lowered rigs.

Chatham Marina's lock from inside. The fuel pontoon is to the left of the office

Chatham Marina entrance – beware strong cross-tides

River Medway looking East towards the Channel Rail Link bridge, the M2 motorway bridge and Rochester Bridge in the distance

Rochester to Allington

Navigation beyond Rochester Bridge is best done on the flood from about half-tide onwards and is very largely confined to motorboats, with only a handful of small yachts to be seen.

Immediately above the bridge there are jetty and pontoon moorings on both sides of the river. The first jetty to

Strood YC's moorings, looking across the river to Rochester Castle and Rochester CC's moorings

starboard belongs to Pelican YC, whose members' only facility is the jetty itself, while over on the port side, once past the towering ruin of Rochester Castle, are the moorings of Rochester CC ☎ 01634 841350.

On the opposite, W shore is the clubhouse of Strood YC, some of whose moorings are on an all-tide pontoon and some on the mud.

The river curves to the S, with remains of the slipways of the old Short Bros seaplane factory still visible on the port side, in front of a mass of modern housing.

Fixed bridge at Rochester, the limit of navigation for most yachts

Past Wickham Point, the river again turns SW towards the Medway Crossing. Just short of this bridge, on the S shore, is the large Medway Bridge Marina where advance booking is requested. There is a mix of all-tide, half-tide and mud berths, engineers, a chandler, and a restaurant in the old Inner Dowsing light vessel. Fuel is available and is the last before Allington Lock.

Beyond the marina, the river runs beneath the two major road bridges and a third carrying the Channel Tunnel Rail Link.

Still heading generally SW, two more marinas swiftly come up on the starboard side, the first of which is Port Medway. This is a growing operation, with engineering and electrical facilities, a dry dock and a chandler. This marina also features a floating restaurant, in the *Rochester Queen*, once a pleasure boat running from Bournemouth.

Port Medway Marina, looking downstream

MEDWAY BRIDGE MARINA

Contact
☎ 01634 843576
Email info@medwaybridgemarina.co.uk
www.medwaybridgemarina.co.uk
Fuel Diesel and petrol
Gas Calor and Gaz
Facilities WC. Showers
Water On pontoons
Electricity On pontoons
Engineers John Hawkins Marine (Volvo dealer)
☎ 01634 840812
GMS (Perkins Sabre dealer) ☎ 01634 844114
Chandler ☎ 01634 844114
Provisions Shops in nearby Borstal village
Restaurant In light vessel ☎ 01634 827194
Taxi ☎ 01634 818777.

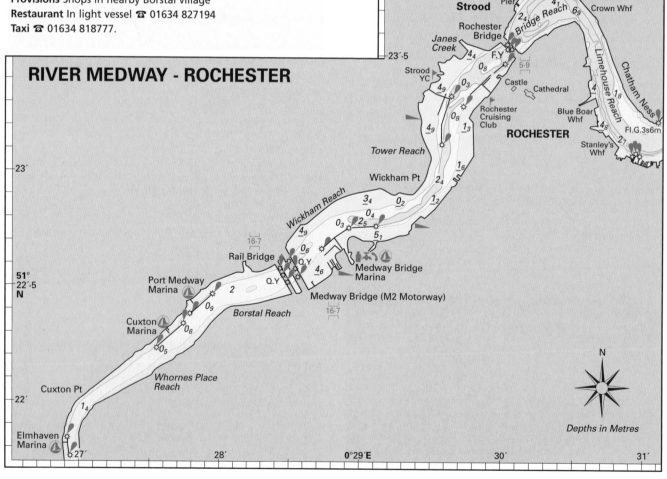

RIVER MEDWAY - ROCHESTER

The view looking upstream from Medway Bridge Marina

Cuxton Marina

PORT MEDWAY MARINA

Contact
☎ 01634 720033
Email jtaylor@portmedway.co.uk
www.portmedway.co.uk
Access HW±5hr
Boat repairs 20-ton and 16-ton cranes, slipway, dry dock
Provisions In Cuxton, 10 mins' walk
Restaurant ☎ 01634 716141
Trains To Maidstone and Strood
Taxi ☎ 01634 720200.

Immediately upstream from Port Medway is a second, smaller operation at Cuxton Marina ☎ 01634 721941, with shipwrights and electricians, a slipway and hoist.

Above Cuxton there is a stretch of the river used for water skiing.

The river runs on through open country, with a chalk escarpment rising to starboard and, at Cuxton Point, the rivers bends S, to the small Elmhaven Marina on the starboard side in the village of Halling, set at the foot of a chalk cliff. Visitors are advised to phone in advance.

From Halling, the river runs through a mixture of rural scenery and considerable industrialisation, although there is nothing left of the commercial traffic that once used the river. The depth steadily reduces and it is important to match boat speed with the flood tide to ensure adequate depth, also that there is sufficient clearance to get under the bridge at Aylesford and reach the lock at Allington within locking hours.

Once past Snodland and New Hythe (where there is a footbridge with an air-draught of 11.2m) the final obstacle before Allington Lock is the ancient stone bridge at Aylesford with only 3.2m clearance at HWS. Like the bridge, Aylesford itself is a pretty little place but there is nowhere to stop by boat.

After a series of bends, the river passes under a major road bridge 1M above Aylesford and just before Allington Lock, the head of the tidal navigation. The lock gate is on the starboard side of the river with a large weir to port. Beyond the lock is Allington Marina, the first stop on the non-tidal navigation.

ELMHAVEN MARINA

Contact
☎ 01634 240489
Email elmhaven-marina@talk21.com
www.elmhaven-marina.co.uk

Electrician On site
Shipwright On site
GRP repairs On site
Provisions Shops at Halling, 10mins
Taxi ☎ 01634 240470.

Allington Lock

Elmhaven Marina

ALLINGTON LOCK

Contact
☎ 01622 752864
Access HW–3hr to HW+2hr

ALLINGTON MARINA

Contact
☎ 01622 752057
Facilities WC. Showers
Water In marina
Fuel Diesel and petrol
Gas Calor and Gaz
Taxi ☎ 01622 690000.

Upnor Castle below Rochester

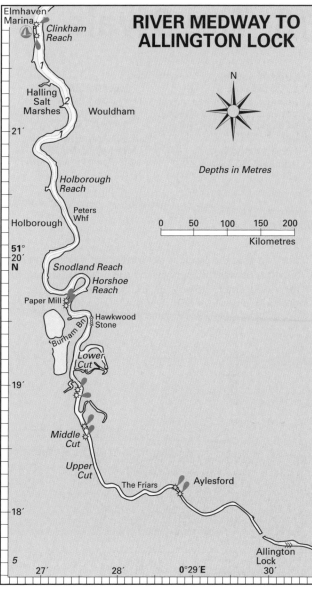

RIVER MEDWAY TO ALLINGTON LOCK

N

Depths in Metres

| 0 | 50 | 100 | 150 | 200 |

Kilometres

Elmhaven Marina
Clinkham Reach
Halling Salt Marshes
Wouldham
Holborough Reach
Peters Whf
Holborough
Snodland Reach
Horshoe Reach
Paper Mill
Hawkwood Stone
Burham Brn
Lower Cut
Middle Cut
Upper Cut
The Friars
Aylesford
Allington Lock

51° 20′ N

Aylesford Bridge

16. The Swale

⊕ **Landfall waypoint**
51°24′.10N 001°01′.73E
(immediately E of line
between Whitstable Street
NCB and Columbine SHB)

Charts
Imray *2100 Series*
Admiralty SC *5606, 2571,
2572*

Tides
(Queenborough)
HW Dover +0130 HW
(Harty Ferry)
Dover +0120

Harbour Authority
Medway Ports VHF Ch 74
Call sign *Medway Radio*

Main hazards

1. Tides

The fact that the Swale is not a river but a tidal waterway between the Isle of Sheppey and the mainland means that the flood enters at both E and W ends, while the ebb similarly runs out of both E and W ends, with a watershed in the W Swale.

The stream runs E for much longer than it runs W, which can be put to good use on a passage E.

At HW Sheerness, the whole Swale is slack. The ebb then begins to run E throughout the Swale for the first hour or so. After that it splits between Queenborough and Kingsferry Bridge, with the W Swale ebbing into the Medway and the E Swale into the Thames Estuary. The separation point gradually moves E towards Elmley and all flows stop at LW, with the exception of a back eddy along the W shore opposite Queenborough.

When the flood starts it comes in from both ends, the streams meeting at about Elmley. Later, the meeting point often moves E towards Fowley.

Although every day follows this general pattern, detailed tide timing and heights are greatly affected by wind, weather and barometric pressure, especially in the E Swale.

Shellness to starboard marks the entrance to the East Swale

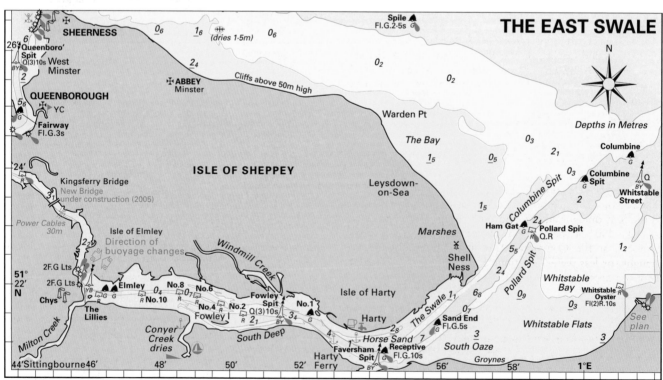

THE SWALE

When it was wider and had greater depth, the Swale was a main route from the English Channel to London, but the channel has narrowed and become shallower by silting and land reclamation to the point where the central section is barely navigable at LW.

With saltmarshes and mudflats on both sides, the Swale forms an area of international importance for breeding and wintering birds. Brent Geese, Widgeon and Avocet are frequently seen, taking little heed of the hundreds of boats kept in the three main creeks – Faversham, Oare and Conyer – as well as at Queenborough.

At low water, the bones of many ships can be seen along the shores of these creeks and in the Swale itself, most of them relics of the hundreds of Thames barges that served the thriving local industries of brick, cement and gunpowder manufacturing, which are all now gone.

If you love the East Coast and the solitude it can offer, the Swale has considerable charm. It brings its own pilotage challenges, especially if you are on the move around low water, but if you run out of luck, the bottom is forgiving and there is plenty to look at while you wait for the water to return.

Hollowshore at bottom left marks the junction of the Oare and Faversham Creeks. Shellness shows at top right of photo

2. Shipping

Commercial shipping uses the W Swale, almost always entering and leaving via the Medway, to reach docks just E of the Kingsferry Bridge. On rare occasions, small coasters may use the E Swale as a short cut on a good tide.

Approaches to East Swale

From E

Make along the coast to the Whitstable Street NCB (Q).

From W

Take the Four Fathoms Channel from the Spile SHB (Fl.G.2.5s), making good about 105° to avoid isolated shoals to the S. If draught allows, and on a rising tide, alter course to make 180° at the 001°E meridian and join the E Swale approach at the Columbine Spit unlit SHB. With deeper draught (or less water) continue E to Columbine unlit SHB for more depth.

From N

Again if draught permits, follow the 001°E meridian past the Red Sand Tower and the Middle Sand beacon. For more water, from the Red Sand make good 120° to pass close by the SW corner of the wind farm, then 215° to pass the Spaniard ECB (Q(3)10s) and on to the vicinity of the Whitstable Street NCB (Q).

Pollard Spit buoy

East Swale

Enter channel by passing between the Whitstable Street NCB (Q) and the unlit Columbine SHB.

With a strong SWly blowing against the flood tide there is often a nasty chop in this area, only smoothing out at the Ham Gat unlit SHB and the Pollard Spit PHB (Q.R). Indeed, any kind of Wly seems to funnel straight out of the East Swale, causing locals to name such winds the 'Swale Doctor', saying it blows away all ills.

From out by the 'Street', the small Pollard Spit and Ham Gat buoys are difficult to locate against the bright sand of

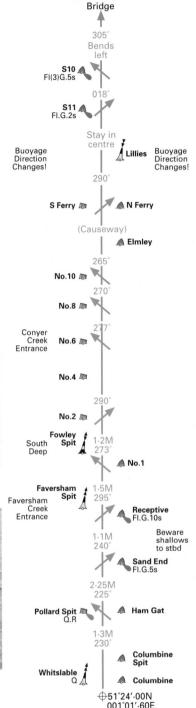

East Swale entrance to
Kingsferry Bridge

Bridge

305°
Bends
left

S10
Fl(3)G.5s

018°

S11
Fl.G.2s

Stay in
centre

Buoyage   Lillies   Buoyage
Direction   Direction
Changes!   Changes!

290°

S Ferry   N Ferry

(Causeway)   Elmley

265°

No.10

270°

No.8

277°

Conyer
Creek   No.6
Entrance

No.4

290°

No.2

Fowley   1·2M
South   Spit   273°
Deep

No.1

Faversham   1·5M
Faversham   Spit   295°
Creek   Receptive
Entrance   Fl.G.10s

Beware
shallows
to stbd

1·1M
240°   Sand End
Fl.G.5s

2·25M
225°

Pollard Spit   Ham Gat
Q.R

1·3M
230°   Columbine
Spit

Whitslable   Columbine
Q

⊕51°24'·00N
001°01'·60E

Harty Ferry anchorage. The longest of the white buildings is the Ferry Boat Inn

Shell Ness, but their bearing is about 240° range 2.1M from midway between the Street NCB and Columbine SHB. Making good that course just scrapes the S side of the deep water in the channel.

With Pollard Spit PHB close to port, a course made good of 225° will take you on another 2.3M to the Sand End SHB (Fl.G.5s), which is again hard to see against the background clutter. In daylight, a good indication that you are heading in the right general direction is the pair of unusually tall electricity pylons that cross Faversham Creek, 4M from the Pollard.

Passing Shell Ness and its collection of remote houses, the N bank of the channel is very steep to, while the S side remains a fairly gentle shelf.

Avoid grounding on the charted shellfish beds in the area.

From the Sand End SHB there is a shallow route WSW passing N of the Horse Sand, but it is advisable to follow the main channel SW to the 'Receptive', a SHB (Fl.G.10s) marking a wreck. Follow a slight curve to port of the rhumb line to the Receptive, to avoid the edge of the Horse Sand. On the S side of the channel is the Faversham Spit NCB, at the entrance to Faversham Creek.

HARTY FERRY

From the Receptive SHB, the Swale turns NW, passing through the anchorage known as Harty, or Harty Ferry. The Isle of Harty, actually now part of the Isle of Sheppey, stands on the N side of the anchorage, with an ancient Saxon church on the skyline, and the white Ferry House Inn ☎ 01795 510214 nestling on the S side of the hill.

The pub is named for the ferry that once ran between here and the mainland, indeed the S shore is also called

Harty Ferry at LW, looking N to Sheppey. The causeway is firm and reasonably clean

Harty Ferry, from where a causeway extends across the mudflats, marked by substantial withies. A dark-roofed building owned by the Kent Wildlife Trust peers over the sea wall here.

Just across the road from the Wildlife Trust building is a fresh-water spring, which is rare on marshland.

The village of Oare is just over a mile from the S causeway, with two pubs but no shop. A longer dinghy trip can take you to the Shipwright's Arms at the junction of Faversham and Oare Creeks (see details for Oare Creek).

On the opposite, N shore, a matching causeway provides landing for visitors to the pub, which has toilets, a shower and laundry for sailors, and also serves food. The landing is a little muddy, but the causeway is hard.

There are a few moorings on the N shore and many more to the S of the channel. These is a mixture of private, boatyard and club moorings, and the usual rule applies that they may be used unless the owner returns. Anchoring either side of the main channel finds good holding in soft mud.

The Harty anchorage in general is very exposed to strong E winds, when it should be avoided if possible. With some N in the wind, you may find shelter under the N shore about a ½M W of the causeway, but avoid charted wrecks on the mudflats.

In general, Harty is a popular overnight stop, but the tide can run hard here and must be considered when going ashore by dinghy. The area teems with bird life that may wake you early on an otherwise peaceful summer's morning.

Faversham Creek

Faversham Creek turns S from the Swale at the Faversham Spit NCB. Leave the buoy to starboard and follow the line of unlit PHBs until the creek bends to port at No.8 opposite a SH post marking a wreck. Give the PHBs room; in some wind and tide conditions they lie over the shallows.

Speed limit in the creek is 6kn and careful progress on a rising tide is advisable. It is about 2.25M to Iron Wharf, the first berthing in Faversham. There is no commercial traffic any more, but it is used by Thames barges.

Telephone ahead to the Iron Wharf Boatyard ☎ 01795 536296 for advice or if hoping to find a berth there.

Once past the final PHB, No.8, follow the centre of the channel S towards the buildings ahead at Hollowshore. Leave moored boats to starboard and be aware that sometimes there are ropes trailing in the water from laid-up fishing boats. Overhead is a high-tension electricity line with a charted safe air-draught of 33m.

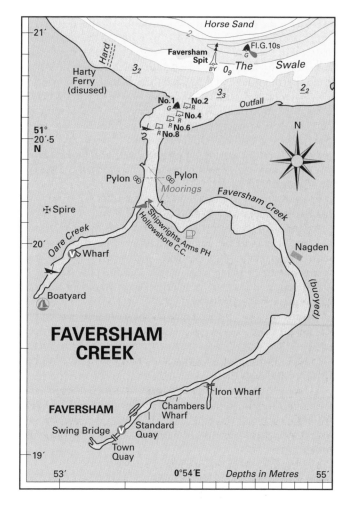

The larger of the buildings at Hollowshore is a boatyard shed and the smaller white building is the Shipwright's Arms pub. These are at the junction of Faversham and Oare Creeks. Here Oare Creek splits off to starboard.

The general rule for going up Faversham Creek when the mud is all covered is to keep midway between the banks rather than hop from buoy to buoy, but it is better to start at half flood, before the saltings are covered.

Enter Faversham Creek proper, with the pub to starboard, follow the line of the starboard bank until abeam the section of stone sea wall. Turn hard to port to bring the nearby pylon fine on the port bow. Pass SHBs 3, 5 and 7; at No.7 stand about 5m off the port bank heading towards a group of cottages. Look to starboard on about 215° for a large rectangular building in the middle distance and a church spire beyond. When these are in transit, turn further to

Faversham Spit buoy at the entrance to Faversham Creek. the long roof to the left is at Hollowshore

Hollowshore

starboard putting the next PHB, No.14, on the port bow. Once past No.14, turn about 30° to port for the next SHB, No.9, then continue mid-channel round a double bend past Nos.11 and 16. From there you will be able to see Iron Wharf ahead. Berthing here and at Chambers Wharf just beyond is likely to be rafted out. The chandler is here at Iron Wharf.

To port above Iron Wharf is Chambers Wharf, home of Alan Staley's wooden boat-building and restoration yard, followed by Standard Quay, home to barges and other traditional craft. Carrying on up the creek, the Front Brents Jetty lies parallel to the shore beyond the modern houses on the starboard side.

Front Brents is run by the local council ☎ 01795 594442 (for berths), dries to soft mud by half ebb and is advertised as suitable for boats up to 8m. Provided there is room, however, it should be able to accommodate shoal-draught boats longer than this. The Jetty has security, power and water, with fees being paid at the Albion pub ☎ 01795 591411 alongside, or at the Corner Shop round in Church Road, just a few steps away.

Slightly further up the creek, on the port side just before the road bridge, is the old Town Quay, which has room alongside for one 10m boat, plus perhaps one more rafted alongside. The bottom is again soft mud and quite flat, but there are no facilities.

Front Brents and the Town Quay are very close to the town centre, with its good mix of shops, pubs and facilities including restaurants. The country's largest independent brewery, Shepherd Neame, is across the road from the Town Quay.

Iron Wharf

Faversham is an excellent little town to visit, with more than 475 listed buildings and the 'best-preserved' mediaeval street (Abbey Street) giving it a general air of history. It also has modern attractions including an indoor swimming pool.

Faversham town quay

FAVERSHAM

Access HW±2hrs
Boatyard Iron Wharf Boatyard ☎ 01795 536296
Boat repairs Crane
Fuel Diesel
Facilities Showers. Launderette
Chandler Faversham Creek Chandlery ☎ 01795 531777
Shipwright Alan Staley ☎ 01795 530668
Supplies The Corner Shop ☎ 01795 532336
Pub Several nearby
Taxi ☎ 01795 538887
Transport Trains to London Victoria or Ramsgate and Dover via Canterbury.

Iron Wharf (top) and Chambers Wharf (centre)

Faversham Creek entrance. Hollowshore is in the centre, where Oare Creek goes off to the right

HOLLOWSHORE

Hollowshore is the old name given to the small area at the junction of Faversham and Oare Creeks. It has one ancient pub (the Shipwright's Arms), a boatyard, a club (Hollowshore Cruising Club), and one private house. Only recently has this area had mains electricity. It is remote and there is no public transport.

The boatyard, Hollowshore Services, where Barry Tester restores and repairs traditional wooden working boats, is one of the many sites where Thames barges were built. Hollowshore Cruising Club is the small building leaning against the N wall of the large boatshed and is generally open at weekend lunchtimes. It's a small, welcoming club for the many boat-owners in these creeks. With permission,

The Shipwright's Arms

HOLLOWSHORE

Boatyard Hollowshore Services (Barry Tester)
☎ 01795 532317
Boat repairs Crane
Pub/restaurant Shipwright's Arms ☎ 01795 590088.

rafting alongside at the yard may be possible, otherwise anchor off N and dinghy ashore.

The Shipwright's Arms has its own ghost, reputed to be a barge skipper shipwrecked one stormy night out in the Swale, who managed to get ashore and stagger to the pub door, but could make nobody hear, and was found dead there next morning.

Oare Creek

Oare Creek is best suited to shallow draught boats and great care is needed with any other craft. Coming in from the sea, keep heading straight towards the pub (The Shipwright's Arms) and look for the end of a low fence that comes down to the shore from the sea wall to port. Look also for a small orange buoy in the entrance to Oare Creek, just off the boatshed. When you judge you are between the two, turn towards the orange buoy and pass S of a shallow patch. Leave the orange buoy, which marks the end of a slipway, close to port.

If going far up Oare Creek, start at about HWN-1½hr or HWS-2hr.

The tide ebbs from the creek faster than it floods and Oare Creek dries entirely after about half ebb.

For its first ½M, the port shore is lined with yachts moored on wooden jetties and some pontoons, all privately owned. The channel here is unmarked. Stand about 10m off

Looking up Oare Creek with Faversham Creek going off East at Hollowshore

Going up into Oare Creek near HW

the sterns of the moored yachts, then pass close alongside the old barge dry-dock on the right-hand bend. Steer gradually out towards the centre of the channel by the time you reach the left-hand bend in the distance and watch the depth.

Around the left-hand bend is an old gunpowder dock to port and the channel moves across close to the moorings. These are owned by Youngboats and there is a visitor's berth on the pontoons by the old red-roofed shed (known locally as the Cylinder House, once a saltpetre store). Power and water is available.

OARE CREEK

Access HW±1½hr
Boatyard Youngboats (Terry Young) ☎ 01795 536176.
   Email info@youngboats.co.uk www.youngboats.co.uk
Boat repairs 8-ton crane
Fuel Diesel
Water On pontoons
Electricity On pontoons (tokens)
Scrubbing berth On site
Chandler On site
Facilities WC
Gas Calor and Gaz from chandler
Pubs/restaurants The Castle ☎ 01795 533674.
   The Three Mariners ☎ 01795 533633
Taxi ☎ 01795 533869
Yacht club Hollowshore Cruising Club.

Boats of up to 1.5m draught should reach here on a 5.0m tide, but from here to the head of the creek, and Youngboats' main base, it gets shallower. Boats over 10m LOA will be hard to turn at the head of the creek. If in doubt, phone Youngboats for advice.

From the Cylinder House onwards, the channel is marked by pairs of withies. There are many more moorings at the head of the creek, where Youngboats has an 8-ton crane and a short scrubbing berth for boats up to about 9m.

Oare village at the head of the creek has two pubs, both of which serve food. Basic provisions are a 10-minute walk from the head of the creek, in Davington, along the road into Faversham. There is an occasional bus service from the village, the bus stop by The Castle pub. Faversham itself is only a couple of miles away.

Conyer and its winding approach channel. Fowley Island is in the middle distance, South Deep lies between it and the near shore

Sunset in South Deep

The Swale – Harty to Conyer

Continuing NW from Harty, the deepwater channel runs close to the Swale No.1 unlit SHB, passing disused remnants of the local gunpowder industry on the S bank. Also to the S, opposite the No.1 SHB (which is very close to the shallows on the N shore) are some scrubbing posts, although these have not been seen in use for a while.

The Swale now opens up into a much broader stretch of water, with a row of narrow chimneys at a paper mill 4M W, but at LW much of the water disappears.

Approach to the village of Conyer

The small Fowley Spit ECB (Q(3)10s) marks the entrance to a quiet anchorage in South Deep, with Conyer Creek beyond.

After passing the Fowley Spit ECB to port, the channel W narrows considerably and is marked with PHBs as far as Elmley.

Boats drawing up to 1m can pass through this shallowest section of the Swale soon after LWS, provided the PHBs are followed meticulously. The No.8 PHB marks the last chance to turn S into Conyer or South Deep.

South Deep and Conyer Creek

South Deep, particularly towards its W end inside Fowley Island, is a quiet and sheltered spot for an overnight stop. The route in from Fowley Spit ECB runs along the mainland shore passing an unlit SHB off the E end of Fowley Island. Carry on past the charted sluice (R. Bn) on S shore and after about 100m there is a hole with 1.5m at LWS.

Fowley Island is low-lying, little more than saltings, and is a wildlife reserve where landing is prohibited. Beyond this secluded anchorage, the route leads on to an unlit PHB and the approach to Conyer Creek.

The creek can also be approached from WNW and Swale No.8 PHB. An islet N of the creek entrance has a post on it and when the islet is covered, with only the post showing, you should find 2m all the way from the No.8 to a point S of the islet, although depths change suddenly as you cross the gutways that meander across the flats.

There are two routes for the final approach into the creek entrance, both marked in daylight with small buoys, although the red and green paint may be worn on some of them.

SWALE MARINA

Harbourmaster Mobile 07742 589845
Marina office ☎ 01795 521562
Email enquiries@swalemarina.co.uk
www.swalemarina.co.uk
Access HW±2½hr

Facilities WC. Showers

Water and electricity On pontoons

Fuel Diesel

Gas Calor and Gaz

Boat repairs 13-ton travel-hoist, 30-ton crane, 30-ton slipway, scrubbing berth

Sailmaker Wilkinsons ☎ 01795 521503

Provisions Teynham village (bus or taxi)

Pub/restaurant Ship Inn ☎ 01795 520778

Yacht club Conyer Cruising Club

Transport Buses or taxis to Teynham and trains to Ramsgate and Dover or London.

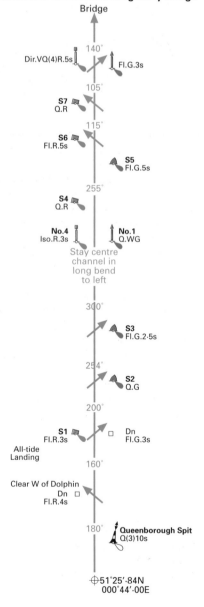

West Swale Entrance to Kingsferry Bridge

The route from E is marked from the unlit PHB at W end of South Deep and is straightforward.

From the Swale No.8, either continue to the start of the E channel or use a W channel called the Butterfly. The first marker for this about 300m NNW of the creek entrance and it leads directly SW towards the sea wall, turning abruptly to port close to the wall before meeting the E channel at a very small NCB.

From this point the channel is marked by more small buoys and posts leading gradually to the W side of the creek approaching a sharp left-hand bend. Around the bend, the channel is nearer to the centre and the village of Conyer comes into view.

Around the next right-hand bend, at the head of the creek, is Swale Marina, providing drying mud-berths alongside pontoons. Access all the way to the marina is about HW±2hr. For advice about getting up there, call the marina on the mobile number for advice. The marina has two waiting moorings out in South Deep.

The Swale – Conyer Creek to Kingsferry

Heading W from the Swale No.8 PHB, past No.10 PHB and the Elmley SHB near LW, the next obstruction is the disused ferry causeway at Elmley. (King James II is said to have fled the country from here, hence the name, Kingsferry.) The deepest point to aim for is slightly N of centre in the gap between two posts on the causeway.

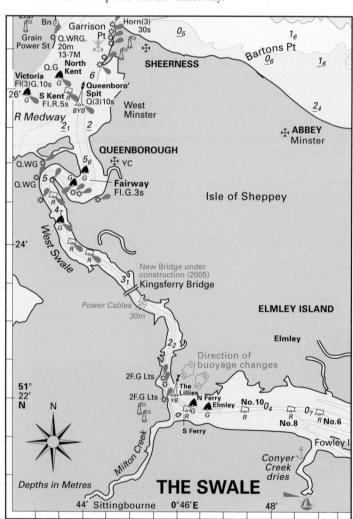

THE SWALE

Kingsferry Bridge with the new road bridge under construction alongside from the East.

From the causeway steer between the North Ferry PHB and the South Ferry SHB. Depth will increase as you head for the Lillies SCB.

At this point, off Milton Creek, it is essential to note that the direction of lateral buoyage changes, because this is the watershed for tides in the Swale.

Beyond the Lillies, on the W side of the channel, is the Grovehurst Jetty used by ships delivering china clay to the paper mill on the shore.

Above this jetty the channel is marked by lit SHBs (to be left to port when heading N), S11 (Fl.G.2s) then S10 (Fl(3)G.5s) in Clay Reach. At S9 (Q.G) it turns NW past S8 (Q.R) and widens into Ferry Reach with the Kingsferry lifting bridge in view less than a mile away.

In Ferry Reach there is a dock on the S shore, Ridham Dock, which takes frequent coaster traffic and it is wise to monitor Ch 10, the bridge operating frequency, both to learn of planned lifts and about ship traffic.

Milton Creek

With its entrance S of Lillies SCB, Milton Creek was once well-used by sailing barges, but it has silted so much that it is of no use to the majority of yachts. However, at the head of the creek is the Dolphin Yard Sailing Barge Museum ☎ 01795 424132, which can be visited by dinghy on the tide. Open Sundays and Bank Holidays, Easter to end of October.

KINGSFERRY BRIDGE

Kingsferry Bridge carries both road and rail traffic, but the road traffic will transfer W to a new fixed high-level bridge in 2006. Trains will continue on the old bridge.

There is no timetable for opening the Kingsferry Bridge, but it is required to lift on request if circumstances allow. In practice, although the bridge is manned continuously, it is actually controlled by the railway signalman at Sittingbourne and the duty bridge-keeper cannot open the bridge without his permission. Additionally, opening can be delayed by road traffic conditions or medical and police emergencies.

The train timetable allows for two lifts per hour, Monday to Saturday. On Sundays there is a lift just once per hour, on the hour. Normal courtesy and reasonableness when requesting a lift by phone or on Ch 10 will probably ease your way through. However, commercial shipping takes priority, but you will usually be allowed through immediately before or after a ship, so monitor Ch 10 carefully.

It is best, when planning a passage through the bridge, to contact the bridge-keeper early to check there is no problem that will delay you or even prevent the bridge opening. (In

Kingsferry Bridge

VHF Ch 10
Call sign *Kingsferry Bridge*
☎ 01795 423627

Lights

Al.Q red/green	– bridge lifting
F Green	– bridge open (29m MHWS)
Q Red	– Bridge lowering, keep clear
Q Yellow	– Bridge out of action
No lights	– bridge down (3.35m MHWS)

very hot weather it is often not opened for fear of unequal expansion jamming it open.)

Approaches to West Swale

Approaches to the W Swale will be from seaward or downriver from the Medway.

From seaward, follow directions for entering the Medway (see 102) then, watching for commercial traffic, make for the W Swale entrance marked by the Queenborough Spit ECB (Q(3)10s).

Heading E down the Medway, the Queenborough Spit ECB (Q(3)10s) can be hard to locate against the Sheerness shore and can be obscured by large tugs on moorings W of it. These tugs are active during shipping movements.

Queenborough

⊕ **Entry waypoint**
51°25′.84N 000°44′.00E (immediately NE of Queenborough Spit ECB Q(3)10s)

Main Hazards

Beware of ruins on E shore marked by dolphins and also keep sharp lookout for occasional commercial traffic.

Tides HW Dover +0130.

Queenborough town is on the Isle of Sheppey at the entrance to the West Swale, a little under 2M S of Garrison Point at the mouth of the Medway. Facilities are limited but it offers a safe and sheltered anchorage with visitor moorings available.

Heading S in the Swale, leave Queenborough Spit ECB (Q(3)10s) to starboard and pass two lit dolphins on the E shore (Q.R and Fl.R) guarding remains of an old pier.

Immediately S of the second dolphin, lines of moorings begin on the E shore, closely followed by more on the W side. Although many of the moorings will be occupied, there are usually some vacant.

There are four large visitors' buoys on the E shore further S, two N of the all-tide landing, and two more S of it. Up to four boats may raft together on each visitor buoy. These buoys are very wide and only have a ring in the centre, so some agility is required to get a line on if you are the first to arrive.

The all-tide landing pontoons stretch across the mudflats from the E shore and end in a hammerhead (2FR) which remains afloat at all times.

Do not anchor in the fairway, because of the commercial

QUEENBOROUGH HARBOUR

Harbour Supervisor ☎ 01795 662051
VHF Ch 08
Call sign *Sheppey 1*
Trot Boat service (weekends/bank holidays) Ch 08
Call sign *Sheppey 1*
Access 24hr all tide landing and causeway

Facilities WC. Showers

Engineer Andre Hardy c/o Harbourmaster

Chandler The Bosun's Store ☎ 01795 662674

Gas Calor and Gaz from Bosun's Store

Provisions In town

Pub/restaurant The Flying Dutchman ☎ 01795 662884

Water On all-tide landing

Yacht club Queenborough YC ☎ 01795 663955

Taxi ☎ 01795 661000

Trains Shuttle to Sheerness and Sittingbourne for connections to London and Ramsgate.

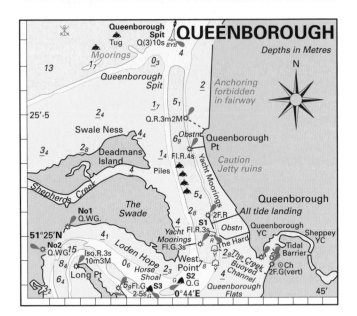

traffic, which operates 24hr through the Kingsferry Bridge, but you might find a place to bring up under N shore of Loden Hope.

Queenborough All-Tide Landing. The yacht club is in the row of buildings on the right

All-tide jetty

Queenborough at HW

The Queenborough YC and the Council share the running of a trot boat service, the Council operating from 0800-1600 in season and the Club covering weekend evenings. If using your own dinghy, note that the tides run strongly here.

The all-tide landing has a turnstile at its shore end, which lets you ashore, but requires a 50p token (per person) from Queenborough YC, the chandler or some stores, to pass seawards again. As a last resort, the night-watchman at the nearby factory, Abbott Laboratories, also has a supply.

Queenborough Creek

Along the south side of the town is the drying Queenborough Creek. Access is across the mudflats closely following the small markers from the S1 PHB (Fl.R.3s),

Queenborough Creek looking downstream from the excellent scrubbing berth

which marks the end of the old hard, then through the floodgate (usually open). The Town Quay can be crowded, but the bottom is flat and free of obstructions, so rafting out is possible, but ask the Harbour Supervisor first ☎ 01795 662051.

There is an excellent scrubbing berth where the bottom is a large concrete slab. Seek permission to use it (at a small charge) from the HM.

Queenborough to Kingsferry Bridge

The passage from Queenborough to the bridge is straightforward, with good depth in the channel, plenty of lights at night and no unmarked obstructions. To help ships, particularly navigating at night, the channel is covered by sectored lights and leading lights.

Call the bridge keeper (Ch 10) before leaving the moorings at Queenborough to find out when the next lift will be.

The channel runs round a right hand bend into Loden Hope, past S2 (Q.G) and S3 (Fl.G.2.5s) SHBs. To port is an old wharf with cranes.

At the end of Loden Hope is a hairpin bend to port with best water midway between the banks all the way round. Do not cut this corner. A lit beacon (Iso.R.3s) stands on the end of Long Point, and there are two sectored lights (Q.WG) on the outside of the bend.

Once round Long Pt, Long Reach runs past S4 (Q.R) PHB and S5 (Fl.G.5s) SHB to S6 (Fl.R.5s) PHB where the channel bends to port past S7 (Q.R) PHB. Do not cut this corner.

From S7, Horse Reach leads past lit beacons on either hand before the final stretch to the bridge on about 140°.

The waters each side of the bridge are the only places in the Swale without an 8kn speed limit, and powerboats and PWCs use the area at weekends. This stretch can be crowded in summer with yachts waiting for a bridge lift and sharing a fairly small area with much faster boats.

17. The North Kent coast

Ramsgate to North Foreland

On passage from Ramsgate N towards the Foreland, you can safely keep as close as ½M from the shore unless you have exceptional draught and it's low water springs. Beware potmarkers in the whole area. There are no charted individual hazards and you can enjoy the scenery of Thanet's chalk cliffs, soon giving way to the tiny haven of Broadstairs.

Broadstairs is a pretty little place and a bustling seaside resort in summer. The harbour dries completely and is not a serious proposition for a visit unless you have a sense of adventure and a suitable craft, and the weather is settled. A lunch-time anchorage stop for a swim a few hundred yards off, or a row ashore for an ice-cream, is something you might consider. Broadstairs SC runs dinghy races just offshore and occasionally hosts large events, which are best avoided by heading a little further out round them.

North of Broadstairs, the cliffs quickly rise again, surmounted by houses most of the way to the N Foreland lighthouse (Fl(5)WR.20s57m19/15M), which was notable for being the last in the country to be manned before it, too, became fully automated.

The cliffs start to descend again as you round the N Foreland and are punctuated by sandy bays. Off the Foreland itself, W winds can produce very rough conditions – it's the meeting place of two tidal streams, where the waters of the Estuary meet the English Channel. In a strong SWly, however, it's sheltered inshore.

North Foreland to Reculver

Boats heading W have a choice here to track along the coast inshore of the mass of sandbanks that fill the Estuary (the 'overland' route) or to make N, turning NW in the vicinity of the East Margate buoy (Fl.R.2.5s) and heading for the Princes Channel

The Princes Channel is a main shipping route and should be treated accordingly. Yachts generally follow its S side taking care to avoid the significant shallows of the Ridge and the Pan Sand. This route has little merit for anyone heading for the Swale, Medway or further W, but could be used en route perhaps to the Crouch or the Blackwater.

Following the popular inshore route along the Kent shore, means heading W towards the South Channel by rounding Foreness Point between the small unlit NCB (guarding the end of a long chalk ledge) and the unlit Longnose PHB three cables NE. This area is particularly popular for pots.

A little less than two miles west of the Longnose, is the small drying harbour of Margate. If planning to take a closer look at it, be sure to avoid the hidden remains of the pier just E, which was destroyed in a storm and is marked by a NCM (Q). The harbour itself, with its single stone arm, has little to offer a visiting yachtsman, being totally open to the

North Foreland around LW, the Longnose rocks in the distance

Broadstairs with the harbour arm to the right

Harbour arm

The East Last buoy, north of Reculver, marks the end of the Gore Channel

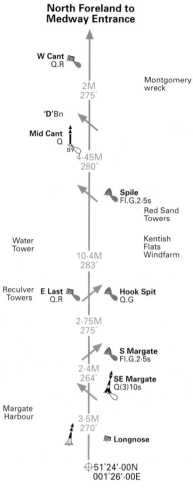

North Foreland to Medway Entrance

W Cant
Q.R

2M
275°

Montgomery wreck

'D'Bn

Mid Cant
Q

4·45M
280°

Spile
Fl.G.2·5s

Red Sand Towers

Water Tower

Kentish Flats Windfarm

10·4M
283°

Reculver Towers

E Last
Q.R

Hook Spit
Q.G

2·75M
275°

S Margate
Fl.G.2·5s

2·4M
264°

SE Margate
Q(3)10s

Margate Harbour

3·5M
270°

Longnose

51°24'·00N
001°26'·00E

Margate

West and drying at least 2m. Like Broadstairs, a trip ashore for an ice-cream might be the only attraction.

Heading on W, the shore beyond Margate rises again as a low chalk cliff, which finally peters out at Minnis Bay. The route on through the Gore Channel is marked to the north

Margate's drying harbour

by the SE Margate (Q(3)10s), then S Margate (Fl.G.2.5s) buoys, and the deep channel is sheltered from the N by the Margate Hook Sand. Beyond Minnis, the coastline sinks to barely more than a sea wall, blocking off the sea from what was once the Wantsum Channel, which separated the Isle of Thanet from the mainland. The Margate Hook beacon is a prominent SCM to starboard, which once housed a refuge for shipwrecked sailors.

Reculver Towers are now seen ahead. These two rectangular towers, linked together, are part of an ancient ruined church that stands inside the Roman fort of Regulbium, whose garrison guarded the N end of the Wantsum. At the Wantsum's S end stands the ruin of the fort at Richborough (Rutupae), which became the Romans' main port of entry into Britain.

The old church at Reculver was built using materials from the Roman fort, but was largely demolished and 'moved' a mile inland in the 19th century when it became clear that the sea would take it if unchecked. That the Towers still stand today, protected yards from the waves by a sea wall, is due in part to their importance as a landmark for mariners. From time to time the towers are floodlit until midnight.

About 1.3M N of the towers is the narrow swatchway at the end of the Gore Channel across the W end of the Margate Hook sand. There is 2m in the approach to the swatchway, which passes between the E Last (Q.R) and

Hook Spit (Q.G) buoys. These are not particularly conspicuous, both being small. Stay on a NW course until 100m or so beyond the E Last, before resuming your W heading across the Kentish Flats.

Conspicuous to NW are the 30 turbines of the Kentish Flats wind farm, 5M off the Kent shore at its nearest point.

Reculver to Herne Bay

From the E Last, if going to Whitstable or the Swale, make for the Whitstable Street NCB (Q), almost 6.5M W. If you plan to go to the Medway instead, the Spile buoy will be your target, just over 10M away on a bearing of 283°.

For Herne Bay, there is a possible short cut inside the E Last Sand, called the Copperas Channel (copperas, or iron pyrites, used in dyeing and tanning, was the basis of a major industry in the area), best navigated on a large scale chart particularly in view of the unmarked 'Black Rock', NW of Reculver, which dries at LWS. Otherwise, pass round to the north of the East Last sand.

About a ½M N of Herne Bay SC, the dinghy club at the eastern end of the town, is a substantial steel dolphin, which is lit Fl.Y.5s.

On high ground inland from the sailing club is a prominent water tower in the shape of a cocktail glass.

Herne Bay

⊕ **Landfall waypoint**
   51°22′.70N 001°07′.20E
Charts
   Imray *2100 Series*
   Admiralty SC *5606, 1607*
Tides
   Dover +0120
Harbourmaster
   Whitstable Harbour office ☎ 01227 274086
   Access HW±2hrs

Herne Bay harbour at half tide

Main hazards

Entire approach is across shoals
Disused pierhead (Q.18m4M) 0.6M NNW
Steel dolphin (Fl.Y 5s) 0.95M ENE
Area used by fast powerboats.

Herne Bay is an entirely drying harbour. A recently built harbour arm acts as a sea defence with no provision for visitors at all, but does represent a possible emergency haven for shoal draught craft that can take the ground.

Approach from the N. The bottom is hard but flat, sand on clay, from some distance out, and the harbour entrance is close to a conspicuous block of flats. The entrance is about 30m wide, the W side being the remains of the shore end of an old pier, lit 2F.G(vert), on which stands a very large white building with a green roof. The end of the new E arm is also lit, 2FR(vert). Turn E as soon as you pass the end of this arm to find the deepest water inside.

Herne Bay's drying harbour

The harbour dries completely to very soft mud, fine for bilge keelers or centreboarders, but not deep enough for fin keels. A number of local fishing boats are moored there and it would be wise to buoy your anchor. You can land by dinghy on the wide slipway at the E end, or on the beach, but do not even think of trying to wade ashore through the mud. Around HW you could lie briefly in at least 2m alongside the S edge of the slipway, but, in season, it's used by PWCs.

Out to the NNW is the other surviving part of what was once the second-longest pier in the country, the old pierhead and landing stage now inhabited only by cormorants, 0.75M from the shore, and lit as a north cardinal.

Reculver to Whitstable

Between the old pierhead off Herne Bay and Whitstable is a popular area for pots, although many are properly marked.

The Whitstable Street shingle bank bars the way W, marked by a NCB 2M from shore. The 'Street' dries for at least 1M from shore at LWS and the Street buoy (Q) is the normal turning point for craft entering the harbour.

Whitstable

⊕ **Landfall waypoint**
51°22′.70N 001°01′.20E
Charts
Imray *2100* Series
Admiralty SC *5606, 1607*
Tides
Dover +0135
Harbourmaster
Whitstable Harbour office ☎ 01227 274086
Whitstable Yacht Club ☎ 01227 272942
VHF Ch 09 (0830–1700 or HW–3 to HW+1)
Call sign *Whitstable Harbour Radio*
Access HW±3hr
Chandler and Rigger Dinghy Store ☎ 01227 274168
Engineer Turf and Surf ☎ 01227 752499

Main hazards

Shallows on approach
'The Street' shingle bank to E
Some commercial traffic.

Whitstable is the third refuge harbour along this stretch of coast, but is again not commonly visited. It is very much a working port, home to the local fishing fleet, plus some gravel and timber coasters. It dries to soft mud at LWS and is not a yacht-friendly place. In emergency it is possible, but contact the harbourmaster before attempting to enter. The walls are high and unforgiving and very long fender boards are needed, unless you can lie alongside a friendly fishing boat. In onshore winds there can be a considerable swell in all parts of the harbour.

The harbour entrance is difficult to make out even in clear weather. It is lit, but in daylight the town behind is fairly featureless. Look for long low roofs and a tall silo, all close to the harbour.

The harbour approach is across shallows. At night, locate the lit Oyster PHB (Fl(2)R.10s) and a sectored light

Whitstable Harbour entrance with the yacht club to the west

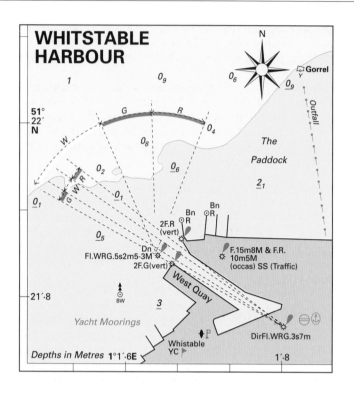

WHITSTABLE HARBOUR

N

1

0₉

0₆

⌐ Gorrel
Y

0₉

51°
22′
N

G   R

0₄

Outfall

W

0₈

The
Paddock

0₂

0₆

2₁

0₁

0₁

0₅

Bn
⊙ R

Bn
⊙ R

2F.R
(vert)

Dn
Fl.WRG.5s2m5-3M
2F.G(vert)

F.15m8M & F.R.
10m5M
(occas) SS (Traffic)

West Quay

21′·8

⊙
BW

3

Yacht Moorings

P

DirFl.WRG.3s7m

Whistable
YC ▷

Depths in Metres 1°1′·6E   1′·8

(Fl.WRG.5s5-3M) on a dolphin close to the West Quay head. At the back of the harbour is a sectored leading light (DirFl.WRG.3s) with the white sector visible on course 122.5°. Traffic signals on the East Quay show F if harbour is open, F.R when closed. The lights of the town contribute to the level of difficulty here.

For a non-emergency visit to Whitstable, the yacht club is just W of the harbour and, although predominantly a dinghy club, also has a cruising section and may have a spare mooring on enquiry to the secretary. When drying out, the beach in front of the club and for 200m W is firm, flat shingle on mud (it was a Thames barge hard) and is an ideal spot for a scrub or underwater maintenance in quiet weather. There is a chandler and rigger close by, and marine engineers locally.

The town is very much an East Coast place, much more like the coastal towns of Essex and Suffolk than its neighbours in Kent, and is worth a visit. There are many small specialist shops and art galleries, plus a number of good restaurants.

SW in Whitstable Bay are oyster beds. These date from Roman times and local oysters, called 'Whitstable Natives', are sold in the town in season.

Whitstable Harbour

Whitstable: scrubbing down

There is no shelter on the S shore of Whitstable Bay in strong SW through N winds, when a far better option is to make for the East Swale. A NWly in particular can make life very uncomfortable with a vicious, steep chop quickly building up.

Reculver to the Medway

On passage from Reculver to the Medway, passing outside the Isle of Sheppey, shape a course of 283° from E Last PHB to the Spile SHB (Fl.G.2.5s) at the W end of the Four Fathoms Channel, just over 10M. This takes you along the 'Overland Passage', an ancient name still shown on charts and referring to the shallow water where least charted depth is around 2.5m.

Off Whitstable another old name takes over, the Four Fathoms Channel, which on Imray's chart has the legend 'at HW' wisely added after it. If tacking through, avoid going

The *Montgomery* wreck is guarded by yellow light buoys

too close inshore off NE Sheppey where there are several shallow patches only highlighted on large scale charts. In particular there is a tricky patch 125° from the Spile buoy, about 1.5M away.

After the Spile, the route crosses an area of continuing shallows called the Cant. The chart warns of 'numerous pieces of wreckage, some submerged' across the Cant, but the most recent will probably be from the Second World War and there is much fishing and trawling activity across it. The route is heavily used by small craft.

The Cant has various substantial posts dotted across it but these do not mark charted hazards. The Mid Cant NCM has obstructions stretching towards it N from the shore, but these stop three cables short of the post itself.

Pass N of the Mid Cant NCM (Q) and post 'D' then, depending on tide and draught, make for either the Medway No.8 PHB (Fl.R.5s) or the West Cant PHB (Q.R) on the SE side of the Medway approach channel.

The infamous wreck of the *Richard Montgomery* lies on the Sheerness Middle Sand NW of the approach channel with her masts still visible. A Liberty Ship on her maiden voyage in 1944 with a cargo of munitions bound for Normandy, she was at anchor when she swung and broke her back on the sands; she was partly unloaded soon afterwards, but bombs and other munitions totalling either 1400 tons or 3500 tons (nobody seems quite sure), still lie there. The wreck is regularly surveyed, but the cargo is considered too dangerous to touch and the wreck is surrounded by an exclusion zone defined by lit yellow buoys.

When approaching the Medway, listen on Ch 74 to Medway Radio for shipping movements and maintain a good lookout astern.

18. Ramsgate

⊕ **Landfall Waypoint**
51°19′.53N 001°30′.27E
(immediately S of 'RA' SCB)

Charts
Imray *2100 Series*
Admiralty SC *5606, 5605;*
323, 1828, 1827

Tides
Dover +0030

Harbourmaster
Ramsgate Port Control VHF
Ch 14

Harbourmaster
☎ 01843 572100
Ramsgate Marina
VHF Ch.80 ☎ 01843 592277
Email
marina@ramsgatemarina.co.uk
www.ramsgatemarina.co.uk

Main hazards

The N section of the Goodwin Sands lies only 4M from the harbour entrance, and passage N of this area, heading E or W, must be undertaken with extreme caution, particularly on the flood tide, which sweeps SW onto the sands.

Shallows lie S of the entrance, the Quern Bank being closest, and the Cross Ledge further S. To the N, the shallows mainly shelve gently with no uncharted hazards, but stand well off the North Foreland in strong E winds as seas build up badly inshore.

Ramsgate has a dredged approach channel (least depth 7.5m) running due W towards the harbour entrance and intended for the frequent large ferries and fast pilot launches. Small craft use the 'Recommended Yacht Track' that runs parallel to the S side of the channel.

No craft may enter or leave harbour without permission from Port Control (Ch14).

Ramsgate's outer breakwaters are low-lying, built of rubble, and are difficult to make out from E. The N pierhead has a G beacon (Q.G 5M); the S has a R beacon (VQ.R 5M).

The tide sweeps across the entrance, roughly NE/SW, at up to 2kn.

Approaches

From N

Follow the coast S from North Foreland keeping ½–1M offshore. There is a 'Small Craft Holding Area' a short distance N of approach channel No.3 SHB (Fl.G.2.5s) and a track S from there crosses the channel just W of No.3 SHB and No.4 PHB (Q.R) to join the Recommended Yacht Track.

Exercise great care crossing the approach channel and, if in doubt, check with Port Control before doing so.

From E

Approach 'RA' buoy (Q(6)+LFl.15s) then join Yacht Track on S side of channel. Keep sharp lookout for commercial traffic.

In daylight, first sighting will be chalk cliffs of the Foreland, N of harbour, and prominent cooling towers at Richborough on low-lying land to S. By night, North Foreland light (W sector) should be identified.

From SE

From SE, approach outside the Goodwins, keeping clear of the Goodwin Knoll, to arrive at 'RA' buoy. Do not risk turning NW across N end of the Knoll, especially when flood tide is setting hard onto the bank.

From S

From S either follow the Gull Stream NE from Deal Pier, turning N towards the No.4 approach channel buoy once past the Brake PHB (Fl(4)R.10s) or stay close inshore through Ramsgate Channel to W of Brake and Cross Ledge.

The inshore route requires extreme caution, especially close to the unlit B2 SHB, which is small and difficult to locate. It guards the Cross Ledge bank, which shifts frequently, and must be left well to starboard. Once past, continue in a wide arc W to pass well W of West Quern WCB (Q(9)15s) to arrive close S of harbour entrance. This route is not advisable at night.

There is a small craft holding area immediately off S breakwater.

Entry

From the No.4 channel PHB, follow the charted 'Recommended Yacht Track' making good 270°. Pass close N of North Quern NCB (Q) to clear shallows.

Call *Ramsgate Port Control* on Ch 14 and ask for permission to enter the harbour. Control lights are displayed (3 vert G – clear to enter; 3 vert R – no entry) at root of N breakwater. They can be difficult to identify against town lights at night. A light (Fl. Or) is displayed on the cream-painted Port Control building on N breakwater during ship movements; do not enter or leave harbour.

On receiving permission, proceed under power through outer entrance. If required to wait, use holding area by S breakwater.

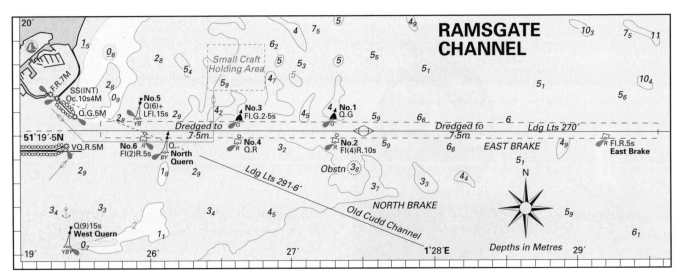

Ramsgate – the marinas clearly visible in the Royal Harbour

Ramsgate entrance to Ramsgate Marina

From the outer harbour, the marina lies to N in Royal Harbour behind stone wall of the old harbour. Leave SHB (Q.G) to starboard and light (F.R) on end of W Pier close to port. Beware drying bank on starboard (E) side and watch for boats leaving. They may appear suddenly round pierhead.

Approaching Ramsgate from the north

Ramsgate entrance. Note the small SHB right of centre

South Breakwater   SHB marks shoal   Royal harbour entrance   N Breakwater

Ramsgate – Royal Harbour entrance and the West Marina

Ramsgate Marina

There are actually two parts to the marina. The newer, and preferable part, is the West Marina immediately to port inside the Royal Harbour entrance. The older part, the East Marina, lies N from the entrance and is entered between two lit dolphins at its W end. Beware the drying East Bank to starboard guarded by a SHB (Fl.G.5s).

Visitors' berths are usually freely available except during large events, like Ramsgate Week. Call Ramsgate Marina on Ch 80. You will not usually be allocated a specific berth, but will be told to find an empty one, on a choice of pontoons, where no 'Reserved' notice is displayed.

In strong winds from N through S or even SW, the marina can be a little rough with the East Marina more affected than the West, but you will normally be allocated a berth in the West Marina anyway, the east section being mainly used by fishing boats.

For long-term stays only, you may be able to berth in the Inner Harbour. This is entered through a lifting bridge and gate open HW±2hr. A red and yellow flag by day, and a single green light by night, indicates that the gate is open. Entrance is beside W end of East Marina.

The marina office is a wooden building immediately W of the lifting bridge. Access to the pontoons and toilet buildings is protected by key codes issued on payment of berthing fees.

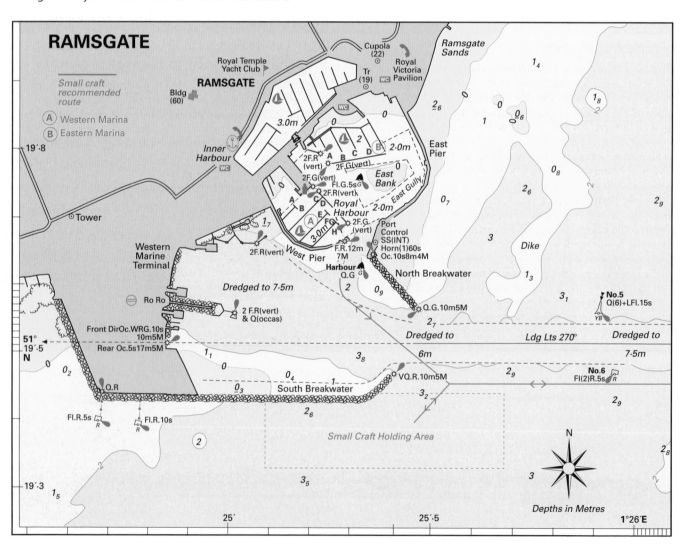

Ramsgate

RAMSGATE HISTORY

Ramsgate Harbour used to consist only of the part that now houses the marina. The great stone piers were largely built by prisoners of war after the Great Storm of 1748, which showed the need for a safe haven near the ancient anchorage of The Downs. The outer arms and ferry terminals were built comparatively recently.

It was granted the title Royal Harbour Ramsgate (the only 'Royal' harbour) by George IV in 1821 when he was made welcome during a visit there.

The famous Victorian engineer Telford was brought in to solve the problem of silting in the harbour and it was he who created the inner harbour. The idea was to fill the basin with water at high tide, lock it off during the ebb, then empty it violently at low tide to flush the silt away. Happily for us this is no longer done. Instead, a dredger is kept busy.

Ramsgate has considerable military and naval history, but in more recent times it has become an important ferry port with a regular service to Oostende and is also a busy home to pilot launches. The marina is a popular stopover for cross-Channel traffic.

Gate to Inner Harbour

West Marina; gate to Inner Harbour is right of centre

Entering the Royal Harbour at LW. Port Control is on the pier to starboard

Royal Temple Yacht Club (with the flag pole) looks out across the harbour

One drawback is the regional airport a few miles W with its runway in line with the town. However, the traffic is not too frequent and is not enough to spoil the ambience.

East Marina entrance between the dolphins

East Marina entrance

RAMSGATE MARINA

Contact
   VHF Ch 80
   Call sign *Ramsgate Marina*
   Harbourmaster ☎ 01843 572100
   Email marina@ramsgatemarina.co.uk
   www.ramsgatemarina.co.uk
   Access 24hr

Fue/ Diesel and petrol from fuel barge by commercial jetty pierhead at N entrance to West Marina. 0800–2000, Ch 80

Facilities WC. Showers. Launderette. (Need gate code in West Marina.)

Water On pontoons

Electricity On pontoons

Gas Calor and Gaz at Bosun's Locker chandler ☎ 01843 597158 in the 'arches' behind the inner harbour

Chandler Bosun's Locker ☎ 01843 597158

Provisions In town

Post office In town

Banks In town

Boat repairs 40-ton boat hoist and slipway Sailmakers Northrop Sails ☎ 01843 851665

Pubs/Restaurants Royal Temple YC and in town

Hospital A&E Queen Elizabeth the Queen Mother ☎ 01843 225544

Yacht club Royal Temple YC ☎ 01843-591766 *Email* info@rtyc.com www.rtyc.com

Transport Trains – mainline station with frequent services to London (Victoria) and Dover

Buses Pass near harbour

Taxis ☎ 01843 595595, 570555, 581888, 592111.

19. Crossing the Thames Estuary

Whatever the conditions, a passage across the Thames Estuary provides a navigational challenge and is certainly not a trip to be undertaken lightly. Weather and sea conditions can change quickly and land will be out of sight for some part of a crossing of the outer parts of the estuary.

Compared with the waters around the Channel Islands, for instance, there may not be any rocks, but there are plenty of charted obstructions, the water is generally shallow, the sandbanks can indeed be as unyielding as rock and are constantly on the move, the tide runs hard, and there is plenty of shipping thrown in for good measure.

But, like any other piece of navigation, provided the passage is carefully planned and executed with due regard for the forecast conditions, it should be without problems.

Hazards

Tides
Tides can run hard in the estuary, approaching 3kn in some areas during Springs. The Admiralty *Tidal Atlas* (NP 249) is an invaluable guide and shows a relatively straightforward flow, generally NE-SW, with some added complications in the SE caused by the flows in and out of Dover Strait. There's also a kind of 'roundabout' effect in the area of the Shingles banks, SW of the Long Sand.

The estuary is, in effect, a bottleneck and this topography, combined with wind speed and direction and barometric pressure, can significantly affect predicted tidal times and heights. These factors must be taken into account when planning a passage, especially if short cuts across some of the banks are to be used.

Timings for passages will often have to be a compromise. For instance, a bank may need to be crossed on the flood near HW, which will mean having to fight the ebb on the final leg up river to a planned destination.

Charted buoys and sand banks
Although the shores of the estuary are mostly soft mud, the banks offshore are most certainly not. They tend to be extremely hard sand and grounding a small craft here on the ebb in rough seas can be very dangerous. Similarly, being stranded on a rising tide in deteriorating weather can be an alarming situation.

But despite their hard nature, the sands are also constantly shifting and the UK Hydrographic Office publishes a constant stream of corrections to the charts of the estuary. Indeed, many of the charts are re-published as frequently as every two years to take account of all the changes. The advice has to be to keep up to date with corrections and buy the new chart versions when they are published. Chart corrections can be obtained from Notices to Mariners on the website www.nmwebsearch.com.

In the same vein, published lists of the positions of navigation marks should be treated with caution. Buoys are frequently moved and occasionally removed altogether or relocated and given new names. A chart corrected up to date should be the primary source of waypoints. The positions published in the nautical almanacs each year are probably the most regularly updated, but unless these books are

thoroughly corrected as well, they should only be used as a 'reality check' for waypoints derived from the chart.

Altered or updated waypoints must also be corrected in the ship's GPS set.

Wind and weather
The NE-SW tidal streams, coupled with prevailing SW winds and frequent NE winds in SE England, mean that rough seas and wind against tide conditions will often be met in the estuary. The 'Thames Estuary chop' can be as unpleasant a sea as you can find anywhere, even in as little breeze as a F4. Many yachtsmen have a rule of not setting off if there's a '6' in the forecast and that is probably an excellent rule to follow in the estuary.

Traffic
The whole estuary is busy with commercial shipping, some of it very large. A good lookout is essential, as is a listening watch on VHF Ch 16 and 69 (the Port of London Authority channel for the outer reaches).

Wind farms
At the time of compiling this book, the Scroby Sands farm was fully operational and the Kentish Flats wind farm was almost complete, while other arrays were in various stages from planning to construction. As they are developed, they will have an increasing effect on passagemaking across the estuary, as is discussed fully on page 3.

Before planning a passage across the area, it would be wise to get the most up to date information about the wind farms and to plan accordingly.

General advice
Work up a comprehensive passage plan before you start, including detailed tidal information for points on your journey. The Admiralty *Tidal Atlas* can be a great help in doing this.

Don't attempt short cuts in bad weather. Short cuts across sandbanks will, by their nature, offer little water under the keel and in rough seas there will be increased danger of grounding in the troughs. Unless certain of adequate depth, the prudent navigator will take the long way round and have contingency plans for using an alternative route or even abandoning the passage.

Use every opportunity and device to maintain an up to date position on the chart. During a passage across the estuary, decisions and course changes will come up very frequently and each will demand precise knowledge of the vessel's position. Such position fixing has been made considerably easier for most navigators with the widespread use of GPS, but nevertheless maintain the log, even every 15 minutes, recording each buoy or beacon identified and passed. Do not ignore the chance to confirm a GPS position by visual identification or handbearing fixes. Everything will be of use should the electronics fail.

E. Swale to Wallet

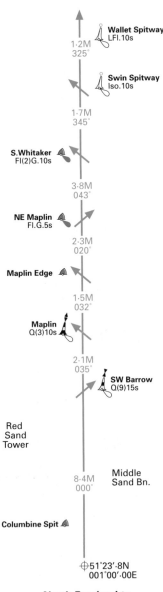

**North Foreland to
Harwich Approach**

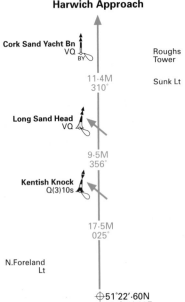

Routes

The inner estuary

Passages between the area of the Medway and Swale and the Essex and Suffolk rivers will follow the 'coastal' route and be able to take advantage of the tide.

A passage from the E Swale to the Blackwater or beyond, for instance, might start from Harty just before HW, push the last of the flood down to the Columbine or Columbine Spit buoys, then head N (with an appropriate W component to allow for tide) to pass the Middle Sand Bn and the Red Sand Towers before entering the SW entrance to the W Swin at the SW Barrow WCB.

The route would then pass the Maplin ECB, cross into the E Swin by the Maplin Edge unlit SHB and head on via the NE Maplin SHB to the S Whitaker SHB. This buoy is some 18M from the Columbine, and the passage will have used at least 3hr of ebb out of a total of little more than 5hr of ebb tide available on this down-tide route.

From the S Whitaker, the route heads NNW to the Swin Spitway SWB, crossing the Buxey Sand directly to the Wallet Spitway SWB before heading for the Blackwater or continuing on through the Wallet towards the Orwell.

Despite needing to cross the Buxey near LW, the Wallet is a better route to use when continuing NE, because the early flood runs hard SW on the S side of the Gunfleet, while the streams in the Wallet are weaker.

This inner estuary route is readily reversible, timing a departure S from the Whitaker area to meet the need for enough depth at the planned destination.

The outer estuary

From N Foreland to Harwich, the simplest route, given a favourable wind, is one that goes around the outside of most of the banks.

Passing N Foreland at around HW Dover –1hr, a track of 010° leads to the centre of the Knock Deep, although wind farm development there may force a track of 025° instead to pass outside the Kentish Knock Sand. In both cases a straightforward route would be taken past the Long Sand Head and NW towards Harwich. A point between the NE Gunfleet and the Sunk Lt is 28M from the Foreland, but there is still a favourable tidal component until about HW Dover –6hr, which should enable entry to the Orwell in the first hours of the flood.

In reverse, a departure from the Orwell on the last of the ebb would give about 6hrs of SW-going stream, but the ebb from the Channel starts heading N off the Foreland at about HW Dover –1hr.

Intermediate routes

Between the N Foreland and the Crouch or the Blackwater, typical routing has in the past used the N Edinburgh Channel or Fisherman's Gat with shortcuts across the Sunk Sand at the SW Sunk Bn. However, shipping route changes have altered some of the options. The N Edinburgh Channel is no longer buoyed and has been replaced as a shipping route by Fisherman's Gat, to the NE. Fisherman's Gat was the preferred route for small craft before that, but yachts are now recommended to use Foulger's Gat, even further to the NE. (See further comment on this in the section on Wind Farms, page 3.)

A route to or from the Crouch via the E Margate PHB, E Tongue Sand Tower ECB and SW Sunk Bn still seems to favour use of the unbuoyed N Edinburgh Channel, because Foulger's Gat entails a long detour NE, while Fisherman's Gat is busy with commercial traffic. Using the N Edinburgh without buoys, however, requires careful navigation.

The short cut past the SW Sunk Bn is particularly shallow when passing, as recommended, close S of it. It should be used within 2hrs of HW to see more than 2m to 2.5m depth, and preferably on a rising tide. Bear in mind also that such swatchways shift and change all the time.

W of the SW Sunk, pass carefully around the NE end of the E Barrow sand, rounding Barrow No.5, and make for the Whitaker ECB, either rounding the N Middle NCB or using the S Whitaker SHB to keep clear S of the shallows marked to the E of the N Middle buoy. From the Whitaker, either turn SW into the Whitaker Channel and the Crouch, or head up for the Spitway and Colne or Blackwater.

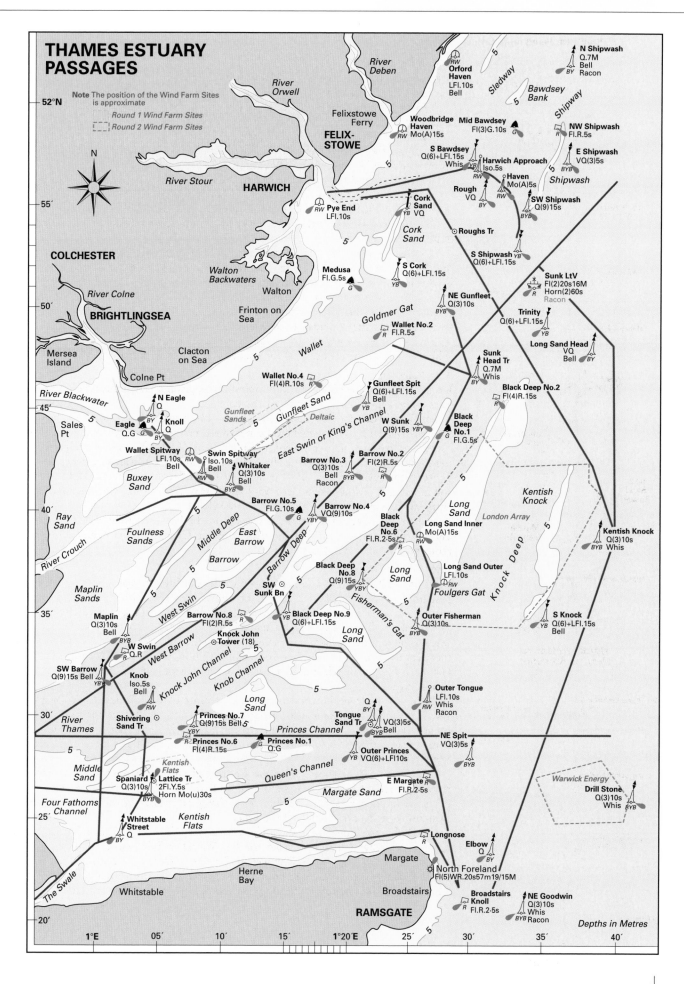

THAMES ESTUARY PASSAGES

Note The position of the Wind Farm Sites is approximate

□ Round 1 Wind Farm Sites
┌─┐ Round 2 Wind Farm Sites
└─┘

52°N

55'

50'

45'

40'

35'

30'

25'

20'

COLCHESTER

BRIGHTLINGSEA

Mersea Island

River Colne

Sales Pt

River Blackwater

Colne Pt

Ray Sand

Foulness Sands

Maplin Sands

River Crouch

River Thames

The Swale

Whitstable

Herne Bay

Four Fathoms Channel

Middle Sand

Kentish Flats

Whitstable Flats

Kentish Flats

RAMSGATE

Broadstairs

Margate

North Foreland
Fl(5)WR.20s57m19/15M

Longnose

Elbow
Q BY

Broadstairs Knoll
Fl.R.2·5s

NE Goodwin
Q(3)10s
Whis
Racon

Margate Sand

E Margate
Fl.R.2·5s

Queen's Channel

Spaniard
Q(3)10s

Lattice Tr
2Fl.Y.5s
Horn Mo(u)30s

Shivering Sand Tr

Whitstable Street
Q

Princes No.6
Fl(4)R.15s

Princes No.7
Q(9)15s Bell

Princes No.1
Q.G

Outer Princes
VQ(6)+LFl10s

Princes Channel

Tongue Sand Tr

Q
VQ(3)5s
Bell

NE Spit
VQ(3)5s

Drill Stone
Q(3)10s
Whis

Warwick Energy

Outer Tongue
LFl.10s
Whis
Racon

Knock John Channel

Knob Channel

Long Sand

Knock John Tower (18)

SW Barrow
Q(9)15s Bell

W Swin
Q.R

Knob
Iso.5s
Bell

Maplin
Q(3)10s
Bell

West Swin

West Barrow

Barrow No.8
Fl(2)R.5s

SW Sunk Bn

Black Deep No.9
Q(6)+LFl.15s

Black Deep No.8
Q(9)15s

Long Sand

Fisherman's Gat

Outer Fisherman
Q(3)10s

S Knock
Q(6)+LFl.15s
Bell

Knock Deep

Kentish Knock
Q(3)10s
Whis

London Array

Long Sand Outer
LFl.10s

Foulgers Gat

Long Sand Inner
Mo(A)15s

Black Deep No.6
Fl.R.2·5s

Long Sand

Black Deep No.1
Fl.G.5s

Black Deep No.2
Fl(4)R.15s

Kentish Knock

Barrow No.4
VQ(9)10s

Barrow No.5
Fl.G.10s

Barrow No.3
Q(3)10s
Bell
Racon

Barrow No.2
Fl(2)R.5s

W Sunk
Q(9)15s

Sunk Head Tr
Q.7M
Whis

Gunfleet Spit
Q(6)+LFl.15s
Bell

Wallet No.2
Fl.R.5s

NE Gunfleet
Q(3)10s

Trinity
Q(6)+LFl.15s

Long Sand Head
VQ
Bell

Sunk LtV
Fl(2)20s16M
Horn(2)60s
Racon

S Shipwash
Q(6)+LFl.15s

Roughs Tr

S Cork
Q(6)+LFl.15s

Medusa
Fl.G.5s

Cork Sand

Cork Sand
VQ

Pye End
LFl.10s

Wallet No.4
Fl(4)R.10s

Gunfleet Sand

Gunfleet Sands

Deltaic

East Swin or King's Channel

Wallet

Whitaker
Q(3)10s
Bell

Swin Spitway
Iso.10s
Bell

Wallet Spitway
LFl.10s
Bell

N Eagle
Q

Eagle
Q.G

Knoll
Q

Buxey Sand

Middle Deep

East Barrow

Barrow

Barrow Deep

Foulness Sands

Clacton on Sea

Frinton on Sea

Walton

Walton Backwaters

HARWICH

River Stour

River Orwell

River Deben

FELIX-STOWE

Felixstowe Ferry

Woodbridge Haven
Mo(A)15s

Orford Haven
LFl.10s
Bell

Sledway

Bawdsey Bank

Shipway

Shipway

N Shipwash
Q.7M
Bell
Racon

NW Shipwash
Fl.R.5s

Mid Bawdsey
Fl(3)G.10s

S Bawdsey
Q(6)+LFl.15s
Whis

Harwich Approach
Iso.5s

Rough
VQ

Haven
Mo(A)5s

E Shipwash
VQ(3)5s

Shipwash

SW Shipwash
Q(9)15s

S Cork

Goldmer Gat

N

Depths in Metres

North Foreland to Crouch

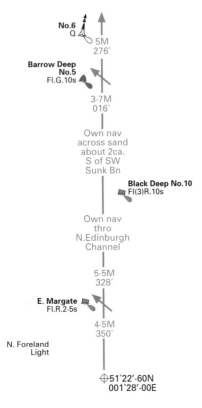

No.6
Q
5M
276°

Barrow Deep
No.5
Fl.G.10s
3·7M
016°

Own nav
across sand
about 2ca.
S of SW
Sunk Bn

Black Deep No.10
Fl(3)R.10s

Own nav
thro
N.Edinburgh
Channel

5·5M
328°

E. Margate
Fl.R.2·5s
4·5M
350°

N. Foreland
Light

⊕51°22'·60N
001°28'·00E

North Foreland to W Swin

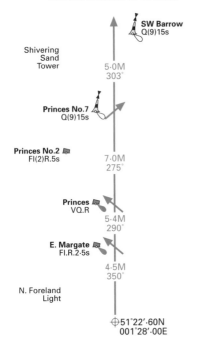

SW Barrow
Q(9)15s

Shivering
Sand
Tower

5·0M
303°

Princes No.7
Q(9)15s

Princes No.2
Fl(2)R.5s
7·0M
275°

Princes
VQ.R
5·4M
290°

E. Margate
Fl.R.2·5s
4·5M
350°

N. Foreland
Light

⊕51°22'·60N
001°28'·00E

On a passage from the N Foreland towards Essex, the timing is difficult overall, because the need for sufficient water at the SW Sunk requires fighting the ebb in the Crouch or Blackwater on arrival. Equally, when departing from either of these rivers it will be against the flood in order to arrive at the SW Sunk in good time.

An alternative is not to take the short cut at all, but to use the E and W Swin, and the Princes Channel, cutting across the shipping lanes between the SW Barrow WCB and the Princes No.7 ECB. This route is perhaps 5M longer than using the SW Sunk short cut, which is not a lot further, but it carries its own tidal considerations.

Personal Pilotage Notes

Personal Pilotage Notes

Index